Christopher Somerville is the author of *Twelve Literary Walks* and presenter of the associated radio series. He is a contributor to BBC Radio 4's 'Bookshelf', writes for the *Sunday Times* travel section and is the author of several other walking books, most recently *Coastal Walks in England and Wales* and *Fifty Best River Walks in Britain*. A former teacher, he is now a full-time writer and lives with his wife and children in Bristol.

By the same author

Coastal Walks in England and Wales
Twelve Literary Walks

Britain
Beside the Sea

Christopher Somerville

GRAFTON BOOKS
A Division of the Collins Publishing Group

LONDON GLASGOW
TORONTO SYDNEY AUCKLAND

Grafton Books
A Division of the Collins Publishing Group
8 Grafton Street, London W1X 3LA

Published in paperback by Grafton Books 1990

First published in Great Britain by
Grafton Books 1989

Copyright © Christopher Somerville 1989

A CIP catalogue record for this book
is available from the British Library

ISBN 0-586-20754-6

Printed and bound in Great Britain by
Collins, Glasgow

Set in Times

To Jane

Contents

Acknowledgements

I'd particularly like to thank Alan Cummings, Lodge Secretary of the National Union of Miners at Easington Colliery; Philip Griffiths and family of the Lizard lighthouse; David Hill, serpentine worker of Lizard Town; Alan Hinks, Alison Boyle and Roy Henstridge, boatbuilders of Appledore; Dan Farson, writer, of the same town; Michael Hughes, Warden of Oxwich Nature Reserve; John Rous of the Clovelly Estate Company; Evan Jones of Barmouth; James McMillan, Tourist Officer of the Isle of Bute; George Milne, harbourmaster at Anstruther; and the crew of the seine-netter *Aurica* at Macduff. All these kind people were prepared to be interrupted at their work and to give up valuable time to discussing the tricks of their various trades.

I am also indebted to Winston Kime of Skegness for his help, and to Arthur Robbins for so trustingly lending me his one and only copy of Mr Kime's book *Skeggy!*; also to Howard Richmond for my original introduction to Cromer, to Jude Howells for sharing Southerndown, and to Henry Sutton of the Lyn and Exmoor Museum for a flood of fascinating talk, some of it publishable, some not.

I am very grateful to Albert Cate of West Wittering for his kind permission to quote from his poem 'Weep for Wittering'.

Terence Wilson at his word processor made short work of some of my manuscript, and Pat Bray added a second bar to her Distinguished Deciphering not-very-Cross by somehow managing all the rest.

32 BANFF & MACDUFF

Inverness

33 CRINAN   31 ANSTRUTHER

Glasgow Edinburgh   1 HOLY ISLAND

30 ROTHESAY

Newcastle-upon-Tyne   2 EASINGTON COLLIERY

Carlisle   3 ROBIN HOOD'S BAY
29 WHITEHAVEN   4 SCARBOROUGH
          5 FLAMBOROUGH
28 GRANGE-OVER-SANDS   York
27 BLACKPOOL   Leeds   Hull
26 NEW BRIGHTON
          Manchester

Liverpool   6 SKEGNESS
Nottingham   7 CROMER

25 BARMOUTH   Birmingham   Norwich   8 SOUTHWOLD
24 ABERYSTWYTH

23 TENBY   Swansea
22 OXWICH   Cardiff   Bristol
21 SOUTHERNDOWN   LONDON   9 SOUTHEND-ON-SEA
20 LYNTON & LYNMOUTH   10 RAMSGATE

19 APPLEDORE   Southampton
18 CLOVELLY   Exeter   11 BRIGHTON
17 PADSTOW   Plymouth   12 WEST WITTERING
          13 SWANAGE
          14 LYME REGIS
16 LIZARD TOWN   15 DARTMOUTH

Introduction

This book began to take shape in the shadow of another, *Coastal Walks in England and Wales*. I spent a long, hard summer walking around Britain's coasts and learning about what today's coastal communities are really like. I already knew about the decline of the great seaside resorts from the golden heyday of the Railway Age, and how the British public, in its living room in January, is far more likely these days to be leafing through the brochure for Marbella than the one for Margate. What I wasn't at all prepared for was the remarkable variety of seaside communities I encountered, dotted around the shores of England, Wales and Scotland. I found Whitehaven, out on an unfrequented curve of coastline in a remote corner of Cumbria, bringing its beautiful Georgian streets back to life after decades of decay; bright, traditional resorts like Blackpool and Southend-on-Sea, and elegant old watering-holes such as Scarborough and Tenby; Clovelly, too pretty for its own good; Easington Colliery in County Durham, where there's never a sniff of a tourist and life revolves entirely round the clifftop coal-mine.

After that rambling summer, I couldn't wait to get back to the coastal communities and begin to put the pieces of the jigsaw together. Chatting to the inhabitants of these towns and villages, one impression stood out above all others: the enormous changes washing over Britain's shoreline settlements. The big, bouncy resorts are no longer able to look to long-stay holidaymakers for their bread and butter. It costs as much (or more) to stay for a fortnight in Ramsgate or Brighton as it does to fly off to the guaranteed sun and cheap fun of the Costa del Sol. With conference centres, theme parks and Radio One Roadshows, the Queens of the Coast are fighting back, but at the expense of their long-established individual flavours. Blackpool is well aware that it's in danger of losing its grip on the loyalty of elderly Lancashire couples who still make their pilgrimage several times a year to the Tower and piers, and that's an unnerving prospect. Southend-on-Sea goes on pulling in crowds from the East End of London, at the same time as the Southend Society tries to point the public away from the rollicking towards the Regency. Cosy small resorts like Southwold and Cromer know that it would take a complete about-face in their appearance and atmosphere to put off their faithful middle-class devotees; but already developers are scratching at the door with money in their hands and marinas up their sleeves. The residents of tiny Southerndown on the Glamorgan Heritage Coast have to pay a price of eternal vigilance in the planning office for their protective buffer of unspoilt green fields.

Only in working communities like Whitehaven and Easington Colliery – never tourist attractions and unlikely ever to become holiday resorts – do people feel free of such pressures; but places like these are fully occupied struggling against economic depression and closure threats. A fishing town like Macduff has its own problems: ever more efficient and specialized catching equipment is pitted against steadily dwindling and ludicrously overfished stocks. There really does seem to be a possibility of virtually all living inhabitants of the sea being scooped out within the next two or three decades. Nothing is deemed useless, nothing is thrown back – unless it's too small, in which case it generally goes back dead. Most trawler skippers will admit privately that they are fully aware of how quickly they are squeezing the life out of the goose, even as it lays the golden eggs that bring them their smart cars, nice houses and foreign holidays. No one dares to be the first to let up, even though their sons may be left with no fishing at all.

Nobody I met around the coastline of Britain seemed confident about the future. The hallmark of today's coastal communities is a kind of grim, half-humorous resignation in the face of change. There's genuine anger in the small towns over what are seen as 'yuppies': second-home owners who leave the place half-empty half the year, inhabitants of exclusive estates newly built on precious stretches of shoreline, purchasers of fabulously costly penthouse apartments in the 'waterside villages' on the edge of marina developments. These so-called villages, ostentatious money mirrors that they are, form the real rallying point for local fury. What the townspeople see are four-storey, quarter-million-pound palaces, usually entirely at odds with their surroundings and the town's established architecture, rising on purpose-built piers and equipped with all the trappings of unreality overdrive: wine bars, pottery shops, expensive restaurants. They regard with envy the smart yachts and smooth cars. They see the occupants of the high-rises staying behind the security fences all weekend, talking to no one except their own kind, visiting no pubs, spending no money in local shops – being stand-offish, not joining in. They hear braying laughter and patronizing comments. Some of this is prejudice and caricature, overspill from the way so many local people feel about second-home owners doing up fishermen's cottages and driving the prices up beyond any fisherman's reach. The town councillors are usually well aware of such feelings – many even share them. But what choice do they have, bearing in mind the state of their crumbling Regency buildings, their rusty old pier or empty hotels, when the development company holds out a cheque to them for anything up to a hundred million pounds? The 'waterside villagers' take a lot of the flak that should be aimed at the development companies behind the marina schemes, waiting like sharks to snap up someone else's tasty bit of coastline.

Seaside residents don't care for the gifte shoppes replacing long-established butchers and grocers in village streets, or the advance of the bleeping, burping electronic-games arcades. What threatens their communities far more, though, is the steady trickle away of local youngsters who have no hope of finding a job or affording a house in the place where they were born and bred. The boys and girls themselves were quite realistic about their prospects when I questioned them. Most of them said they didn't want to stay, anyway. It was much too boring, nothing to do, dead as a dodo, hopeless in winter, too full of wrinklies. The wrinklies, on the other hand, seemed almost without exception happy with their havens, and their havens with them. 'Know what we call this place? God's Waiting Room' was a joke I heard in more than one place. Retired settlers are seen by locals as polite, pleasant, grateful to be in their chosen anchorages, great joiners-in and members of clubs and societies. They keep the place ticking over all year round, was the general impression.

Attitudes to the tourist are a bit more ambivalent. 'Bloody grockles', always leaving their litter behind them, tanked up and shouting their heads off at three o'clock in the morning, asking bloody stupid questions, look at those sticky fingermarks all over the lifeboat, grumble grumble. The prettier the place, the more tight-lipped the inhabitants. To conduct a proper, unguarded conversation often took several minutes of clambering carefully over the obstacle of being another grockle asking grockles' nosy questions. Yet everyone admits quite unsentimentally that without the revenue the tourists bring in, their home communities would curl up and die. And at least the grockles take themselves away at the end of the day.

Such prickly comments are probably to be heard anywhere where towns and villages feel themselves put upon by outside pressures. They do ring especially loudly around Britain's coastline, however, where no community can escape facing up to change. Seaside residents tend to look askance, if not with foreboding, at the future. But on the other side of the coin are the Devon boatbuilders who allowed me to wander, sniff, poke and pry to my heart's content; the Macduff trawler-hand, tired out after a week's rough trip, who cheerfully spent his first hour in harbour showing me all over his boat; the lighthouse-keeper's family at the Lizard who gave me tea, biscuits and a guided tour; the elderly miners in Easington Colliery with a whole afternoon's worth of stories about old times in the pit; the tough young Southend barman prepared to talk long and hard about the problems of the town he loves and doesn't want to see go any further down the slide. As I went round the coastline of Britain I began to see, below the uncertainty and insecurity, a framework of traditional livelihoods still in place, prized more and more by the communities that sustain them as touchstones of reality and continuity. To listen to an Anstruther trawler skipper moaning about the terrible state of today's fishing industry while his brand-new Volvo waits at the kerbside, or to Alan Hinks of Appledore discussing boat-building timbers with his daughter, is to hear the heart of the coastal community still beating strongly. The fishermen of Flamborough, out on their East Coast headland, have all but abandoned their beautiful cobles, proved to perfection over a thousand years, in favour of the guaranteed catches and wage-packets of big-ship fishing; but when a Force Ten is blowing no good for some unknown crew at four o'clock on a freezing January morning, they'll leap from a warm bed and race through rain or snow for the right to a place in the lifeboat. While such a spirit continues to burn in these places, the winds of change are unlikely to blow the whole house down.

I have arranged this book in the form of a journey, travelling clockwise around the shores of Britain, starting on the unfrequented Northumbrian coast and travelling down the East Coast and westward along the South Coast; then turning north around the toe of the West Country, up to Wales and the north-west before ending on the Scottish coast. The only deviation from this clockwise pattern is at the end, where I dodge across from Rothesay to Anstruther and Macduff before doubling back westward to finish at Crinan. It seems appropriate, having started with an island on a remote coast, to end here on the lonely edge of western Scotland where the mainland faces the Western Isles.

This isn't just a guidebook to the attractions of Britain's sunny seaside resorts: the Regency splendours, the piers, the golden sands, the picturesque views. Such towns already have helpful museums, libraries, town trail leaflets and brochures in abundance, doing that job superbly. My aim is to highlight the richness of history and strength of character, the enormous variety and vitality of the communities, large and small, around our coastline; also to point to some of the changes that threaten their identities and ways of life as change sweeps over all of them. And, of course, to take you on a journey of rediscovery to the too-long-neglected towns and villages of Britain-beside-the-Sea.

EAST COAST (North)

1. The Holy Island of Lindisfarne
2. Easington Colliery
3. Robin Hood's Bay
4. Scarborough
5. Flamborough

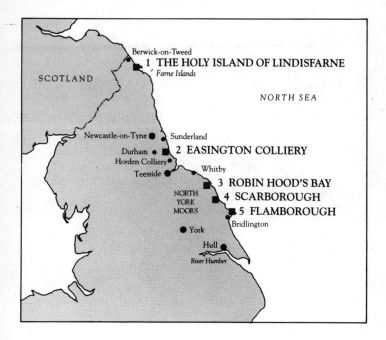

1. The Holy Island of Lindisfarne

I went down to the mainland to wait for the arrival of the cart . . . I made out, approaching across the sands, a slow black dot which I knew was the cart from Holy Island. I sat on the dunes and wished that the black dot might take two hours to reach me . . .

The moving dot, now near, resolved itself into a Ford car. The indomitable thing, rust red, its mudguards tied with string, splashed and slithered towards me; and at the wheel was a handsome young girl with blue eyes and a soft Scots voice.

So we splashed over the sands to Lindisfarne.

(H. V. Morton, *The Call of England*, 1928)

These days, when the tides are right, you can drive yourself from the Northumbrian mainland over the sands to Holy Island on the hard surface of a new causeway. But the islanders – and many of their long-time visitors – still feel a nostalgic affection for those battered old taxis, rusted almost to pieces, that used to ply the ancient route across Holy Island sands. A thousand years of pilgrim feet had trodden those watery, dangerous miles marked out by lines of poles. If the incoming tide caught you halfway across, you had to scramble up into the refuge towers that stood by the crossing, and watch your taxi, or horse and cart, slowly disappearing under the water. The crossing may have changed its position and surface, but the threat from the tides is no different: there's still a white-painted wooden refuge like a dilapidated signal-box waiting in the middle of the causeway to receive the unwary.

As soon as Holy Island comes into view from the narrow mainland road, the heart lifts. The island lies across the gap of sea in a long green hump, rising gradually from grassy sand dunes in the north to the cluster of houses in Holy Island village squatting together at the southern end under the fairy-tale castle atop its shoulder of rock. Until the Benedictine monks arrived shortly after the Norman Conquest the island was known as Lindisfarne, 'land of the Lindis stream'. It's a lovely name to hear and speak; but the whole essence of the place is caught in the title of 'Holy Island' which those unworldly refugees gave to their green retreat among the waves. Here the first spark of Christianity and its attendant art and culture had glowed in the Northumbria of the Dark Ages, and from here it

3

burned its way across mainland Britain. The monks who built the superb church and priory here at the beginning of the twelfth century were part of the most powerful and splendid organization on earth, yet one that looked with humility on the tiny island where that spark had been kept alive against all the odds.

The receding tide leaves pools of water and green hanks of weed that squelch under your tyres as you drive across the causeway, looking ahead to Holy Island over miles of sand and mud-flats dotted with wading birds returning to their newly uncovered feeding-grounds. The road under the shaggy green dunes brings you suddenly to the village, a handful of old houses and a few new ones spaced out around a network of lanes on the south-western tip of the island. There are two or three hotels and pubs, a market place with an ancient central cross from which the lanes radiate out, a post office, a few shops, a couple of gift emporia. Holy Island gets its fair share of tourists in the summer months – more than a quarter of a million of them in a busy year. The new causeway has done away with much of the isolation. But tourism here is a muted affair. The drink-driving laws have put an end to the parties of city drinkers who used to drive the sixty miles from Newcastle in order to maroon themselves and get wrecked in the pubs if not in the next tide. Such noise and litter problems as there are come mostly from the parties of schoolchildren being shepherded round the priory ruins and castle. Holy Island is treasured by Northumbrians as a retreat, albeit a secular one nowadays, where fishermen still trudge up the street in tall seaboots, with lobster pots slung across their backs.

Standing low on the flat tip of the island, the outlines of those great Benedictine buildings are well hidden as you walk among the houses of Holy Island village. From every other viewpoint around the island they stand out prominently, but from the village you have to walk down into Church Lane before they claim attention. The centrepiece of this ruined religious township is the enormous priory church – massive walls, Norman arches, thick columns, great windows full of sky instead of stone tracery – all of dull red sandstone. One slim arc of stone, the 'rainbow arch', leaps lightly across the transept crossing nearly fifty feet above the grassy stones of the nave floor. Otherwise it's all solid Norman dignity. To the south are the plainer stone remains of the monastery walls, spreading down the bank; to the west, St Mary's Church whose outside stonework has been smoothed and pitted by the rough weather of nearly a thousand years.

These are magnificent achievements by the medieval masons, testaments to powerful faith and powerful skill. But they don't hold the real heart of Lindisfarne. That lies a few yards further to the south-west, Holy Island's own holy island of Hobthrush, a knob of rock marked by a tall cross, cut off from Lindisfarne every high tide. From here there's a wide, peaceful view over the low mainland shoreline to the blue backs of the Cheviot Hills rising inland. The prospect hasn't changed much in the 1,300 years since the little chapel whose foundations you can still make out in the rock was built as a refuge by Cuthbert, prior of the pioneer community on Holy Island. Hermit, mystic, healer, miracle-worker: soon to be a bishop, later a saint; the further Cuthbert turned away, the more desperately the world tugged at his sleeve. The shepherd boy from the Scottish lowlands could stir crowds with his oratory and kings with his counsel, could save lives and cure sickness with a touch. But he wanted to serve his God in prayer and solitude. Soon he had abandoned Hobthrush for the greater remoteness of the Farne Islands, a few miles further away from the Lindisfarne community.

Cuthbert chose Inner Farne, a tiny slab of rock a couple of miles off the coast, as full of devils as a cheese is of maggots. In AD 676 devils were to be reckoned with in everyday life, something to be wrestled with in the flesh as well as the spirit. It took great physical courage, let alone moral strength, to set up on a bleak, spray-swept rock with the reputation of Inner Farne. Such mysteries are beyond our modern rationalism. All we can do is point to loneliness, fasting, exposure and hardship every day and night of the year, allied to rigorous soul-searching, as devil-like tormentors of the hermit of Inner Farne. Bede reports him as reflecting: 'How often have the demons tried to cast me headlong off yonder rock; how often have they hurled stones as if to kill me; with one fantastic temptation after another they have tried to disillusion me into retreating from this battlefield; but they have never yet succeeded in harming either soul or body, nor do they terrify me.'

The Farne Islands are easily seen from Holy Island: a group of flat platforms canted upwards out of the sea like a fleet of surfacing submarines. Grey seals breed out there, the only place along the east coast remote enough for them. Looking across to the islands on a stormy day, their low, bare outlines blurred by spray, it isn't hard to appreciate why the

Northumbrians peopled them with devils, or why Cuthbert felt drawn to them as a spiritual and corporal battleground.

He conquered the demons, inside and out, but in the end the world needed him too badly to allow him his solitude. Bede again: 'The King himself and that most holy bishop, Trumwine, with numerous devout and influential personages sailed across, knelt down and adjured him by the Lord, and wept and pleaded with him, until at last he came forth, very tearful, from his beloved hiding-place and was taken to the synod. Very reluctantly he was overwhelmed by their unanimous decision and compelled to submit to the yoke of the episcopacy.'

There's a fine picture in the chancel of St Mary's showing King Ecgfrith and Bishop Trumwine in their finery pleading with the sackcloth-clad hermit, his hand raised as if trying to ward off the world. On 20 March 687, two years after becoming Bishop of Lindisfarne, Cuthbert died, worn out by mainland travelling. At least he had been able to die where he so much wanted to live, back on Inner Farne. The Lindisfarne monks buried him on the south side of the altar in their little church on Holy Island. There was rest at last for his soul – but none for his body for the next three centuries. Dug up, re-buried, inspected at intervals to verify the assertion that it remained whole and uncorrupted; removed to the mainland with the monks as they fled the marauding Danes in 875; carried around the North of England with them as they searched for a permanent home: it wasn't until 995 that Cuthbert's remains finally came to rest at Durham. Even then the world couldn't leave him alone. He was exhumed again in 1104, re-inspected, re-buried, disturbed again at the Reformation, investigated once more in 1827. The passing of time couldn't abate that insatiable need to pin down and possess the hermit saint of Holy Island.

Cuthbert's body was not the only treasure rescued from the Danes by the Lindisfarne monks. They also took with them a book of rare beauty, adorned outside with jewels, gold and silver, and decorated inside with illuminated pages of exquisite artistry. The Lindisfarne Gospels bring together the work of the artist and craftsman in perfection. Colours, shapes, symbols, bird and animal forms intertwine on the pages that preface each Gospel. This wonderful book was created to the glory of God and his servant St Cuthbert a few years after Cuthbert's death, and still survives today in the care of the British Museum. Even after his death Cuthbert went on performing miracles, and it was just as well for the

Lindisfarne Gospels that he did. The book fell overboard from a boat during its journeyings, but the saint caused it to be washed ashore the following morning with not a water-stain on it. In St Mary's Church is a copy of the Lindisfarne Gospels, and on the altar steps lies a beautiful carpet which re-creates one of its pages. Over three-quarters of a million stitches went into that carpet, worked in by eighteen Holy Island women over two years.

Down below the priory buildings lies the island's harbour, well sheltered from all winds but south-easterlies. The six or seven boats that make up Holy Island's fishing fleet ride near the small jetty, dominated by the castle perched on its basalt crag. Holy Island's fleet numbered more than thirty boats at the turn of the century when the herring were still there to be caught. The upturned hulls of those old herring boats have been cut in half, their sawn ends filled in with doorways, their skyward-pointing keels tarred against the weather, and now they do duty around the harbour as fishermen's huts. In those days more than a thousand people were living on the island, fishing, farming, quarrying lime and burning it in the kilns that now lie empty on the far side of the castle. The inshore fishermen, relying on oar and sail, might go seven or eight miles out to sea and have to spend the best part of two days rowing back to harbour against wind and tide. Their long lines held sixty hooks apiece, and each hook had to be baited individually by the fisherman's wife. (If you were unmarried, you paid someone else's wife or daughter a shilling to do the baiting for you.) The fish were taken by horse and cart over the sands crossing to catch the fish train that stopped at Beal, the nearest mainland village, on its way to London, or to be bartered around the farms for eggs, vegetables and fruit. You saved what money you could against the stormy winters when the boats stayed in the harbour and the days were spent making and mending.

Some things are easier for today's Holy Island fishermen. Echo-sounding devices, radio and diesel engines, synthetic materials for gear and clothing have done away with some of the discomfort and danger. But it's harder to make a living when the catch has narrowed down to crab and lobster. Some of the old herring curing sheds still stand by the harbour, but these days the herring are hoovered up well out to sea by bigger ships than Holy Island can compete with. What income there is for the few remaining fishermen comes through the heaps of netted pots and the stacks of wooden trays in which the crabs and lobsters are piled for market.

'They work very hard for what they get, the fishermen here,' Jean told me as she picked crabs one by one out of a tray and transferred them to a plastic basket in the boot of her car. 'Sometimes in the summer the boats go out at four in the morning and aren't back till nine o'clock at night. One of these boxes will fetch £10 or £12, and a good catch might be seven or eight boxes. Not much for two men for eighteen hours' work. In the winter most of the fishermen go on the dole. Young lads who have a boat to go to when they leave school can stay on the island, but everyone else has to leave.'

Jean showed me one of the crabs, gripped across the shell in her fingers, its little pink mouth bubbling and hissing indignantly as it searched around with its one remaining pincer.

'Wicked little devils, these are. My daughter had her finger pinched and the bugger wouldn't let go. My husband had to fetch the poker and prise that claw open. Bruises? Ee, you should just have seen them.'

Some of the Holy Island boats are lucky enough to be awarded a salmon licence by the Ministry of Agriculture, Fisheries and Food. From April until August they can catch salmon offshore during the daytime. These crews keep themselves going a little more easily than the others, who have to rely entirely on crab and lobster, but no one does very well from fishing here.

The increasing number of young people who have to leave their home village to find work and housing is nothing new in the north-east, and nothing strange among small seaside communities. There are fewer than a hundred born-and-bred Holy Islanders living there at present. Most of the adults leave the island to work during the day. Children over the age of nine stay away from home all week, boarding at a hostel near their mainland school. The younger children attend the little school on Holy Island on days when the causeway is covered by the tide during school hours; but at other times their teacher takes them with her over to the mainland. The compromise works well enough, but it's another wedge between the islanders and their home.

No one wants to see the Holy Island traditions watered down any further, but everyone recognizes that times are changing for idiosyncratic communities like theirs. Second-home owners have been eroding the stock of old stone-built cottages where, only sixty years ago, families of twelve and thirteen were being brought up by the fishermen and quarry workers. These weekend islanders tend not to buy their food in the island shops or drink in the pubs, but to bring their own supplies with them. The Holy Island pubs were the focus of entertainment when the fishermen used to come in the evenings with a couple of bob and eke them out over halves of beer and tots of rum. Sunday night was sing-song night, and each member of the company was expected to entertain with a song or tall story. These days the pubs and hotels are run mostly by incomers, as are the shops. A dozen people work at The Lindisfarne Liqueur Company's mead distillery by the village car park, but this most traditional of industries – dating back to the days of the monks – employs only one island girl. The mead, a sweetly fiery concoction of honey, spirits and pure well-water, is very popular – coachloads of tourists come to taste free and buy reasonably cheap. Since 1961 when mead-making was revived on Holy Island, production has steadily gone up to several thousand gallons a year, most of it drunk at mock-medieval banquets around the country. Just as you are duty-bound not to leave Lizard Town in Cornwall without a serpentine ornament, or Blackpool without a stick of rock, so you mustn't cross the causeway from Holy Island without a bottle of mead, or packet of mead fudge, or jar of mead honey, in your car. It's another strand in the tapestry of tourism, discreet but essential, that keeps the place alive.

There's a fine story about the capture of Lindisfarne Castle in 1715 by one Launcelot Errington, a ship's captain and ardent supporter of the Old Pretender. While being shaved one morning by the Master Gunner of the castle garrison, Errington became aware that most of the defenders had gone ashore to the mainland. He slipped away, returned with his nephew Mark and relieved the Master Gunner of the castle with the economical phrase: 'Damn you! The castle is ours.' By next day the intrepid twosome found themselves in Berwick Gaol, from which they soon tunnelled their way to freedom.

The castle draws visitors to the island by the car-full and school party-load. There can't be many forts with such a striking, eye-catching position. Its sheer walls seem to grow out of the top of Beblowe Crag, an outcropping shoulder of the Whin Sill that runs across northern England, forming such dramatic features as High Force in Teesdale and the great inland cliff under Hadrian's Wall. Begun in 1549 as a border fort against the Scots, Lindisfarne Castle still retains a formidable air along with its prettiness. From the top there's a wonderful view south over the equally striking and much larger Bamburgh Castle on its headland, north to Berwick's houses and harbour, inland to the distant Cheviots and seaward over the rock slabs of Cuthbert's Farne Islands.

It's the other end of Holy Island, however, away from the priory, castle and hotels, which draws visitors who are looking for the feeling of peace and remoteness that an island retreat should give. Here on the long arm of sand dunes, a National Trust Reserve, there are uninterrupted sea views to the north. The sands below the dunes are the feeding grounds of tens of thousands of curlews, dunlin, turnstones, godwits and oystercatchers. During especially cold winters, upwards of 30,000 wigeon take refuge among them. Light-bellied brent geese spend the winter here, too, the only place in Britain where they do. Cowslips grow under the shelter of the dunes; and in the open bowls of the old limestone quarries, now powdered over with sand drifts, it's impossible to walk in spring and summer without crushing orchids beneath your feet. Eleven species of orchid have been recorded here. Their short, conical heads, pink, purple, pale mauve and deep red, cover the sand and rough grass so thickly that you literally can't step between them. Sometimes it can be hard to plot a course between the upraised bottoms of botany students, too.

The arm of dunes runs landwards towards The Snook, a snub-nosed sand headland where a gibbet used to swing in Jacobean times. In those days The Snook formed a vital part of the island's economy as a rabbit warren. A tower near Snook House – it must be one of the remotest houses in the country – bears witness to an attempt to mine coal here. But only the squawking of sea birds and an occasional exclamation of triumph from an orchid-spotting student break the peaceful silence of these dunes today. It's a place to stand, sniff the wind and absorb the view. From the top of the dunes you get a good impression of the emptiness and remoteness that still characterize the Northumbrian coastline as they did in Cuthbert's day: long yellow beaches, rocky headlands and coves, stark low islands and the blue hills and grey sea horizon bounding everything. If the hermit spirit of Cuthbert lives anywhere, it's here.

2. Easington Colliery

This country all about is full of this Coale the sulpher of it taints the aire and it smells strongly to strangers . . .

(Celia Fiennes, 1698)

A strange procession is coming up the cliff-path from Easington shore. In the lead are two elderly men, their faces, hands and trouser legs plastered with black filth, pushing hard at bicycles. Behind them comes a woman, wheezing with the effort of shoving a battered old pram up the sodden path; behind her, a boy and a girl pulling a wheeled trolley after them. Bikes, pram and trolley are loaded down with plastic bags and buckets full of coal. Below the little straining group lies the black beach from which they have been salvaging coal for the past hour. Sluggish brown waves wash the stuff ashore, breaking on the beach in a line of grimy grey foam. Standing out on tall legs above the water, a run of conveyor housing dribbles a continuous shower of colliery waste and small coal down into the sea.

Coal-picking is one way to keep the wolf from the door in Easington Colliery. You can either use it on your own fire at home, or – if the Social Security are looking the other way – you can sell it onwards for a few pounds. There's no shortage of beach coal at Easington Colliery, for the seams run out ten miles or more under the North Sea; and no stigma attached to supplementing your income in this way, either. It makes a useful small economy, and it passes the time for retired pitmen and jobless lads.

This East Durham coastal landscape is one of sharp contrasts. The red-and-yellow cliffs around the bays are topped with cornfields and cattle meadows and cut with wooded valleys or denes that run down to the sea. But under them lie thick seams of coal, with all that that implies for the landscape.

In the cornfields above Easington beach stand the enormous pit-head buildings, conveyor housings and winding wheels of the coal-mine around whose yard cluster the short terraced streets of its village. When Easington Colliery was opened in 1910 it created an instant community drawn from pit villages all over County Durham. The Easington Coal Company covered the green fields on the cliffs with sloping streets of brick houses standing back to back across narrow roadways. The inhabitants of the little farming village of Easington, above and inland of the colliery, were less than delighted to see their fields ripped up, and not entirely happy to welcome several thousand colliers. A fine but definite line is still drawn these days between the two places: wary tolerance is the mutual feeling. The pit village set-up, where no family could avoid sharing its squabbles, noise, pleasures and troubles with the neighbours, gave rise to a tightly knit community fiercely protective of its members. The men – anyone over the age of fourteen – worked their ten-hour shifts in the pit, driving out into the seams under the sea and coming home at the end of their stint filthy and exhausted. According to one locally produced booklet of verbatim interviews:

> 'They never got bathed at the pit, you know, they came home all black. And you had to have a bath and put it in front of the fire there for him to get washed in the tub . . . They had to take their pit clothes off and go outside and dadd them against the wall, you know. And you had to take their shoes and scrape all the dirt and thick off. They were tired and weary, poor things; and, mind, they reckon it was different work to what it is now, they had to work scandalous hours, poor things.'

In those pre-war days the hewers or coal cutters were still paid on the traditional system according to how much coal they could cut. If you happened to be assigned to a face where the coal was hard and had to be hacked out inch by inch, or where there was a lot of loose rock which would be disallowed in your quota, you could be a strong and competent worker and still go short on your weekly wage. Conditions in the Easington pit were hard, too. Some seams were sweltering hot, others chilly. The atmosphere was always damp: the limestone that overlays the coal to a depth of 500 feet is sodden with water, and the sides and roofs of the workings trickled and ran. Lungs pumping hard to drive bodies at full stretch were clogged by the dank atmosphere 1,500 feet below the sea; and they gradually filled, year by year, with the powdery coal-dust hanging in the air.

Things have changed for the better in many ways for the men who work in Easington pit today. Powerful booster fans keep fresh air circulating through the workings, and the levels of dust are carefully monitored. If there's too much, the miners stop work. The deadly methane gas that lies in almost every mine is piped off and burned to heat the water for the pit-head baths into which the men can step as soon as their shift is over. The coal is cut these days by machine instead of by a muscle-powered pick, ensuring a predictable output and a steady wage; face-masks are available to cut down the intake of dust. But the fundamental nature of pit work stays the same. It's still a damp, dusty, demanding job. And the coal faces are now more than six miles out to sea. There's always the thought, pushed far to the back of every miner's mind, that they are working far from land and rescue.

To walk around the streets of Easington Colliery is to take on board an object lesson in the power of a continuing tradition. Close to a thousand village men work in the colliery, and they still live in the same houses that their grandfathers first occupied. The dark brick terraces run up the slope of the ground, each slate roof stepped higher than the last. There's a rigid perspective in the converging lines of roofs, chimney stacks, window sills and outside lavatories or 'netties' in the back yards. Telegraph poles and wires loom large in these foreshortened views. Windows and walls are filmed with fine coal-dust. Take away the twenty-year-old cars and this could be Easington Colliery before the First World War. The children skip around in the alleyways, and the pitmen's wives trudge up and down between the small shops in the steep main street of the village. The men walk to and from the pit in their orange working suits and donkey-jackets, coal smears clinging to their boots and knees. The retired pitmen labour slowly along the streets, taking their dogs for a walk or going up to the Black Diamond pub or the Welfare Club for a couple of pints, a game of cards and a 'bit crack' with their cronies. The generations are closely in touch with one another here, men, women and children stopping to pass the time of day with the old men. If you are over fifty in Easington Colliery, the chances are that heart, lungs and skin will all be suffering in one way or another from those underground years of dust, heat and damp. Many of the pensioned-off miners can show tanned, plump faces. These are not the results of a blow-out on a Spanish beach – cancer and heart treatment, more likely. Only a few years ago a young miner in Easington Colliery could look at his father and see exactly how he was fated to end his days. The likelihood of an old age of disease and decay is receding year by year as conditions improve, but the retired miners of the village still carry their infirmities around with them as an everyday reminder of the way things used to be.

Back in the 1920s, when these men were in their prime, the village sat in the heart of some of the most beautiful coastline in the North East. There were more pits open then, each one with its spoil heaps and tight bunch of terraces; but the beaches below were still clean enough to be the destinations of a day out for the miners and their families. The beach below Horden Colliery, a couple of miles down the coast, was a wide stretch of golden sand where people went to picnic and listen to waltzes from the bandstand. Easington beach, now a black and sludgy wasteland, had a natural rock pool known as the Twelve Foot where village lads stripped off and went diving; though things weren't squeaky clean even then.

'We would dive under all the shit and sewage that was floating on the top, and come up on the rocks the other side,' remembered a Black Diamond regular. 'Then we'd get some winkles off the rocks and boil them up in an old tin can – they frothed up and bobbed all around – and then eat them in our fingers. You wouldn't want to eat anything off the shore now, with all the tipping and the pollution. Another place we went was Hawthorn Dene, just under the railway line there. You could have a run-about on the beach there and then have a picnic in the woods.'

A footpath runs from below the colliery along the clifftops to Hawthorn Dene, still a favourite place to spend a sunny afternoon. The great arches of the railway viaduct stride over the dene, a narrow valley running inland, full of birds, trees and plants. A black-and-red beach lies at its mouth, surrounded by cliffs whose outermost feet have been worn by the waves into rocky arches. It's a green and quiet spot – together with the much more spectacular Castle Eden Dene below Horden Colliery, the lungs of the district. Not for much longer, though, if local builders continue their advance into the top of the dene and British Coal carries on polluting the bottom end. A small amount of beach coal comes Easington Colliery's way through this cavalier dumping of waste a few yards out to sea; but all the villagers agree with local conservationists that there's no excuse at all for continuing the practice. The tides do not carry the spoil out to sea; they simply deposit it with the following wave back on Easington Colliery's doorstep. It looks horrible, it kills the fish, it poisons the winkles and cockles, it smears the landscape. But it's quick, and it's cheap.

The Easington coal is won these days far beyond the polluted fringe of the sea. Out there under the water it's not just the possibility of a sea inundation that threatens the lives of the miners; a spark can set off the methane gas in the workings and cause a disastrous explosion. No one knows for sure exactly what touched off the gas on 29 May 1951; but eighty-one men were killed that day, and two rescue workers died while trying to reach them. Most of the victims were buried in a mass grave in Easington Colliery cemetery, and each man had a tree planted in his memory in the park behind the Welfare Institute half-way up the village. Easington Colliery, like all mining communities that suffer such wounds, somehow absorbed the tragedy. A fund was set up and swelled by donations from all over Britain and overseas. The village rallied round the bereaved families. Life carried on.

Everyone knows, of course, that sooner or later the coal will run out. That's the reality that lies behind the tradition in every colliery village. Easington Colliery people only have to look along the cliffs to the neighbouring pits at Blackhall and Horden (both closed in the 1980s) to know their ultimate fate. Easington pit produces over a million tons of coal a year at present, a healthy state of affairs, and employs 2,000 men; but more than half of them come each day to the colliery from villages to the west whose own pits have closed. There's no resentment between natives and foreigners – it's just a fact of twentieth-century mining life.

The two sets of men have nicknames for each other: 'woolly-backs' for the up-country pitmen and 'cod-heads' for the miners who live on the coast. But under the banter lies the knowledge that the only pits still working in County Durham are the few that can get at the coal under the sea, and that there are a dwindling number of jobs to go round. British Coal is reluctant to take on Easington Colliery youngsters; it takes nearly three months to train a school-leaver, compared with the forty days an experienced man needs to work himself in at a new pit. With fewer village men working in the mine, Easington Colliery people are becoming reluctant to live in the old tied colliery houses near the pit, cramped, damp and shabby as they are. Corbett Street, Cook Street, Chandler Street, Camp Street – the windows and doors are filling with boards and the pavements with weeds. Unemployment among Easington Colliery's teenagers, unknown a few years ago, is beginning to be a problem. All over the North East these days there are young men kicking their heels on street corners; but Easington Colliery, with its pit and its pit tradition, was always an island of security. Now the foundations of this solid father-to-son work-succession are starting to quiver. That numbing, deadening depression that has settled over so many northern industrial towns has not yet got its hooks into Easington Colliery, but the warning signs – empty houses, shuttered shops and young people hanging around – are slowly creeping in.

It was this background that made the 1984 miners' strike such a traumatic experience for the people of Easington Colliery. More than any other event in the life of the community – more than the disaster of 1951, or the General Strike of 1926 – the year of 1984 shook the village to its roots. The hardships of the miner's way of life and the uneasiness of his relationship with the colliery owner had from the outset formed a community very much dependent on self-help. The Union, the Welfare Club, the various miners' societies were supports created by the pitmen for the pitmen. Through disputes with their bosses, through sickness and poverty, the miners looked for their salvation not outwards but inwards. The issues were essentially local issues, to be resolved locally. In 1984 things were different. The newspapers, radio and television arrived in Easington Colliery to record every incident, word and deed, at the pit-head and on the doorstep, for the whole country to judge. This time it was not just a pay claim at the heart of the dispute, but the accelerating closure of uneconomic pits. Easington pit could be vulnerable. The newly appointed chairman of the National Coal Board, Ian MacGregor, was the target for the miners' resentment.

Their fears were summed up by the leader of Easington District Council, John Cummings: 'He wants to take away our independence and our cultural heritage, our village life and our club life. All this is our heritage, and I'm not prepared to let him take my heritage away from me.' Negotiation and compromise were out from the start of the strike. It was 'them and us' as never before.

When the Easington Colliery miners agreed to strike in March 1984 they were determined to stay out as long as possible. In spite of the fact that winter was nearly over and stocks of coal were high, everyone was convinced that they had taken the right decision. But as the months went by, the miners began to realize that this Government was not going to give way. The event that turned the dogged, even-tempered cold war into a real battle was the arrival in the village of the police in numbers no one had dreamed of. In retrospect, given the state of mind of both sides in the dispute, it was inevitable; but in Easington Colliery the blame for the invasion is laid squarely at the feet of one man, a miner who had come to Easington pit from another village with a reputation for being a difficult loner. His name is well-known and reviled in Easington Colliery – you can still see it sprayed up in angry letters on walls all round the village, fading with time, usually accompanied by a threat or curse. The pamphlets produced by the strikers that year carry it prominently. This man was the first to go back to work – driven there, according to some accounts, by desperate poverty, or by his own weakness of purpose, according to others. Hundreds of police were drafted in, most of them from other counties, to protect him on his terrible journey to the pit – a journey vividly described to me by a council secretary who saw it all:

> I could hear the chanting – awful, it was. The men found out that he'd been sneaked in round the back. They were just like ants running towards a piece of bread, surging round there to get at him. His wife was spat at when she went to the shops. His windows were put in. Every morning the glaziers were sent round to his house by the NCB, and every evening the windows went in. He moved – he had to. People won't speak to him where he lives even now.

In Easington District Council offices there is a set of photographs taken during the strike. One shows the blackleg miner shambling to work, head down and bait bag over his shoulder, surrounded by tall policemen, their solid boots tramping along the village streets. Others record the street disturbances that went on, striking miners locked in the grip of riot-helmeted policemen, women shouting and crying as their men are dragged away with shirts flapping from trousers and hair tangled, children open-mouthed on the tops of walls. There are no pictures to show the bricks and bottles flying, the bleeding policemen or the places of origin of some of the pickets. Those images, transmitted daily by the news media, are not ones that Easington Colliery wants to remember. People will show you the posters, the 'Coal Not Dole' badges, the photographs of miners' wives serving out food to the moneyless men and their children. The women of Easington Colliery grew ten feet tall in 1984; and they gave the old 'men in the pit, women in the kitchen' tradition a shaking from which it hasn't yet recovered. But the sense of pride and togetherness solidified by the strike is mixed with a deep feeling of shock at some of the emotions that surfaced and the actions they led to. The mining life doesn't make for a soft community. There have always been pay-night scraps and hard words given and taken. Those old pitmen playing cards in the club enjoyed bare-knuckle fights on Easington beach in their younger days. But it's a condition of such a way of life that you don't overstep the accepted bounds in anger, and that at the end of it you make up and start again. The passion and violence of 1984 have been relegated in most Easington Colliery people's minds to the drawer labelled 'Do not open' – but such emotions, once unleashed, leave their mark. In the end, the men achieved what the village still regards as a victory: the Union seen by the whole country to be leading its members honourably back to work under Lodge banners rather than being forced to agree to the return of beaten and demoralized men. Wages were improved. But the shadows of Blackhall and Horden Collieries loom as large over Easington Colliery as they did before the strike, and lads leaving school still can't get work in the pit.

There's no doubt that the events of 1984 gave Easington Colliery a tremendous shot in the arm. The community's pride in its resourcefulness, its resilience and 'stickability' is sky high. The scars are still there: real bitterness against the police, a loss of faith in the justice of the courts, an unyielding anger against those who went back to work during the strike. It's the confidence born at that time, however, that keeps the village's collective head above water as it faces up to the limited future that the pit can expect. The tradition, the pride, the bonds of the coal-mining life are still rock solid, gathered around the pit. As long as that continues, so can the village. People know that it can't go on for ever, but that doesn't stop them fighting for it and for their community: 'Nobody wants their sons to go down the pit, my dad didn't want my two brothers to go down. But that pit is the centre, the pulse of Easington Colliery. Without that pit we have nothing. We must keep that colliery alive because I want this place to be alive, with a living pulse, not to be something that is just floating through time, like suspended in space.'

3. Robin Hood's Bay

Crammed into a nook of the cliffs south of Whitby on the north Yorkshire coast, Robin Hood's Bay doesn't reveal its secrets all at once. The view from the car park is charming enough, looking out round the bay's circle of cliffs over red-pantiled roofs that stand at every conceivable angle to one another. It's only when you begin to walk down the bank, however, that you appreciate why your car has to be left at the top, and why there are red faces and labouring lungs coming in the opposite direction.

The bank drops three feet in every ten, a slope steep enough to have you leaning well back on your heels even on the stone steps that flank the roadway. The gradient eases as you cross Kings Beck at Bridge End and continue down New Road towards the harbour, but gravity goes on tugging at your upper half until the bottom of the hill. Every few yards of the narrow roadway between tall buildings opens up a fresh view of wall-angles, house corners, chimney-pots and red roofs, all squeezed together and bending with the valley left and right as they fall towards the sea. And if the self-respecting writer has to keep his hand clamped tight over his quiver of clichés here, how much more they clamour to be used among the roadways that run east and west from the main street of the village. They just are quaint and picturesque, there's no getting away from it. Cobbled or flagged, twisting and turning, plunging from one level to another by worn stone stairways, wriggling between tiny gardens and hanging flower baskets, climbing and falling, framing views of sea and cliff under crooked archways, some so constricted that you have to walk in single file, graced with such evocative names as Fisherhead, Sunny Place and Bakehouse Steps – you have to be prepared for an aching camera finger here.

At the bottom of the village – known locally as Bay Town – everything suddenly spreads out wide, opening from The Dock, where the fishing cobles are drawn up in front of the shops, on to the broad curve of the beach bending away under the cliffs. Three miles to the south, the blunt nose of the 600-foot South Cheek cliff closes the view, rising to the dramatic block of the Raven Hall Hotel sitting in high and mighty isolation on the land horizon. If one of the frequent sea mists or 'frets' has come creeping inland, however, the hotel is likely to be hidden within a grey band of vapour whose lower edge is sliced off with razor sharpness half-way up the cliffs.

Standing up there on the southern heights and looking down into Robin

Hood's Bay, there's a strong impression that one good push would have all those toppling houses on the beach. The village seems to hold together as one solid lump, rammed into its cleft and clinging on grimly there. Down the centuries it has maintained this balancing act against the efforts of the sea to dislodge it. The high cliffs that form the boundaries of Robin Hood's Bay are of hard enough rock, though even that is ground down eventually by the unremitting action of the waves. The scours or eroded ribs of rock on the beach that curve obliquely against the curve of the existing cliffs are remnants of ancient cliffs, and testament to the long-term effectiveness of the sea as a demolition agent. These rocks were bent into undulations by volcanic pressure and the resulting hollows filled with a soft, unstable mixture of clay, sand and peat. Underground springs course through this doughy blanket; after rain you can see them trickling out of the stuff on to the beach between the village and South Cheek. It's good land for growing crops, but fatal for building on. There are places in the bay where erosion has bitten more than twenty yards inland since Edwardian days. During the last two centuries, 200 houses in Bay Town have fallen from their perches. King Street, which now climbs northwards past the village post office to peter out on the cliff edge, was part of the main road from Whitby to Scarborough until a great chunk of it, along with twenty-two houses, collapsed into the sea in 1780. The Bay Hotel on The Dock was built as a replacement for an inn which foundered in a storm in 1843. The Quarterdeck promenade, constructed in 1975 as a retaining wall under the cliffs where King Street used to run, is already showing signs of erosion damage. One day the sea will be through it and ready to take a bigger helping from the houses stacked so temptingly above.

In the days before the waves claimed the old King Street, outsiders had to be pretty determined to get to Robin Hood's Bay. The journey involved a bumpy ride over rough lanes, then a steep descent into the village, followed by a stretch along the beach – impassable at high tide – and a climb up the cliff track at Stoupe Brow that necessitated getting out of the carriage to lighten the load for the horses. Not that many people wanted to visit Bay Town; a self-contained, insular little fishing community, it had few attractions (according to a seventeenth-century guidebook) apart from its 'grotesque appearance, the houses being strangely scattered over the face of a steep cliff and some of them hanging in an awful manner on the projecting ledges of the precipice'. The steepness of the surrounding cliffs, the poor state of the roads and the isolation of this whole North Yorkshire coast combined to keep visitors away, as they had done since the Vikings settled here. The Bay Town men and their wives were entirely wedded to the sea and to fishing. The village, overlooked by the outside world, rode on the silver backs of the herring to a peak of prosperity in the early nineteenth century, when it was the most important fishing community for nearly a hundred miles.

In recent years the last Bay Town native to carry the Norse surname 'Storm' has left the village, but the Storms were the lynch-pins of Robin Hood's Bay for possibly as long as a thousand years. In the cramped, crammed little museum in the old reading rooms at the bottom of Fisherhead they dominate the display. Here are the knitting patterns of their ganseys, fishermen's jerseys whose distinctive family stitchings helped to identify the bodies washed ashore after disasters out at sea – on Storm ganseys a criss-cross pattern represented a fishing net, a plaited one the ropes of their boats. Photographs of Oliver, Reuben, Will and Tom Storm round the lifeboat that they coxed and crewed, and of their children carrying baskets of fish through the lanes, show the same characteristic long, dark, serious family face. There was no love lost between the Storms and the Dukes, incomers from Flamborough, who also fished and crewed the lifeboat. In winter, when the steep lanes to the village were glassy sheets of ice and no one could get away even if they wanted to, such rivalry could make life difficult for everyone. Notwithstanding the dilution of that tight, time-hallowed village spirit, in some ways it was a blessing when the Whitby to Scarborough railway line reached the top of the bank in 1885 and brought the wide world with it. At that time the herring were being cornered by bigger boats further out to sea than the Bay Town fishermen could compete with, and the tourism engendered by the railway gave the isolated village a new lease of life. Visitors came in to present the fishermen and their wives with an alternative source of income. New houses were built near the station, on level ground and in enough space to include a garden. Bay Town families began to move up the hill, putting their damp, dark, poky old cottages on the market. Artists, writers and lovers of the picturesque moved in. They had the money to improve the drains, the lighting and water supplies. The unevenness of the cobbled lanes was a delight to them, the steepness of the climb up the bank a thrill. As for the Bay Town men and women – the fishing was in decline, and the tourist trade could employ only so many of them. The new influences were undercutting the closed community and its traditional way of life every bit as irresistibly as the sea was nibbling away at the bay cliffs. Young folk began to move away, and their parents followed them. By the outbreak of the First World War, there were only two families, the Storms and the Dukes, still fishing out of Robin Hood's Bay where a hundred years before there had been nearly fifty boats and 130 fishermen.

Crab pots and pairs of long seaboots still hang up to dry on nails outside the doors of Bay Town fishermen's houses; and in The Dock the wooden cobles lie on the tarmac between fishing trips, high-prowed and wide-bellied like the Viking boats which were their original pattern. The lifeboat station was closed in 1931, taking with it a cornerstone of the old village tradition, but the fishing still goes on, albeit mostly for the luxury crab and lobster trade that most small fishing communities like Bay Town rely on these days. Many of the fishermen are incomers, and most work their boats part-time – one man is a driller on a North Sea oil-rig, another does odd jobs around the village, and a third works as a fitter up at the Early Warning Station at Fylingdales. All agree that fishing is still a drug-like habit that gets into the blood. They don't resent the visitors: 'We must have them, otherwise the village would die. Mind, there's times they leave their bloody brains behind, getting in the way of our tractors and letting their kids scramble all over the gear. I catch the crab and lobsters, my wife dresses them and the visitors buy 'em, so I'm easy.'

Bob has been a fisherman all his life, moving here from Grimsby to buy a coble and divide his time between boat and oil-rig. 'You wouldn't do this work unless you were born to it. In winter we fish for cod with long lines, four if we're single-handed and six if we've some help. There's 220 hooks to each line. The wife has to bait each one of them hooks with mussels. That's when the hard work starts, when you get home. We've only a narrow landing here and the sea breaks across it, makes it hard to get in and out if there's a north-west wind.

'It's hard work, but it's something you wouldn't do without. There's been times when I could've cut the bloody line and let the fish go just for the pleasure of catching it again. Then of course there's times I've gone out with six lines and come back with six fish and more than a thousand hooks to bait. This isn't a living – it's a bloody way of life.'

The second-home owners who snapped up the dilapidated cottages in the village lanes are not really resented, either. There's a feeling among the elderly folk that the responsibility for the disappearance of the native Bay Town community spirit can be laid at the door of the incomers; but in general they're seen as maintaining the old streets that would otherwise have decayed to extinction, as well as bringing a spark of life and colour to what can be a very claustrophobic place, especially during the winter. It's the short-stay, long-profit shopkeepers, here as elsewhere, who raise the hackles of the locals. There aren't as many nice little village shops as there used to be, and those that there are have grown too showy. The owners tend to move in, stay a couple of years and then take their money away with them. The shop-fronts change from year to year, giving the place an unsettled look. The fly-by-night shopkeepers don't join in with village life. Some are foreigners from down south. These are the bones of contention you hear being chewed over in the pubs and the old-established shops. As far as the day-visitors are concerned, it's only the crisp-papers left by the children that bother the village people. These casual tourists arrive, spend their money, have a chat and go away. Many are on their way through, walking the long-distance Cleveland Way. Others are rambling or driving around the superb North Yorkshire moors that lie in long purple swells behind Robin Hood's Bay, and have only come for a scamper on the beach, a cup of tea and a quick look around. The Bay Town folk know which side their bread is buttered, and most of the butter comes in this easily digested form.

'The museum? Oh, it's just around that corner, up the steps and turn left, and it's a big stony house on your right.'

I spent a good half-hour looking for the Bay Town museum, and came across it only by accident. Squeezed into that little room, the old Robin Hood's Bay lives on. Here are the unsmiling, dark-faced Storm men in cork lifejackets; their wives in aprons collecting 'flithers' (limpets) on the scours for bait, knitting and chatting round the cottage doors. There's a photograph of William Turnbull, the town crier, 'Will the Bellman' who could neither read nor write and gave local wags a lot of malicious fun. His employer would write out a note for him to learn, and Will would have to ask someone more literate to tell him what it said – so the message he cried often bore no relation to the original. There are accounts of the wild day early in 1881 when the Whitby lifeboat had to be dragged overland for six miles through snowdrifts, assisted by teams of horses from local farms, to rescue the crew of the brig *Visitor*, wrecked in the bay. Here is Joseph Parnaby, the first Robin Hood's Bay station master, who would write out a weather forecast, embellished with wise sayings, on a blackboard for the edification of railway travellers. The theme is of a community held in upon itself with very tightly drawn strings.

In the large Congregational Chapel just below the museum hangs a painting by J. Ulric Walmsley, father of the novelist Leo Walmsley who based several of his books – notably *Three Fevers* – on Robin Hood's Bay. Ulric Walmsley didn't make much money out of his pictures, though at the age of ninety he finally got one into the Royal Academy. The painting in the chapel shows the bay as it was a few years after the railway arrived and at a time when the village celebrated in the museum exhibition was starting to feel the influence of the outside world. The red-tiled roofs in the picture pile down their green cleft as they do today. The oyster-like, self-absorbed little community may have been diluted beyond recognition since Ulric Walmsley's day – but, unpalatable though some of the Bay Town old folk may find it, the truth is that it's the incomers with their money and taste for the past stripped of its discomforts who have kept that beautiful scene unchanged.

4. Scarborough

'Scarborough is a very pretty Sea-port town built on the side of a high hill,' wrote Celia Fiennes, that inquisitive and honest traveller, arriving on the North Yorkshire coast in 1697. 'On the sand by the Sea shore is the Spaw Well which people frequent . . . there they drink, its something from an Iron or Steele minerall [of] a brackish and saltness which makes it purge pretty much.'

That was about seventy years after the mineral spring across the beach had been discovered, and three years before the first spa buildings were put up to guard the vital source. Twenty years later, Daniel Defoe admitted: '. . . it is hard to describe the taste of the waters; they are apparently ting'd with a collection of mineral salts, as of vitriol, allom, iron, and perhaps sulphur.' Two centuries after Defoe's visit, H. V. Morton (a kind of romantic Celia Fiennes, ever ready to have a go at anything) tasted 'a mild and pleasant drink, but slightly earthy, as if someone had drowned a mushroom in it'.

Personally, I found Celia's description nearest the mark. Scarborough's mineral spring is a rather sad affair these days, dribbling out of an alcove in the beach wall from the remnants of a leaden hood to smear the stonework bright orange as it oozes away down the steps on to the sand. The spring has been declared unfit for human consumption but, with the shade of H. V. Morton at my shoulder, I brought a cupped handful to my lips and poked the end of my tongue in. Not recommended. The water was so strongly flavoured with rusty iron that it instantly dried the mouth like blotting paper and had me gagging and spitting. It tasted like a dredger's bucket. I spent that night being purged pretty much.

On the map, Scarborough has the look of a face – a boozer's face, veined red with roads and with a bulbous nose sticking out into the sea. It's an appropriate image. As Lancashire mill-town workers go to Blackpool, so people from the industrial towns of Yorkshire come to Scarborough for a seaside holiday. Groups of men settle down for a week's drinking in the pubs and clubs in the central part of the town, and things can get pretty lively there on a Friday or Saturday night. But Scarborough's boast is that it has something for everyone. As well as the bands of likely lads, families come for a traditional bucket-and-spade holiday on the sands. People use the town as a base for walking the nearby North York Moors, or for fishing trips on hired boats out into the North Sea. Elderly couples come for the floral gardens that stretch under the cliffs, and for the shows. Literary pilgrims visit the grave of Anne Brontë in St Mary's churchyard up on the hill, and wander round the house and terraced gardens of Woodend where the Sitwells spent their childhood. The Scarborough Cricket Festival in September brings in fans from all over England. Theatre buffs arrange their holidays so as to be in town when Scarborough's own Alan Ayckbourn has a new play premiered at the Theatre in the Round. There are splendid, well-maintained Regency and Victorian crescents and terraces, hotels and houses lining the cliffs of both the town's long, sandy bays. The fishing is doing better than in most East Coast places. The air of despondency and resignation that has settled over so many seaside resorts doesn't get a look-in here. Scarborough is proud of its popularity and confident about the future. It's an attractive atmosphere to be in.

The castle ruins on the nose-like headland are a constant feature of Scarborough views. Some 300 feet above the sea the long, jagged wall of the barbican runs back to the 85-foot-high keep, built in the middle of the twelfth century and regularly battered through the years by Scots, turbulent barons, Roundheads and a couple of First World War German cruisers. The steep old fishing town sprawls down from the castle in a mass of red roofs and tight, twisting alleyways, to reach the harbour sheltering under the south flank of the headland. Here a strip of bingo halls and slot-machine arcades runs behind the beach to end under the Grand Hotel. This 'swaggering building', put up in 1867, trumpeted ostentation all over the bay by cramming as many windows as possible into its frontage and sprouting a giant samovar at each corner of the roof. 'Look at me! I'm rich!' bawls the Grand; and the same message, infinitely more subtly, comes from the massive yet graceful curve of the Esplanade rippling along the edge of the South Cliff. This is Scarborough's Kemp Town, built at the same time as Brighton's pride and joy was being completed in the 1850s, and just as Regency in effect.

Viewed in the most pleasant way imaginable – from a sun-warmed seat in an old wooden fishing coble, rocking gently out in the bay – you can absorb the whole story of Scarborough's growth and development in one easy lesson. There to your right is the headland where Bronze Age people settled, where the Romans put up a signal station and the Normans their castle. Down below tumbles the medieval town and port that grew up on the site of a fishing village named after one Norse invader, Thorgil Skarthi or Hare-lip, and laid waste in 1055 by another, Harald Hardrada. (He got his come-uppance eleven years later, at Stamford Bridge.) To the left below the South Cliff trickles that rusty little spring of mineral water which first brought the quality bumping over the bad moorland roads to Scarborough; above the spring stand the arcades and cupolas of the last in Scarborough's long succession of spa buildings, the Grand Hall of 1880, looking like some splendid Indian colonial railway station. Between South Cliff and the Grand Hotel is a wooded cleft, spanned by the elegant green iron-work of the Spa Footbridge of 1826 that finally linked the town with its medieval waters. Filling the valley between cliff and old port is the town that grew behind the beach and up the inland slope as Scarborough became the 'Queen of Watering Places' and the most fashionable resort in the North.

The coble *Adventure* in which I sat to gaze on all this was a sturdy boat, clinker-built in 1962 for inshore fishing and still powered by the original clattering old engine. Bill Wood, her owner and helmsman, munched a ham sandwich with his gums before reaching into the pocket of his faded old blue smock for his teeth so that he could talk to me. He named the headlands – White Nab, Osgodby Point, Yons Nab – running south to the distant line of Filey Brigg, and gave me directions to the boatyard, 'up t'snicket from t'Golden Ball', that still makes these wooden cobles. Bill's brown face was pickled and seamed with three-quarters of a century's daily anointing of spray and wind. Like most elderly fishermen along this coast, he'd seen the herring fishing die, but things at Scarborough weren't too bad compared with some places. He was making ends meet with his trips for visitors around South Bay at £1 a head, and still taking pleasure in work he'd been doing for a lifetime.

Back on the quayside, standing by the fish market's long sheds, among the strong smells of fish and tar and the piles of wooden crates and heaps of drying nets, I heard another side of the story. 'The young lads, they just aren't interested,' Harry said in his fast, clipped voice from under a heavy black moustache. 'They can get more up at the f—ing Social Security. Me, I was born and raised to fishing. The visitors like their coble trips, but they don't know the half of it. Now these EEC quotas have come on, you might get your 160 kits [1,600 lb] a week in one or two good hauls. Then that's it for the rest of the week. A fellow round here tried to land some fish one night and got fined £2,000. They tell us, "Go and catch haddock," but that's no use to us. They're too far out for small boats.'

Harry pointed to a line of trawlers moored by the quay wall. They were stumpy, tough-looking boats, rusted by deep-sea weather.

'These keel boats are all right. They go forty or fifty miles out and can fish for cod all the year round. It's the small fishermen who struggle. Mind you, prices have doubled, so we just about make a living by the time we've paid for gear and the bank loan. We fiddle by, you know.'

The proprietors of the amusement arcades to the south of the harbour do more than fiddle by – they make a very good thing out of teenagers bored with the beach. Here and up in Eastborough, the street that threads the downmarket centre of the town, the youngsters come to the honeypots of bright colours and instant fun. Eastborough is a bazaar of knick-knack places, tattooists and fortune-tellers with their testimonial letters ('His Royal Highness has instructed me to reply to your letter, which he found most interesting . . .') standing shoulder to shoulder with chemists, grocers and clothes shops. Here are the hard pubs and nightclubs where the city lads go for the girls and promise of a punch-up. There are quieter corners, too, especially in the old part of the town, like the Leeds Hotel up behind the harbour with its hanging flower baskets and lounge of well-stuffed benches. In the cool gloom of this bar sit old men on holiday, having dropped their wives for mid-day shopping, chuckling the early afternoon away over pint glasses. In the Gents they've solved the problem of graffiti artists by the master-stroke of providing both blackboard and chalk. Even here, though, there's a notice hanging in the bar threatening would-be rioters with a ban.

Walking from Eastborough up into Westborough, you walk upmarket. Big-name stores and classy clothes shops and jewellers run up to side-turnings going south into the elegant Scarborough of crescents, terraces and tree-lined Victorian streets. Beyond the Sitwells' Woodend, now a natural history museum, the bridges over the valley lead down to the Spa's Grand Hall, a conference centre and show theatre these days. There are plans to re-open the mineral spring and pipe it away from its present beach trickle into a smart new pump room. Here you can sit on the slatted wooden benches of the cliff lift and enjoy a widening view as you rise up the cliff-face, over the Grand Hotel to the sands of South Bay, the keyhole enclosures of the harbour and the old town and castle beyond. At the top of South Cliff stretches the Esplanade, tall and white, with the Corinthian pillars of the Crown Hotel massively in the centre; further south, the

Cleveland Way long-distance footpath runs above the formal Italian gardens in the cliff and out into open clifftop country towards Filey Brigg.

Up above the castle on the north side of the old town is St Mary's Church, the churchyard still containing the pinnacles of masonry that are all that remain of the section of church destroyed during the seventeen-month siege of the castle that ended in 1645. Across Church Lane is a favourite place to bask on benches under the graveyard wall that overlook the splendid sea view. One grave always has fresh flowers on it, placed under the funerary urn on the headstone by the world's Brontë-worshippers. Anne, the baby of the family, had watched her older sister Emily die of consumption in December 1848. She shared her bedroom at Haworth Parsonage with Emily, and soon came to share her fatal disease as well. On 25 May 1849 Charlotte Brontë and her friend Ellen Nussey brought the ailing Anne to Scarborough to see what the salt air could do; but in three days she was dead.

Over the headland there's a different Scarborough, never quite part of the main town – not as elegant as the South Cliff residences, not nearly as rowdy as the town centre. Marine Drive is the best way to approach North Bay, a curving causeway that rounds the seaward face of the headland (this can be an exciting place when storms throw enormous sheets of water over the roadway) to come suddenly on a spectacular sight. The cliffs are higher here than round South Bay, their flanks threaded with paths through bushy gardens. On top is an almost unbroken run of tall Victorian hotels and terraced houses – Blenheim Terrace and Queen's Parade – seeming at first glance to be one huge Regency curve completely encompassing the bay. It's like the scene in a Western where the entire Sioux nation floods as one man to the rim of the canyon. There's no arcade strip here behind the sands, only a line of sober black beach huts.

Under the end of Queen's Parade, the narrow mouth of the valley of the Peasholm Beck brings the road inland past the snaking blue slides of Water Splash World and the rides in the theme park above. These are the only concessions to money-spinning visitor fun here; there is a zoo, a boating lake and a kiddies' activity park under the pagoda on the island in Peasholm Park's lake, but enjoyment around North Bay comes in the shape of paths, parks and floral gardens. One of these gardens, stiff and exact, lies behind the Floral Hall Theatre which in 1987 I found shuttered, boarded up and weed-grown, waiting for some saving scheme to rescue it from demolition. Peasholm Park climbs inland from the lake through the fulsomely named Tree Walk Wonderland up to a deep, wooded glen with a splashing stream falling through its upper reaches. This is strollers' Scarborough, surrounded by well-spaced, wonderfully neat residential roads with immaculate semis and private hotels, built later than the tourist expansion of the southern part of the town and still maintaining a cool distance. Lucky Scarborough, to have all those bright attractions and this quiet haven as well.

As for the spa waters and their planned revival – I wish you joy of the worm.

5. Flamborough

Flamborough village sits at the centre of a spider's web of roads and lanes out at the end of the great chalk truncheon of Flamborough Head. You could slice off Flamborough Head neatly by running a sharp knife south and east down the A165 from Scarborough to Bridlington. The Head sticks out over Bridlington Bay like a wart on the flank of the Yorkshire coast – though nowadays Flamborough perches uneasily just inside North Humberside, much to the disgust of the villagers, Yorkshire men and women in the bone if not on paper. All round the village flattish corn and grass fields roll away across their chalk platform a couple of hundred feet above the sea. Walk north, east or south out of Flamborough and you come to the edge of the cliffs that encircle the village. On the north they rise to 400 feet, eaten away into caves and arches by the sea that comes pounding on to Flamborough Head in northerly and easterly winds. To the south they are lower and smoother, guarding small beaches and well sheltered from the weather. The thousands of sea-birds that nest on the Head have their main colonies on the northern cliffs, preferring the cracks and ledges in these battered chalk faces to the shelter of the south side. It's an edge-of-the-world place where ships have regularly come to grief, driven on to the cliffs and rocks as they try to round the Head and make the safety of Bridlington's enclosed harbour in the ferocious storms characteristic of this stretch of coast.

Wind, waves and constant vigilance – those are the facts of life here. It was possible for the *Skegness* to run on to the cliffs at nearby Speeton in 1935 and for its entire crew to die while the would-be rescuers stood helplessly by. The lighthouse on the easternmost tip of Flamborough Head warns off most potential victims. But when things do go wrong, perhaps in enormous seas and with a Force Ten gale on a freezing pitch-black winter's night, sailors off the Head know that their safety depends on the determination of the fishermen from the headland village and the skill with which they handle their lifeboat. That skill is hard learned through long experience of manoeuvring small fishing cobles around the suddenly shifting currents that suck at the Flamborough cliffs. People have been fishing these difficult waters and farming the high cliff lands of the Head for a long time. The Norsemen gave Flamborough its name ('settlement on the headland') and left their own memorial of fear and respect in the name of Danes Dyke; but that great collar of an earth bank that runs right across the neck of Flamborough Head, barring entry to invaders from the west, was built by an Iron Age tribe two thousand years before the longships beached under the cliffs. Rather than a base for inland exploration, the headland has always been a stronghold where men could keep the mainland world at bay and wrestle in isolation with the wind, soil and sea.

Flamborough village is based round a cluster of squares and open spaces from which the streets run outwards. Chapel Street and Tower Street form the north-south axis, centred on a wide open space where two memorials bear witness to the dangers that Flamborough fishermen accept as the background to their everyday lives. A tall obelisk commemorates the bravery of George Gibbon, Melchior Chadwick and Thomas Leng Major during the Great Gale of 5 February 1909. In their coble *Two Brothers* they went to help the Cross brothers and their father whose coble, *Gleaner*, was foundering. All six men died. Beside the obelisk is a slab to the memory of three more Flamborough men who drowned on 7 May 1984 while taking part in a fruitless search for four Bridlington men missing in their coble. The seven names are carved side by side, uniting the victims of the tragedy.

Before brick became a commonplace building material in this solitary corner of the country, most of the village was constructed either of flint cobbles and clay or of blocks of chalk. At the northern end of Chapel Street is an old barn whose thick walls consist of lumps of white chalk, knitted together at the corners and round the slit-windows with bricks. Just below it is the enormous Wesleyan Methodist chapel, built in 1889 when there were bricks and tiles aplenty to put up such an elaborate monster, more suited to an industrial city scene than to a small fishing village. There were nearly two hundred Methodists in Flamborough then, while St Oswald's Church could attract only a dozen or so Anglicans to its communion services. Expansion was all northwards, from the original village centre around the church towards the part of Flamborough where the fishermen preferred to live, closer to their harbour out at North Landing. Dog and Duck Square lies just east of the memorials at the bottom of Chapel Street, a long terrace of fishermen's small brick cottages running up High Street away from the eighteenth-century Dog and Duck Inn. Here life and labour, like religion, were hard and practical affairs, always under threat from the unpredictable sea. In the long brick-and-slate terraces on long streets there's a hint of the severity of mining and cotton-working communities.

Such a close society produced its own individual customs and traditions. There were the ghost stories of drowned girls in ponds and White Ladies haunting Danes Dyke. There was the Ribbon Dance – more of a scramble-cum-scrap – in which village lads would race to the bride's house after a wedding in order to be first to grab a ribbon left there by her before the ceremony, and thus have the privilege of giving her a kiss. There was a kind of informal ritual for raising the herring, in which the women would dress up in their men's clothes and dance and sing round the streets to charm up a good catch. And there was the Flamborough Sword Dance, performed round the village at Christmastime and on Filey sands in summer. The fishermen, dressed in blue jerseys and caps, white trousers and black shoes, and sometimes with blackened faces, wielded wooden swords to dance 'a very picturesque kind of pantomime, somewhat after the fashion of the old Morris dance'. Two 'beggars' went round with them collecting money. Cecil Sharp visited Flamborough in 1910 and suggested a new tune; but the villagers were happy to stick to the old 'Buffalo Girls', known to them as 'Old Johnny Walker', which had done them proud for centuries. (For the edification of traditional-dance fanatics, the progression was: Ring and Lock – The Clap – Threedling and Double Threedling – the Straight Hey – Ring and Lock.)

Tower Street connects the fishermen's quarter on the north side of Flamborough with the older, more widely spaced and haphazardly sited farming village scattered in larger buildings round St Oswald's Church. The atmosphere is quite different here, with tall old trees overlooking chalk-built farmhouses, long farmyard walls and big gardens. But the two communities join in the churchyard, where hundreds of drowned sailors lie buried – some Flamborough men, others nameless, shapeless corpses washed ashore. There are always fresh flowers around the slab by the south door, memorial to the seven victims of 1984. The church holds many treasures beside the outward-leaning Norman chancel arch: a round Norman font, some old brasses and the tomb of Sir Marmaduke Constable who died in about 1530, reputedly of swallowing a toad which ate his heart away. You can still just about make out the rib-cage, heart and munching toad in the fragment of his effigy that remains. There's also a wonderful swivelling display of water-colours by a local artist, showing the many activities through which village people helped win the Second World War: the lifeboat rescuing three airmen from a giant wave, fire-guards putting out fires, volunteers bandaging the wounded and bringing them trays of tea, the pillbox on Flamborough Head, cobles in the sunset.

Sir Marmaduke Constable was a member of the family that held sway in Flamborough for nearly 500 years. They began in Norman times with an illegitimate son of the Constable of Chester, and nearly ended themselves and their village when Sir Robert Constable put down his Roman Catholic marker in 1537 by taking part in the Pilgrimage of Grace. King Henry VIII had him executed and his body hung in chains from Beverley Gate. The manor was forfeit, and Flamborough declined to a decayed village of tumbledown houses. The remains of Flamborough Castle, the fortified manor house of the Constables, can be seen in the field over the wall in Tower Street − a crumbling angle of chalk blocks and a few grassy hummocks.

Three roads lead out from the village towards the cliffs. Lighthouse Road goes due east for a couple of miles to the tip of the Head where the two lighthouses stand near each other − the present one (built in 1806) and the old tower it superseded, an octagonal finger of grey chalk by the golf course, put up in 1674 and still used as a landmark by the fishermen. Beside the lighthouses is the large Greenacre Caravan Park, but it's nothing in size compared to the Thornwick Holiday Camp out on North Marine Road on the way to North Landing. While Flamborough caters for visitors with pubs, shops, a post office and garages, and has a number of boarding houses and small hotels, most holidaymakers don't stay in the village itself. They go to the caravan park or the holiday camp, to the thousands of neat little boxes in neat little gardens that cover large areas of the headland. On the sites there are shops, bars, cafés, playgrounds, cabaret and dancing joints and all mod cons laid on. Thornwick is rather sniffy about Sea Farm Holiday Camp next door, but will recommend the Greenacre site. Greenacre returns the compliment. Sea Farm doesn't give a damn about either. Flamborough village accepts the money of all three, grins and bears it.

If a nineteenth-century Flamborough fisherman was baiting his lines and anyone happened to mention a hare, rabbit, pig or fox, he would curse the speaker and give up on the day's fishing. If he was unlucky enough to meet a woman or a parson or a hare on the road to North Landing, he might as well go home again, for there would only be trouble and a poor catch waiting for him. The ensuing hundred years have done away with the superstitions; but nowadays all the Flamborough women dancing together couldn't raise a good catch of herring where a coble could reach them. They are trawled up well out in Bridlington Bay, and most of the village men work away from home on the trawlers. In the 1850s there were thirty herring boats in Flamborough, drift-netting for herring from summer until early autumn. By the turn of the century there were twelve, and shortly after the First World War they were all gone, beaten by steam trawlers and dwindling stocks. The village had more than 150 fishermen in the 1920s, and many of them had to humble themselves in the soup kitchen queues. Motor-powered cobles came in, and tourists eager for a trip round the cliffs, bringing a little prosperity back. Salmon-netting in the 1960s helped to keep things going. But the number of boats steadily declined: sixteen in 1940, nine in 1947, seven in 1968. In 1987 there were just three cobles working out of North Landing, selling their crabs and lobsters to Bridlington and taking holidaymakers on fishing trips and scenic cruises.

The Flamborough fishermen draw their cobles up on the ribbed slipway by the lifeboat shed, high prows towards the narrow entrance between the high chalk cliffs. A rusty old caterpillar tractor drags the cobles out into the water, past the dark crevices and caves in the cliffs where children test the echoes with shrieks. The lines of each boat swoop down from the bow to the bulging midriff, then up again to the narrow stern which is designed to allow them to be retrieved from rough water in constricted harbours. Amidships is a square box containing an old diesel engine, in the bows a pair of oars in case the engine breaks down. A winch and pulley for the salmon nets stands in the stern, where the decking is covered with old bits of carpet to give a warm, dry footing. The outside wood of the coble is varnished and plain, the inside painted bright orange to help a helicopter pilot to spot them if they're in trouble. The whole boat is only about thirty feet long, but it rides beautifully in the water. The lessons of a thousand years' seafaring have been thoroughly learnt and incorporated into the design and equipping of the Flamborough cobles. They are unimprovable, perfectly adapted to their work.

The lifeboat that sits high above them at North Landing, however, is only the latest in a long line of design refinements. It can communicate with land, sea and air, batter through almost any sea and roll through 360° to right itself if it capsizes. As it stands gleaming in its shed, surrounded by admiring tourists, it looks like a highly polished giant toy. But on those winter nights it comes into its own as a precision instrument. Its efficiency has always been founded on an intimate knowledge of conditions around Flamborough Head gleaned by the fishermen who crew it, through their everyday work in cobles close to the cliffs. Trawler work denies a man this close daily contact. Is the lifeboat's efficiency impaired by the decline in purely local fishing? The Flamborough lifeboatmen won't hear of it. The lifeboat is a totem for them, especially now that they disperse so far afield to their work; it's something round which village pride gathers as all other traditions fall away.

There's a crew of thirty-five men for the *Will And Fanny Kirby*, all of them Flamborough fishermen and all desperate to get a place on board. When the alarm goes, they race down to North Landing on anything that moves. Seven men can go to the rescue, including the three whose berths are guaranteed: the Coxswain, the Second Coxswain/Mechanic and the Second Mechanic. The four remaining places go to whoever can get their boots and jackets on and be there before the rest. The oil-stained orange suits and long boots hang up in the shed, ready to be snatched down and put on. When the seven men are at their stations on board, the boat is run out by winch on to the turntable at the top of the launching ramp, then tilted downwards. This ramp is the steepest in Britain, and at high tide the lifeboat hits the water at something like 50 mph. The shock jars the arms of those on board and sends up an enormous, thick sheet of water all round the boat. Three tons of seawater are sucked in immediately as ballast. If the launch is at low tide, an immense, dark-blue battleship of a tractor pulls the lifeboat out to where the cliffs end, chugging in up to its windows in the sea. Then those who came worse than fourth in the race to the shed have to stand by and wait until the boat comes back again with the survivors – all wet, cold and exhausted, some hysterical, some numb, some euphoric. The photographs round the shed walls capture the helplessness of their blanket-wrapped figures and the sheepishness of their grins as they hobble up the steps by the slipway. Then there are the times when the lifeboat comes back with bodies, or with no one. Everyone knows that there may come a night when the boat itself won't come back; but they don't talk about it, or about the work they volunteer for and risk everything to do. It's seen simply as duty, and nothing remarkable.

The service boards hanging in the shed are full of coble rescues, some boat names appearing two or three times on different dates. There are also a good number of 'man over cliff' entries, witness to the dangers of the headland. These cliffs don't shelve into the sea; they get there by the quickest route, straight down. Before the Wild Birds Protection Act came into force in 1955, egg-collecting among the seabird colonies of the cliffs was a thriving business. The 'climmers' put on a harness and were lowered by pulley and rope to dangle on the ledges while they collected the eggs. The puffins were reckoned to be the fiercest defenders of their broods, but a handful of straw stuffed into their nesting place would usually occupy them long enough to allow the climmer to rob the nest. 'These eggs find a ready sale,' enthuses a 1937 guide to Flamborough, 'for they afford good rich food.' Ten years earlier H. V. Morton had watched Sam Leng, the egg-gatherer of Bempton, being hauled up the cliffs by three friends and bearing 'as pretty a basket of eggs as I have ever seen', fruit of guillemots' nests. The eager Morton couldn't resist having a go – good copy for *The Call of England*, the book he was writing at the time – and soon found he'd bitten off more than he could chew:

> I found myself on an almost perpendicular ledge of rock. I braced myself against it with my feet as I hung passionately with both hands to the rope, so that I was at right angles to the rock. I felt like a fly on a ceiling. Above me was the rough grass edge of the cliff against the sky and the voices of the egg-gatherers shouting to me: 'Let yourself go!'
>
> My problem, which was one of gravity plus pure funk, was solved for me when something gave way, leaving me swinging at the end of the rope, kicking the cliff for a foothold. Voices from the sweet world above said that I was 'getting on fine!'

He got out of it by having himself hauled up again, eggless and 'in an agony of self-contempt'. Those who have frozen halfway up the first staircase of the Eiffel Tower will know just how he felt.

From Flamborough village the third cliff road, South Sea Road, runs down to South Landing, another tiny cleft and beach. The difference here is that the wind and waves are shepherded away by the curve of the headland, making it easier and safer to launch a coble or lifeboat. A lifeboat station was established here in 1871, at the same time as the one at North Landing, so that a rescue could be made whatever the state of wind or tide. It closed in 1938, and its brick shed is now used by the fishermen as

37

a convenient storage place for their equipment. There is still a little fishing from the beach, most of it tourist trips or by private boat owners. Trees grow thickly here, unlike the wind-scoured north side of the headland, and wild flowers can get a sheltered hold. The excellent Heritage Information Centre in the car park just above South Landing has an exhibition on the geology, history, wildlife and village traditions of Flamborough Head, beautifully laid out in a small area. They also organize guided walks with all kinds of themes, and have a good stock of leaflets and books. What a sensible idea this is, helping visitors to get the most out of their visit without damaging either themselves or the place they've come to enjoy. In 1979 the Countryside Commission designated Flamborough Head a 'Heritage Coast' area, and here they are doing something practical and enthusiastic about it. As long as visitors continue to want trips by coble, leave the crab-pots alone and don't smear their ice-creams on the lifeboat, the Flamborough fishermen like to see them. Provided they don't run all over the crops and break down the fences, the farmers can live with them. The fabric of the village itself doesn't suffer from the hundreds of thousands of people who come to Flamborough Head every year – it's a place to fill the petrol tank and buy a paper, rather than the main attraction. The Heritage Coast's footpaths, guided walks and imaginatively presented information displays can only help to preserve these amicable arrangements. But what most of the villagers think about the caravan colonies on their green fields is better left imagined than recorded.

EAST COAST (South)

6. Skegness
7. Cromer
8. Southwold

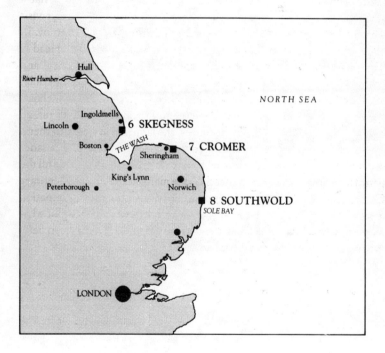

6. Skegness

'I was flying back from Spain,' said the receptionist in the Skegness tourist office. 'That plane was full of people from all over Britain, but as we came over the coast they all went to the windows and called out, "Oh, look – we're coming over Skeggy!" Then everyone had a little grin.'

There's something about Skegness that strikes that chord with most people. Any comedian dying the death in a Midlands club can get the audience on his side with a crack about a wet weekend in Skeggy. It's a paradigm of flat misery that you don't have to have experienced for yourself to recognize. Skegness is so familiar to so many generations, such a well-worn holiday rut, that it's reached the ultimate position possible for a British institution – a running joke, hedged about with affection. It's very much a Midlanders' preserve, a place where people from Nottingham, Leicester and Derby still feel they must have a week or two, even if their main holidays are spent under the spell of Spanish sun and wine. Skeggy commands as much loyalty as Blackpool, and as many grumbles: it's too far, too windy, too cut-off, too old-fashioned.

Skegness is an archetype, a cornerstone of British seaside mythology. There's one image above all others that symbolizes Skegness: that rotund old salt in the Great Northern Railway poster, prancing along the sands through the puddles and flapping his arms like an overfed pelican trying to get airborne. 'Skegness is *so* bracing' trumpets the slogan, making the best of a bad job. South coast resorts promised you sunshine, northern ones touted their cliffs and mountains; Blackpool guaranteed you non-stop fun and larks, Cornwall offered sandy bays and quaint fishing villages. John Hassall, the artist who dreamed up that most famous of all seaside advertisements, had never been to Skegness when he produced the Jolly Fisherman in 1908; but, like everyone else, he had the general idea. Dear old Skeggy, out on a flat, windy East Coast limb, did you good. The public agreed with him: his poster, displayed for the first time over the Easter holidays in 1909, brought the customers flocking. Hassall did finally get to Skegness in 1936, to be given a civic reception, an illuminated address and the Freedom of the Foreshore. His masterpiece may have set the town up for the twentieth century, but it didn't bring him much reward. The Great Northern's fee for the original poster was twelve guineas; and when Hassall died in 1948, aged eighty, he was destitute.

There are Jolly Fishermen all over Skegness, plaster models waving you into theatres and funfairs, painted versions with café menus across their bellies, all with arms waving and mufflers a-trail, their crimson faces bulging with glee. There's something grotesque about their combination of grandfatherliness and wild hilarity. The expression on the face of Hassall's own tar (now on display in the front lobby of the Town Hall), studied carefully, reveals grim determination rather than mirth. He looks as if he's leapt into the air for the purpose of squashing the starfish that lies on the beach under his descending seaboot. In spite of the caper he's cutting, he's a no-nonsense figure, like the invigorating breeze that's blowing him along. Today's Jolly Fishermen have no such forcefulness – they are just too frolicsome. And they don't really do justice to a town where you can step from a shrieking funfair straight into a quiet floral garden, where right next to a busy prom is one of the most peaceful parks I've ever dozed in, where the streets leading inland from the seafront are wide, lined with trees and full of small shops under fine Victorian cast-iron arcades.

The flatness of the Lincolnshire coastline has always made Skegness vulnerable to the sea. Before the thirteenth century great sandbanks offshore ran right down this coast, separated from the land by a brackish lagoon, like the Fleet behind Dorset's Chesil Bank. Then the progressive downward tilting of Britain's easterly edge – still going on today – dragged the sandbanks under the sea and opened up the coastal marshlands to centuries of flooding. The old town of Skegness, a couple of miles out to sea from the present shoreline, was washed away in about 1526, as John Leland noted when he visited the area in 1540: 'The old toune is clene consumid and eten up with the se. For old Skegnesse is now buildid a pore new thing.' It was still pretty pore when the Hon. John Byng came to the Vine Inn two and a half centuries later. He turned up his aristocratic nose at this 'vile, shabby bathing place . . . we had some miserable smelts, and some raw, rank cold beef . . . no garden, no walk, no billiard room; nor anything for comfort, or temptation! . . . From all these miseries, and a kitchen stinking of strong mutton and a roasting hog, we hurry'd away.' But within fifteen years the Vine, a notorious smugglers' meeting-place in Byng's day, had transformed itself into a smart hotel where lords and ladies could sit down sixty strong to dinner and entertain themselves afterwards with 'dramatic performances'. By the middle of the nineteenth century Skegness was a well-established member of that club of respectable small seaside resorts where the middle and upper classes could safely holiday. Tennyson knew the town well, and as a young man would wander along the sands bareheaded and in his shirtsleeves, muttering poetry. The visitors found him rather enchanting, but the locals thought he was crazy. Everything was quite genteel until 1873. Then came the new-fangled Bank Holiday, and hot on its heels the railway.

Richard Lumley, 9th Earl of Scarbrough, owned Skegness and its environs. His agent, Vivian Tippet, realized what could be done with the town now that it was connected to the factory cities of the Midlands by railway. There was no shortage of examples for the Earl and his agent to study of what could happen to nice little seaside towns once the trains began to call. Together they planned and built Skegness into a model resort – partly so as not to miss out on a golden financial opportunity, partly to have all the reins in their own hands. The grand plan, in full colour, now hangs near Hassall's Jolly Fisherman in Skegness Town Hall. It shows wide grids of regularly spaced streets around the large green square of Tower Gardens, a seafront lined with gracious, spacious hotels, the pier carried on hundreds of spindly legs, bathing machines, gentlemen scorching round a track on penny-farthings, crinolined ladies and sailor-suited youngsters wandering down the middle of the broad, leafy streets. What a dream town! In the end it wasn't all built, but you can make out the basic design as you stroll around the shopping streets. There's no other way to see how the heart of Skegness is laid out – the dead level ground where the town stands prevents you from getting an overall view of the place. You have to narrow your horizons and take it piece by piece: wide Lumley Road running west from the landmark of the Clock Tower, the arcaded shops and shady trees; the old stone lion who used to stand on the roof of the Lion Hotel at the corner of Lumley Road and Roman Bank and who now prowls the pavement, his back hollowed by the bottoms of nearly a century's riding children; the parallel strolling thoroughfares of Algitha Road and Ida Road with their tall brick Victorian houses; St Matthew's Church on Scarbrough Avenue, whose stained-glass windows are well worth a linger. (Stories I don't know but would love to: the one behind the window to Ruth Farmer which shows a sulky elder brother turning away from the prodigal son's homecoming party, captioned 'And he was angry & would not go in'.)

Right in the middle of this neat locals' town is an overgrown garden, full of birdsong and butterflies, marsh marigolds growing in its boggy lawn and unkempt yews, ashes and oaks drooping low over the grass. Here on

Roman Bank stands The Hall, fallen into decay since it ceased to be the Earl of Scarbrough's estate office. Rambling roses climb up its walls to roof level, and ivy smothers the windows. There's a crumbling stable block beside it, a ruinous dovecot on the waste ground behind. It's a heart-touching sight, soon to be obliterated under new development – an estate of small houses, perhaps a supermarket.

'Skeggy could do with a few wild places like this,' said Frank, who was on his hands and knees in the long grass looking at the butterflies. 'We used to have a big patch of wilderness called The Jungle along there by the Town Hall. It was a great place to get lost when we were kids – lost and muddy . . . and wet. But they built it up eventually.'

He sighed, looking around the overgrown garden.

'Do we need a supermarket, we ask ourselves. Skegness is all small shops – that's the attraction. Soon we'll be just another bloody Doncaster. However . . . this is prime building land, I suppose, and the house isn't listed. So there you are.'

Down on the seafront the amusements are as big and bright as seafront amusements ought to be – coloured lights, cut-out dolphins, manic Jolly Fishermen, a Big Wheel, a Big Dipper – but they stand with their flashing feet in floral gardens. The atmosphere's local and familiar. Strangers nod 'G'morning' to each other, and proprietorially stroke the donkeys who belong to teams differentiated by the colour of their nosebands.

'They're green donkeys today, look.'

'Oh – particular, are we?'

'Aye, well – they're not *our* donkeys.'

The advertising bills for the wrestling at the Festival Pavilion have that same local touch. You can go and cheer your home-town favourite or boo a well-known villain (see opposite page).

The Embassy Centre, to the north along the seafront from the Festival Pavilion, specializes in good, safe family shows featuring stars of yesteryear who can be relied on not to upset anyone. In the winter the Embassy gets in on the conference business, but its heart is firmly rooted in showbiz. With its square columns and 1920s' dignity it's a shining example of the second great phase in the development of Skegness. By the time the First World War ended the town centre planned by the Earl of Scarbrough and Mr Tippet had come as much into being as it was going to; and now the seafront was revamped with a new boating lake, bathing pool and the

Sheffield's **ALAN KILBY**

- The Champion - Brilliant Deaf Star -

Versus

KING BENN

- The Challenger - Keighley -

Fitness Fanatic - Spirited - In There To Win!

Embassy Ballroom. Young Billy Butlin set up his amusement park below the Embassy, the first outpost of a mighty empire. A waterway was laid out up which you can still travel by motor boat, past the sad remnant of Skegness Pier (opened in 1881 and split into three isolated sections during a storm in 1978 – only the shore portion remains), past the paddling pool shaped into the word 'SUNSHINE', to the small amusement park on the North Shore. Here Sea View Road meets North Parade and continues seaward into a car park. This was the site of a beach ramp known as Sea View Pullover, where on 26 July 1937 the holidaymakers gathered to see the erstwhile Vicar of Stiffkey doing his popular act as Daniel in the lions' den. The poor half-crazed Reverend Harold Davidson had been thrown out of his living on the North Norfolk coast after being accused of 'immoral conduct' with London prostitutes (he claimed he was only interested in their souls); he joined the circus as an outlet to vent his feelings about the church authorities to the public at large. His customary speech went well that summer day in Skegness, but the second half of his act, during which he entered the cage to gambol with the lions, went drastically wrong. Mr Davidson was so badly mauled in front of the onlookers that he died two days later, having delivered himself of the immortal plea: 'Telephone the London papers – and don't miss the first editions.'

Notwithstanding such dramas, Skegness survives and retains its public's affection by taking the moderate line. It's not so quiet that seekers after sensation won't come, and not so strident that its many elderly clients are put off. Three miles out of town to the south are the lonely sand dunes and salt-marshes of Gibraltar Point Nature Reserve, crammed with sea-birds, waders and marsh plants. The views from the marsh edges and dunes are immense, right down the throat of the Wash over miles and miles of water or shining mud-flats, clear across its mouth to the North Norfolk cliffs around Hunstanton. In sunshine it's heaven – though rather too bracing if you've come in beach attire, and one of those chilly easterlies whips in from the sea.

You have to go north of Skegness for a couple of miles on the A52 towards Ingoldmells to get the true brassy tang of modern seaside overkill at the Funcoast World leisure centre – known to millions as Skeggy's Butlins until that image was deemed too tarnished to be helpful. Here along the shore that natural showman Billy Butlin set up the first of his holiday camps in 1936 – Redcoats, chalets, 'Good Morning, Campers', drilled meal-times, queues, PT and all. Britons were happy to be bossed about on a cheap holiday before and after the Second World War, and Butlin's intuitive grasp of what exactly it was that they wanted made him a many-times-over millionaire. But soon that mixture of garish entertainment, genial bullying and institutional fare began to stick in the customers' throats. Skegness camp, the pioneer and chief source of legend among all Butlin's establishments, gradually declined – or rose – to the status of a national joke. People might laugh affectionately at Skeggy's Butlins, but they weren't prepared to put up with the regimentation, bad cooking and rain once the Spanish resorts began to open their new airports to cheap charter flights. By the time the Rank Organisation took it over in 1978, the camp was in a bad way.

Since then there have been big changes. The good old Redcoats have been retained, along with the all-star shows, but the trend is away from the flimsy chalets towards luxury caravans and self-catering flatlets. A huge new undercover entertainments complex is planned to defeat the worst enemy Billy Butlin ever had – the British weather. Holidaymakers who can jet away to the sun and foreign fun have higher expectations than yesterday's obedient droves of chalet-fodder. The statistics are staggering. Funcoast World gets upward of 100,000 day-visitors each year. Some 10,000 people are resident at any one time. All told, the leisure complex attracts not far short of 200,000 customers annually. What do they all come to this place for? To be one in a crowd, says David, a senior member of the staff.

'They come for live entertainment, which they get here with a big bang. But mostly I'd say people come to be together. They come here so as not to be noticed. Everyone rushes everywhere all together – like a pack of lemons.'

The economy of Skegness benefits from all these spenders on its doorstep, and it gets another boost from the 800 or 900 employees, of whom less than a tenth are permanent staff. The rest drift in at the start of the season and drift away in the autumn, enticed by the free bed and board, the free shows and the casual sexual encounters that have always been one of the strongest attractions of a Butlins holiday – remember 'chalet rash'?

Butlin himself would probably be pleased to see how well the old place is doing, but dismayed at its lack of style. He was not exactly loved by his staff, but was admired for his energy and his flair. When word got round that the boss had landed at Skegness Aerodrome in his private plane, the Redcoats would shake in their shoes and the wages clerks pile their desks with paper in order to look busy. Butlin would stalk round the camp, demanding to know why that dripping gutter had not been fixed. Like the king that he was, he carried no money. The manager would follow him round, paying his bills as they cropped up. The great man never wasted time being wined and dined by his subordinates. Cheese-and-onion and ham sandwiches would be ordered in advance, together with a thermos of soup, so that Butlin could eat and drink while running meetings. Those present got soup and sandwiches too, whatever their rank in the Butlin empire. The boss liked to crack on, and you were no use to him if you couldn't follow suit.

David started working at the Skegness camp in 1963, when Butlin was at the height of his power. He's realistic about the old despot, but still a Butlin man to his fingertips.

'The thing about Billy Butlin – he knew what people wanted. He was smart, too. He built all his camps in areas of low employment so that he could get plenty of cheap labour. Rank are in this to make money, pure and simple; but Billy was a showman. He wanted to make money, yes – but he wanted to please people as well. Time and again he'd have a hunch about some ride or entertainment, a silly thing. Everyone would say "Good Lord, no, that won't work." But it did.

'Like, he'd say, "OK, put a spinning wheel in the dining room. The number it stops at, that's the table that gets a free bottle of champagne." Cheap champagne, of course, but it worked. The Redcoats would march down there with the champagne in a bucket and glasses on a tray – the people at the table all proud and embarrassed and everyone clapping.

'That's what we want here now – a little bit of that champagne.'

7. Cromer

'You'll love Cromer,' my friend said. 'You can leave your watch behind. When I'm there I never look at mine from one weekend to the next. It's that sort of place.'

He could have added: You might as well tear the calendar up, too. It's certainly that sort of place. Getting to the town from Norwich or King's Lynn takes a long time, and with every mile of the empty roads you slough off another year. By the time you reach the 'Gem of the Norfolk Coast' you're back in a pre-war seaside atmosphere, if not a Victorian one. Everything slows down or stops. Shopkeepers twinkle and gossip. Directions and advice come served with a smile. Well-mannered children play soberly on clean sand, with never a flicker of neon to lure them away. Cromer, like a dear old nanny, breathes reassurance. It even smells like everyone's childhood seaside holiday: warm, salty and fragrant.

To look at, too, Cromer is a dream of a seaside town. Dropping downhill past dignified Georgian and Victorian houses and hotels, you find yourself drawn into streets that become ever narrower till they squeeze you out into the open square below the tall flint tower of the church. Even narrower streets twist down to the seafront, where zigzag steps lead to the beach and a beautiful view. Cromer's houses are heaped up on their cliff above the pier, grey, white and red angles of wall and roof stacked between the 159-foot tower of St Peter and St Paul and the copper and terracotta of the Hotel de Paris. From this angle you can't see where the streets and lanes thread through; the houses and hotels seem to have grown like some conglomerate sea plant round the church. They are piled up like this to keep their feet out of the water. Cromer's cliffs are some of the most unstable in Britain, regularly crumbling in acres of landslip. Back in the Middle Ages there was a prosperous trading port and harbour town known as Shipton-juxta-Mare directly below today's Cromer, but by the seventeenth century the sea had swallowed the entire place, church and all. Cromer, left alone on its perch above the shore and deprived of its deep-water harbour, declined to a tiny lobster- and crab-fishing community, often the scene of shipwrecks and losing hundreds of yards of cliff to the sea every year.

Looking to left and right you soon spot the signs of instability in the cliffs: sagging and receding at the top, running with water in the middle, heaped with the loose clay of old falls at the foot. A couple of miles to the east, a large part of the clifftop village of Overstrand is quietly slipping over

49

the edge, year by year. No one would think of building anywhere near these cliffs, though up by the lighthouse the Cromer Country Club has plonked down a hundred or so luxury time-share holiday chalets in a forbidding rampart of flaring red brick, only a few hundred yards inland. With luck the sea will have got to them before the end of the next century. The cliffs around these parts of the North Norfolk coastline are strong enough to support caravans, though, thousands of them in an almost unbroken line for three miles between Cromer and Sheringham. You can always move a caravan as the cliff edge comes closer. Cromer people have learnt to put up with the caravans that cover their fields; but they don't like the time-share chalets at all, for exactly the same reason as Swanage, Ramsgate and Brighton people don't like those towns' marina developments, existing or planned. The incomers they attract are too rich, too remote, too cosmopolitan. The developments are too insular and self-contained, offering too little extra income to the town to justify the sacrifice of so much ground or such a view. The actual effect of developments such as these is usually less drastic than was feared. They serve as aiming points for the anxieties of small places with a big, bad world knocking on their door; especially so in Cromer, where outside influences have always had to push against firmly closed and stoutly defended barriers.

Just as the houses of Cromer huddle up round the central pillar of the church tower, so do Cromer people jealously guard their privacy. Born-and-bred inhabitants are proud to call themselves 'Cromer Crabs'. Like natives of anywhere, they love running Cromer down, but it's entirely a locals' sport. Cromer Crabs are famously touchy on the subject of their town. So are the many long-term settlers who move among the true Crabs, their lives touching but rarely interlocking: outsider families whose roots in Cromer go back through the decades. These people own or rent the old fishermen's cottages and the town houses near the seafront, or the solid villas behind along the roads leading away from the centre of Cromer, which they inhabit for weeks at a time, coming armed with playing cards and Scrabble to pass away rainy days. They use the shops of the town, join the clubs, attend meetings, take part. They greet the shopkeepers and fishermen as old friends, shedding the comfortable glow of satisfaction of those who know Cromer in and out of season and whose children feel at home here. The town is a time-capsule for these long-established visiting families, the same cherished and secure haven that it was when their great-grandparents first put down a marker here. Their voices are quiet in the street, loud in council meetings and planning offices; formidable opponents of change in Cromer, as many would-be developers have found out to their frustration. The Quaker cousinhood that scraped Cromer off the floor two centuries ago would be proud of them.

When the Reverend Robert Barclay bought Northrepps Hall, two miles inland from Cromer, in 1790, he was laying the foundation stone of a Quaker dynasty. 'Barclay, Buxton, Gurney, Hoare – and then God,' said the locals. John Gurney, Barclay's brother-in-law, came to stay with Farmer Terry in Church Street. The combined Barclay and Gurney children numbered twenty-two; Cromer beach was big enough for all of them. Samuel Hoare bought Cliff House in 1801. Thomas Fowell Buxton rented Cromer Hall in 1809. More Gurneys settled at Northrepps and in Cromer. Everyone exchanged visits, banking news (the cousinhood in its various branches formed a mighty banking empire) and sons and daughters in marriage. They bought up land all round the district and began to spend as much time here as in their London residences. Cromer acquired, painlessly and swiftly, a squirearchy which was to direct its affairs for the next hundred years. The Norfolk villagers that the Quakers discovered were deep in the doldrums, scraping away at subsistence farming and fishing, with only the coal boats that beached at high tide and the occasional carrier's cart from Sheringham or Mundesley to remind them of the outside world. That was the way the cousinhood wanted it – to keep that close-knit, hidden-away feeling, while also enjoying the civilized amenities of life that sophisticated London bankers were used to. The four Quaker families presided as benevolent despots over the development of Cromer into a select resort with a salt-water bath-house, a subscription room off Tucker Street and a few bathing machines. The lower orders were debarred from visiting Cromer by the difficulty of getting here – bad roads and no railways. Throughout the first half of the nineteenth century the cousinhood tightened their grip on Cromer's social life, happy in the knowledge of good works done and good lives led. By 1860 they had established the custom of Sunday readings at Cliff House. Up to forty members of the clan would gather for recitations of scripture and hymn-singing by their younger representatives, while the frail old dowager Hannah, Lady Buxton, held court on the ottoman in her black silk dress. These gatherings cemented the agreeable feelings of permanence and worthy well-being that kept the cousinhood firmly in control of Cromer.

It couldn't last – not when the East Norfolk Railway arrived at Cromer in 1877, followed six years later by the sprightly Clement Scott and his purple prose. Scott, on secondment from his job as drama critic of the *Daily Telegraph* to write a few nice holiday pieces, found Cromer a bit of a bore, crowded and rushed off its feet, petty-minded and grabbing. Out along the poppy-strewn cliffs lay the hamlet of Sidestrand, however, where in the crisp, white sheets and country cooking of the miller's daughter Scott found what he was looking for. He christened the area 'Poppyland', and the fashionable world came running to discover the North Norfolk coast. Cromer sat contentedly in the slipstream of Poppyland's popularity, drawing its quotient of fine folk. There was a new generation of upper-crust families: Lord Suffield of Gunton Park, who spent most of his fortune entertaining King Edward VII; the Locker-Lampsons at Newhaven Court above the Norwich road, who played host over the years to a galaxy of stars including Oscar Wilde, Alfred Lord Tennyson, Sir Ernest Shackleton, Winston Churchill and Suzanne Lenglen. One of his guests remarked of Frederick Locker-Lampson, 'One does not notice his affected way of talking when one is used to him'. But these people were already relics of a bygone age, with their huge houses that depended on armies of servants, their meetings of the Primrose League and afternoon drives to tennis and tea at each other's residences. Behind their elegant backs, Cromer settled comfortably into its role as a resort for the middle-class family, and stayed that way. The Barclays, Buxtons, Gurneys and Hoares, meanwhile, having sold a good deal of their land in the town, loosened their grip on Cromer. The Quaker families dropped out of local social life and retreated to a group of fine houses encircling the town, where members of the cousinhood still live their harmonious corporate family lives.

The middle-class holiday settlers of Cromer don't like talk of change to the town, and neither do the Cromer Crabs who still fish and man the lifeboat. As further up the east coast at Flamborough, the lifeboat here is more than just a means of getting accident victims to dry land; it's a symbol of continuity. Cromer lifeboat station was established in 1804, only fourteen years after Robert Barclay arrived in the district, and the lifeboat has been manned by local fishermen ever since. These extremely brave and modest men are quick to detect and brush aside any attitude approaching the patronizing, or the wide-eyed. 'Just a job,' they shrug if asked about their lifeboat work. At the first alarm, whatever the season, weather, or time of day or night, they are ready to abandon plates, nets, pints or beds, run to the shed at the end of the pier and take their place in the self-righting lifeboat: ready, literally, to give their lives at a moment's notice. The strongest tradition of the service is that no one boasts, brags or makes a song and dance about it. Coxswain Henry Blogg of Cromer was the pattern for all lifeboatmen. The statistics of his service stand unequalled by anyone else – fifty-three years in the Cromer lifeboat, thirty-eight of them as Coxswain (1909–47); three gold medals of the RNLI (the Victoria Cross of the lifeboat service), four silver medals, the George Cross and the BEM; assistance at the saving of 873 lives.

'He would rather go to three wrecks than make one speech,' wrote A. C. Savin, Cromer's historian, in 1936. 'He is not a talker, but a worker; with the gift of leadership. When "Ry" says "We will go" or "Do so and so", his crew follows; they have supreme confidence in his judgement.'

In the summer months Henry Blogg turned to the deckchair and bathing-hut business, and refused to be drawn by eager visitors on the subject of his other calling. His reserved style on the rare occasions when he did talk about his work is well illustrated by his clipped, rather testy account of the wreck of the Dutch oil tanker *Georgia* on 21 November 1927. Reading his words, it's hard to realize that the rescue was in fact carried out in mountainous seas and a howling gale, during which the lifeboat was actually thrown on top of the wrecked tanker and all but capsized. If that had happened, the entire lifeboat crew and the rescued men from the *Georgia* would have died. To the assembled newspapermen back on the shore, Cox'n Blogg described their hair's-breadth escape, due entirely to his experience and quick thinking, in these ultra-laconic words:

'What's all this fuss about? We have to do it. I saw that the job had to be done in daylight, so we went straight at the wreck. There was no searchlight, there were heavy seas running, but we quickly ran alongside the steamer and threw lines aboard, which made the lifeboat fast. The remainder of the crew of the *Georgia* jumped into the lifeboat one by one, but when it came to cut the rope the strong cross-currents and seas lifted the lifeboat on to the bulwarks of the *Georgia*. For a moment I thought we were in a fine mess. Had the boat moved further on to the wreck it would have upset. The engines on the lifeboat were reversed, and she responded so quickly that it carried the boat clear before the next wave came. It was a minute or two before we got clear, and then we went to Yarmouth, and that's all there is to say about it.'

When Cox'n Blogg died in 1954, a bronze bust of him was put up in North Lodge Park where it still stares ruminatively out to sea. A better idea of the kind of man he was can be got by going into the public bar of the Red Lion Hotel at the bottom of Jetty Street on a weekday at lunchtime and quietly listening to the conversation of his successors. Surrounded by photographs of the craggy face of Henry Blogg, and of former lifeboats and their crew members, the Cromer fishermen discuss the previous night's catch and the state of the weather, something of crucial importance to men working inshore on one of the most dangerous coasts in Britain. Conversation is slow and drawling. Some of the young fishermen who look as if they can hardly have left school have known wild nights and desperate danger aboard the lifeboat; but neither they nor their fathers enjoy being questioned about the work. The freckled, sandy-haired, broken-nosed barman, John, gave me a timely word of warning: 'The old fishermen, they take their time. You can't pump 'em. If they think you're genuine they'll talk to you; but if they think you're an aaasshole, they'll tell you so.'

With this in mind I kept quiet and learnt a lot. The younger fishermen, moustachioed tough lads in smocks and jeans, sipped their lager and listened deferentially to their fathers and grandfathers laying down the law over bottled stout. There was a lot of effing and blinding over herring unsold at market – in this trade, goods that are not shifted quickly are a total loss. Cromer's family tradition of fishing goes on from year to year, father-and-son teams landing their glistening, already-gutted catch on the beach in the early morning when only the gulls are about. Salt-rusted tractors haul on the hawsers to beach the boats in place of the horses of yesteryear; but in most other respects one could easily be witnessing a pre-First World War scene. Sepia-tinted old photos produced by the locally based Poppyland Publishing Company show identical character-istics in turn-of-the-century Cromer fishermen: hands knobbled by a lifetime's pickling in brine, deep facial wrinkles, a stolid stance to talk, with one hand resting on the gunwale of the boat. These wide-beamed, clinker-built wooden boats still go out nightly for herrings and the famous Cromer crabs which are advertised on hand-painted boards outside the fishermen's homes. The Cromer fishermen are a tight, enclosed order, proud to man the lifeboat and get their livelihood from the sea. But there are fewer than a dozen working boats in the town now, and an increasing tendency for private boat-owners to make occasional solo trips and sell the catch to supplement earnings from regular jobs ashore. Some of the full-time fishermen speak of their determination to carry on regardless through economic recession and hard winters, dwindling stocks and competition from outside trawler fleets; others fear that they are a dying breed, and that tomorrow's Cromer boys will grow up ignorant of hard-won satisfaction such as barman John describes:

> 'Herrin' fishing – it's beautiful. I reckon I've had the best times of my life herrin' fishing. You go out on a sea that's prett' nearly calm – just a lap-lap-lap against the boat – a brilliant sky up above with the stars out. You put your head down below the side with the wind going over the top of you. There's not a word spoken – no conversation, if you know what I mean – just a word every five minutes.
> 'In winter you can lose your nets easy if it's rough. The fishermen use the long line as well – maybe a thousand hooks. You let it down, wait a couple of hours and pull it up. If there's nothing on, you let it down again. If there's a couple on, you pull 'em in quick. The boats work in twos and threes, so there's always someone close by. The fishermen stand by each other. They've got to.'

What the Cromer youngsters are expected to do for a living if they are not lucky enough to have a boat to go to – that's a problem no one has a solution for. There's only one small industrial area in Cromer, and no employment base. Some small industries have left the town because they can't find a workforce. Young men and women move away to find work, and few of them move back again. There's little entertainment in Cromer for a lively teenager. Most go gratefully to the warmth and light of the pubs, to yawn at the old folk and be chaffed by middle-aged drinkers. It's not much of a life. None of the Cromer youngsters I chatted to expected to get satisfying work, or any work at all, without getting out to a bigger town inland.

Cromer is really incapable of further development. Its physical position in a bowl between unstable cliffs prevents any sideways spread, and being in a designated Area of Outstanding Natural Beauty it's not allowed to break the skyline to the south. The town is well and truly stuck with its success as a haven and a bastion, a comfortable time-capsule. Second-home owners with a lot of money and no emotional ties to Cromer are beginning to buy up houses round about. No mid-February visits for these new short-stay Cromerites. Many villages along this North Norfolk coast have become two-or-three-weekends-a-year rich men's toys. Others have been all but smothered by their encrustations of caravans and chalets. While Cromer Crabs and traditional cousinhood-style families continue to bare their teeth at the outside world, the 'Gem of the Norfolk Coast' can probably go on keeping the barbarians outside the gates. Who will rally round the flag and man the defences in the next generation, though? That slow but steady trickle away of town youngsters is a mortal wound that no one has any idea how to stanch.

8. Southwold

The old man had fixed me with a glittering eye as I was wandering down South Green. Wearing an overcoat that had obviously seen a very large number of better days, his fingers, eye-whites, and long tangled beard all bright orange with nicotine, he'd given me a shock when he had first fallen into step alongside and begun to expound on the habits, natures and bank balances of the owners of some of the beautiful old houses round the green. My teacher turned out to be a retired baker, 'Born in that house there – see? Seventy-six years, three months, two weeks and a day ago!' His house stood by the green like a tired old dog, head down and almost on its knees, the only shabby mongrel in a well-groomed pack of pedigree show winners.

'Of course, Southwold has always been a place where rich people buy houses. See that one over there? That's Higgs, the wool people. And that one with all the brickwork around the windows? Thomson, that is – got a house in Bahrain as well, and one somewhere out East too, I hear.' He put his hand on my sleeve and pointed down South Green to a group of ordinary-looking cottages. 'All those little cottages down there were lived in by the fishermen when I was a young boy here. They were nothing special then, just working men's houses. Do you know how much one of them was up on the market for, the other day? *A hundred thousand pound!* Well, you've got to admit it, Southwold's the best place to live, anywhere on the Suffolk coast. People fall for this little town. Jack Parnell, the bandleader – he was just visiting Southwold one day and he liked it so much that he went straight off and bought himself a house here.'

That's it, in a nutshell. You find yourself walking round Southwold in a daze of envious longing, with one harmonious, seductive vista, nook or corner succeeding another. The local people look unbearably self-satisfied and pleased with life as they gossip on street corners in the shadow of Georgian inns, or duck in and out of shops that are the way shops ought to be: dark and crammed to the rafters behind ornate wood-and-glass Victorian shopfronts. Every building style, from medieval farmhouses onwards, rubs shoulders in the gently curving old streets and along the sides of the charming greens that are dotted all over Southwold. Dutch and Flemish influence has floated across the North Sea down the centuries and settled benignly side by side with Elizabethan, Jacobean, Georgian and Victorian. These days the delicious savour of malt floats equally happily on the breeze, wafting from the Adnams' brewery which supplies the South-wold pubs and hotels with one of the tastiest and most distinctive beers brewed anywhere. No wonder Southwold people look like the cat who's got the cream. Their town looks, smells and feels marvellous. It's a place that visitors discover and then return to year after year, hopelessly in love with its unique atmosphere. Southwold's admirers vow to come back and live here one day. Some of them do – the town has a very high proportion of retired people. The rest just dream about it, myself included.

Southwold's atmosphere of isolation and self-containedness forms a big part of its charm. From a point just west of the town, two watercourses separate, Buss Creek running north and the River Blyth south to enter Sole Bay a couple of miles apart, pinching off a triangle of land between them on which Southwold stands. Only one road enters the triangle, straggling in over Buss Creek after four miles of wandering east from the A12 Suffolk/Norfolk through-route. There's no coast road bringing passing trade to Southwold. On this northern Suffolk coastline, the settlements – all of them medieval centres for fishing and trading, most now declined or declining – are widely separated by many miles of salt-marsh, carr and intensely cultivated fields, looking out across high shingle bars into the enormous East Anglian sky and sea panorama. The sea, champing away at the soft clays of this shore, goes on making its way steadily inland. 'Sole Bay' is printed on the OS map on an area of sea indistinguishable from what lies all around; but back in medieval times this was Southwold's sheltered bay and anchorage, protected by two projecting horns of land at Easton on the north and at Dunwich to the south. Easton Ness was the most easterly point in Britain in those days, the town of Dunwich one of the most prosperous with its great fleets of fishing boats and trading vessels, its two monasteries and nine beautiful churches. The sea took the lot, slowly but surely, leaving today's handful of remains at Dunwich and nothing at all at Easton Ness. Southwold stands on its triangular island hemmed in all round by water, skirted by marshland; a remote town on a remote coast.

As at Dunwich, the sea gave plentifully to Southwold by way of fishing and trade with Dutch and Flemish ports, before sealing the harbour approaches with the sand and shingle that killed off the sea commerce of most small east coast towns in the seventeenth and eighteenth centuries. Daniel Defoe, coming to 'Swole, or Southole' around the start of the eighteenth century, found a town thriving on sprat catching and curing. The silted-up old harbour had been abandoned a hundred years before, and a new one cut straight through the already re-grouping shingle banks. The same fate was waiting for the new cut, however. Defoe quotes a rhyme made up by northern coasting seamen about the narrowness of the River Blyth entrance:

> 'Swoul and Dunwich, and Walderswick,
> All go in at one lousie creek.'

For a time Southwold fishermen prospered again, this time on herrings caught under the noses of their Dutch rivals; but more silting had killed off the enterprise by 1800. Luckily Southwold was perfectly placed to take on new colours as an agreeable watering-place and seaside resort. In came the gentry intent on bracing sea air; up went their lovely elegant seaside residences. Southwold expanded as far as the marsh edges, and settled into respectable stability.

The legacy of these shifting fortunes and Southwold's ability to adapt to change is a wonderful richness and variety of building eras and styles, even more impressive when you consider that nearly 250 houses and numbers of other buildings were burned down in a disastrous fire in 1659. One beneficial effect of the catastrophe was in clearing the ground for bigger, better and more beautiful buildings when the Georgian era got under way. The layout of the town is hard to grasp at first acquaintance, and this helps to invest a stroll around Southwold with a sense of excitement and discovery. You find yourself confronted with unexpected corners, flashes of green, country lanes next to busy town streets, glimpses of the sea framed in walls of brick and flint cobbles. There are pre-Tudor farmhouses, frontages with Elizabethan windows and doorways, Jacobean cottages, Georgian town houses, Regency elegance along the cliffs, Victorian magnificence beside South Green. The small but splendid Town Museum in Victoria Street has a curly gable-end that could have been lifted straight from across the North Sea. Pinkneys in Queen Street has a wood-framed, large-windowed Victorian shopfront with a dark old catch-all store behind – many of these in Southwold. Child's Yard off the Market Place is like a Beatrix Potter illustration, narrow and further narrowing, full of ladders and sawdust. And so on. The town has literally hundreds of interesting, handsome old buildings, but it's the way they stand, lean and curve together in small groups that gives Southwold its magical appeal. Every so often you come across one of Southwold's greens, quiet squares or triangles of grass among the streets, with sufficient space to let you appreciate the charms of individual buildings. It's no good coming to Southwold to take in the four or five major attractions in as short a time as possible. Above all it's a strolling, sauntering, time-wasting town, in the style of the rackety little railway that ran from Halesworth to Southwold until 1929. According to legend, drivers and firemen would stop the train to get down and pick groundsel for the canary, or push stray cows off the line.

Once launched on a ramble round Southwold, it becomes impossible to keep any shape in mind – though the excellent (and cheap) booklet *Discovering Southwold*, as pithy, learned and idiosyncratic as any Pevsner, does its best to lick your peregrinations into shape. You keep being seduced into going round the next corner to see what's there. The best plan is no plan at all – just abandon the day to the town. By following your nose, however, you'll arrive outside Adnams Sole Bay Brewery on East Green, my personal favourite among the greens of Southwold. Brewery employees sit on the bench under the central wych-elm, waiting for the hoarse snort of the hooter to drag them back to work. The neat, spick-and-span Sole Bay Inn on one corner of the green serves Adnams beers that couldn't be fresher – they only travel a few yards from source to mouth. Fishermen's cottages and large red-brick houses line two sides of the triangular green, while the third is filled with the tall but graceful bulk of the brewery, hissing steam and giving off that rich, malty brewing smell. Southwold is proud of Adnams, founded in 1890 and still owned and run by the Adnams family, employing nearly 150 local men and women. The draught beers, famous for their flavour and consistency, reach the glass by way of a hand pump. Around Southwold they are delivered to the pubs and hotels by traditional dray-horses. Old malt grounds are taken away to feed local pigs in tractor-drawn containers labelled 'Adnams' pigs are happy pigs'. Large as it is, the brewery enhances East Green – though its modern office-block nearby is a hideous aberration, completely out of place. Peeping over the roofs into East Green from the south is Southwold's tall white lighthouse, while to the north stands the magnificent flint tower of the fifteenth-century church of St Edmund. You'll need an hour at least to take in St Edmund's. Among many glories the chief one must be the pre-Reformation rood-screen with its wonderfully fresh paintings of gold-feathered angels and stiffly posing saints. Every face has been savagely scored out, the Puritan gougings as sharply slashed across as the day they were done. All other details were left alone. How disturbing the zealots must have found those calm smiles and eyes raised in bliss.

To sit on the bench on East Green, sniffing the brewery and savouring its product, surrounded by so many fine buildings and with the sea just over one's shoulder, is to taste Southwold summed up. The sea frontage itself, devoid of pier and pierrots, gets crowded on hot summer days when families from a radius of perhaps twenty miles come to lie out along the strip of sand below the pebble bank. At all other times of year it's a great place for lonely, stormy walks accompanied by that half-dreamy, half-threatening rush and click of waves sucking at millions of pebbles. Amber in large brown chunks is thrown ashore from time to time, a memento of the submarine forest offshore. Staring out over Sole Bay from the doorway of the Sailors' Reading Room on East Cliff (nautical periodicals, ship models, marvellous photos of long-dead Southwold salts with names like Sloper, Brushy, Winkle and Slummy) you can easily turn the clock of the imagination back to 1672 when the bay was the scene of a fierce though inconclusive battle. Not that you'd have seen much from East Cliff, anyway, as the set-to was soon shrouded in a thick East Coast sea-fret.

The Dutch had enjoyed centuries of intercourse in one form or another with the East Anglians. Dutch building styles, Dutch dykes, Dutch names all still abound in these parts. However, when it came to encroachment on what they considered theirs, the Dutchmen could be tough adversaries. For ten years, from 1665 to 1674, the English navy was based at the anchorage in Sole Bay, supposedly ready to deal with the Dutch at a moment's notice. In 1672 the Lord High Admiral was James, Duke of York, brother of King Charles II. He billeted himself at Sutherland House in Southwold's High Street (now a restaurant) in command of a fleet of 101 fighting ships, a mixture of English and French vessels that was bound to cause problems, given the history of Anglo-French relations, even when combining to see off a common enemy. For a number of reasons – dilatoriness, mutual distrust, arrogance, difficulties in communication – the joint fleet was not properly ready for action when on 28 May the Dutch fireships came drifting into Sole Bay. One name stood out in the ensuing fight – that of the Earl of Sandwich, who had cleared from the bay as soon as the fireships were sighted in order to give his colleagues more elbow room to dodge the blazing hulks. Somehow Sandwich got hold of the idea that his courage was being questioned, and he seems to have spent the rest of the day in a frenzy of action and blood-letting (including among his victims the Dutch Admiral, Van Ghent, whom he personally ran through with his sword) before leaping to his death from the burning deck of the *Royal James*, his flagship, in full dress including his Star and Garter and three diamond rings, rather than fall into the hands of *Mynheer*. Can't you just see Douglas Fairbanks in the role? The Anglo-French fleet lost only the *Royal James*, the Dutch a couple of their fighting ships. 'Not to be too partial to ourselves, the English fleet was worsted', reported Daniel Defoe. As 600 English sailors were lost, he was probably right.

The seagoing side of Southwold's present-day life is centred along the narrow mouth of the River Blyth. Leaving South Green's pleasant spaces down Constitution Hill, the road crosses the town marshes, wide and flat, with the red roofs and church tower of Walberswick standing tall across the Blyth. Southwold's own roofs and church tower on their rise of ground compel the eye even more strongly as you view them from the sheltered harbour at Blackshore, a mile south of the town. Here is a thriving yacht club and an inshore lifeboat; also Southwold's fleet of working fishing boats, more than twenty of them. There's still a living to be made for the crews in trawling and line fishing, and the occasional setting of pots. Each small, salt-scabbed boat has its own wooden jetty festooned with drying nets, where the fishermen in yellow waterproofs and industrial gloves unload the catch. From their tarred huts beside the jetties you can buy, cheaply, fish that were in the sea a couple of hours before. The profits are not enormous; the labour is. While there are people prepared to grapple with such long hours, danger and hard graft as a way of life they wouldn't swap for any other, the harbour will go on being a fishing concern in spite of its narrow, difficult entrance. Had one recent 'improvement' scheme come to fruition, the entire area would have been transformed – and not for the better, was the unanimous verdict of the Southwold fishermen. The townsfolk, the very large majority of them, felt the same way.

The trouble began with the harbour defences, always shaky, which during the 1980s had shown signs of crumbling away altogether. Marine consultants were called in, and prescribed a three-million-pound repair scheme. The council was in despair, wondering where on earth such a sum was going to come from. Suddenly up popped a fairy godmother in the shape of a development company. The bill would be footed, if the council would agree to allow some classy waterside homes to be built – not many storeys, no – around a marina-style development on the site of Southwold's harbour. A new cut would be necessary from the River Blyth north-eastwards through the town marshes, turning the whole area into a little island. There would be some nice new creeks for the yachts that would be attracted here, and a nice artificial windmill, just to make the whole thing look authentic. And, of course, people would come flocking into Southwold to enjoy the new amenity. (As at Ramsgate, Brighton, Swanage . . .)

A packed and seething public meeting had to be transferred from the meeting hall to the church, to accommodate everyone who wanted to throw objections at the councillors and the development company's representative. The scheme had stirred up all the feelings well-settled ants have towards a boot descending on their cosy nest. What on earth did the company think would be the effect of tall, modern buildings in a landscape whose intrinsic beauty begins and ends with flatness? What would happen to the fauna and flora of the marshes? What benefits could accrue to Southwold from a development a mile to the south? Where, on the plans, was there provision for the fishing boats that would be displaced in the upheavals? How dare they even think of attaching such a carbuncle to a long-established, entire place like Southwold? The killer blow turned out to be something quite different, however: a quiet enquiry as to whether there might be any truth in the rumour that there were connections between the development company and the marine consultants who had originally recommended the expensive repairs.

The mere fact that such a scheme could be proposed from outside brought the community together with a crunch. A lot of rich people live in Southwold; a lot of people not nearly so well-off, too. Some come only at weekends, some for the summer, some every school holiday. There are incomers flushed with romantic love for the place; families like the Adnamses – brewers, estate agents, lifeboat crewmen – who have lived in Southwold for generations. Here they are luckier than in most comparable places, for pride in this loveliest and most harmonious of seaside towns has created a closely knit community. If incomers pull their weight and put on no side, they are soon part of the beating heart of the place. Southwold is the sort of place that engenders loyalty strong enough to keep its schools open, buildings secure and harbour free from 'improvement' as far as its people want to look into the future: a fortunate town.

LONDON'S COAST

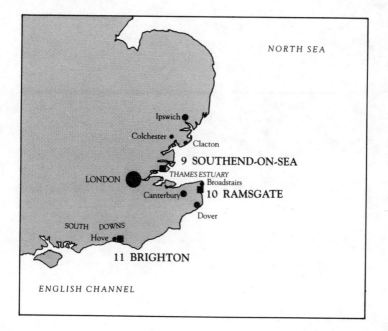

9. Southend-on-Sea

At nine o'clock in the morning on Spring Bank Holiday Monday, the only figure I could see on Southend's Marine Parade was an elderly man in slept-in clothes stooping low in a doorway, inspecting the rubbish thrown down on the pavement by last night's revellers. It took him a minute or so to find what he wanted, a bundle of chip papers. Chewing a fist-full of cold chips, he wandered off towards the pier: a fitting symbol for Southend-on-Sea, still the archetype of seaside seediness in public mythology.

The town council would give its right arm to get rid of that image. So would the Chamber of Trade and Industry, the Hotel and Catering Association and the Southend Society. Look at our thriving cultural life, their booklets and brochures say; come and see our Regency architecture, our medieval halls, our parks and gardens, our theatre, our fringe of beautiful historic villages. Visit Southend in early spring or in the autumn and discover the quiet and elegant resort we know we really are. *Please* don't be put off by all that old stuff – fist-fights on the seafront, hordes of trippers invading the beach, Bethnal-Green-beside-the-sea. That's all in the past. Terribly unhelpful.

Such image-building brought me to Southend determined to see the very best in all things and all people, to ferret out the lovely crescents and terraces, to savour the sophisticated and wide-ranging pleasures of the town. I would choose Bank Holiday Monday, to show that Southend was well and truly shot of those parodically raffish, dangerous, highly coloured East End wide boys and fast girls who, the tabloids said, were still taking over the town on such occasions. In the early hours of that windy, cold spring morning, strolling from the deserted amusement arcades of the front up into the well-polished Regency smartness of Cliff Town, it looked as if my preconceptions would be borne out. By the evening, with Marine Parade a solid block of rattling and flashing arcades, 20,000 people choking off all movement along its pavements, police dogs moving in on groups of hilarious, defiant boys, the beer beginning to shout, beatbox rhythms clashing from rival ghetto-blasters, cheap perfume sweetness and chip vinegar tartness jarring in the nostrils, I knew I didn't have a hope in hell of making out a case for the respectable face of Southend.

On the map, Southend-on-Sea forms just the central and seaward chunk of a sprawling blotch of building that covers a good seven miles of the Essex coast where the Thames broadens out to meet the North Sea. Two hundred years ago Southend didn't even exist. A flat expanse of open shoreline ran east from the fishing and ship-building village of Leigh-on-Sea all the way to Shoebury Ness, where the coast turned north towards the watery marshes of remote Foulness Island. A string of small villages lay inland: Eastwood, Prittlewell, Southchurch, North and South Shoebury. Southchurch had its Norman church and moated, timber-framed fourteenth-century hall (now open to the public); but Prittlewell, a settlement since at least Roman times, was the chief village of the area. Prittlewell Priory, founded about AD 1110, had housed the black-gowned, black-hooded, grimly quiet and prayerful Cluniac monks until the Dissolution of the Monasteries in 1536. Nearby stood the old brick house known as Porters, built round a great hall and solar at about the same time as the Tudors were establishing themselves at the top of the tree.

Prittlewell, like Southchurch and the other nearby villages, was quickly swallowed up in the enormous expansion of building in the district as the seaside boom got a grip in the early years of the nineteenth century. These days Prittlewell village is a small haven of quiet respectability away from Southend's seafront razzmatazz, both Priory and Porters pleasant refuges to be explored at leisure. Porters does duty as the Mayor's Parlour, while the Priory house stands as the centrepiece of a peaceful garden layout. Splendidly detailed booklets give you chapter and verse on these survivors from the district's unfrequented past. A Bank Holiday Monday hour or two in the Priory grounds is a great recharger of batteries, but it has nothing at all to do with what's going on at the business end of the town.

It was oysters that brought Southend into being at the south end of Prittlewell. All this Essex coast, from the Thames Estuary right round to the Suffolk border, is good oyster-growing territory. The Romans knew it; so did the Normans, and the medieval oystermen supplying rich towns like Maldon and Colchester. The Essex shore of the Thames went bullish over oysters at the beginning of the eighteenth century. Between Leigh-on-Sea and Shoebury the oyster fishers built their shacks, many of them along the shore where Southend's Kursaal dance-hall now stands. The Ship Inn was built about the middle of the century, at the same time as the fishermen were putting up more solid and permanent cottages. The upper classes were becoming avid for salt-water resorts, and the Ship became the centre of a rapidly expanding nucleus of new houses and lodgings. Southend was only a short journey by sea from London, though in those early days visitors had to be carried ashore piggy-back by brawny fishermen. Soon they were settling here in the stylish splendour of Regency terrace and square. The Terrace was built on the clifftop to the west of the Ship Inn in 1791, to be dignified after the turn of the nineteenth century as Royal Terrace – Princess Caroline of Brunswick, already deeply out of love with her husband George, Prince of Wales, had stayed there in 1804. Southend remained respectable and fashionable for another half-century; the eminent railway engineers Peto, Brassey and Betts thought it worth their while to oversee the building of Cliff Town, Southend's own version of Brighton's Kemp Town, in 1859. Three years earlier, however, their London, Tilbury & Southend Railway had stretched its long iron finger out over the flatlands of Essex to point Southend away from the guineas of high society towards the coppers of London's working-class masses. A short journey and a cheap ticket – those were Southend's selling-points in an era when ordinary folk had no right to a fixed-term holiday. When the Bank Holiday slid into common acceptance in the 1870s, Southend was made. Commuters, too, found that they could live out here by the river, yet be at their desks in the City in less than an hour's journey time. In the 1830s the population of the town was still under 2,000. By 1891 it had swelled to 12,000, by 1921 to over 100,000. In the late 1980s it is well on the way to double that figure. Five million visitors arrived in the season just before the Second World War. Far fewer people stay for a complete summer week nowadays – here, as in most British seaside resorts, Spanish sun has creamed off the best of the trade. But millions still do come every year, and Bank Holiday in Southend continues to exert its magic.

There's nothing self-effacing about Southend Pier. 'The longest pier in the world' announces the signboard. It's the single biggest selling-point of the town. The paddle steamer *Waverley* visits Southend for a fortnight every year from its home base on Clydeside, puffing away from the pier every day laden with sightseers. You can embark here for trips to Harwich, Clacton, Whitstable and the Goodwin Sands. Smart little trains, decked out in crimson and cream livery, rumble along to a terminus a mile out from the shore above the cold and muddy waters of the Thames. The locomotive that pulled my train was named *Sir John Betjeman* – how that lover of the matter-of-fact would have enjoyed recording the stolidity of the teenage fishermen on the train. Overloaded with rods, tackle-boxes and newspaper packages of ragworms, blown sideways by the wind the moment they stepped out of the carriage, shivering in T-shirts as the breeze

69

whipped up the white horses around the legs of the pier, they wedged themselves in the angles of the railings and settled down for a cold, hungry, day-long vigil. From the train terminus there was still another couple of hundred yards to walk to the very end of the pier, a mile and a quarter out from the seafront, where the Southend lifeboat is housed. The grey-green water sucked greedily at the timber baulks supporting the pier. Most of the timber was charred and blackened, legacy of the fire that burned the pierhead buildings to ashes back in 1976. No one has got round to doing anything to remedy the mess. The views out here are immense, stretching across to the Kentish shore of the Thames, down west to a horizon of oil-storage tanks and refinery chimneys around Canvey Island, east to the big ships inching their way into and out of the mouth of the river. These are not classic resort views, however. No one, bar the fishermen, seemed inclined to linger at the tip of the pier. By train or on foot, the visitors made their way back down the pier's narrow corridor of planking to the ten-pin bowling emporium on the shoreward end.

This bright place reinforced the notion of Southend as a family resort. Enthusiasts from eight to eighty were grouped in chairs around computerized consoles which recorded what was going on down at the other end of the alley. Contraptions that looked and sounded like Victorian bottle-capping machines cleared away the toppled pins and set up new ones with mathematical exactitude. The whole hall was clean, cheery and hearty, ringing with the clashing of the resetting machines, plasticky click of falling pins, thump and rumble of bowling balls on the wooden runways. Smug eight-year-olds swaggered about, grinning, after knocking down all ten in one go. Dads missed them all and shrugged it off. Hulking lads stuck their hands in their pockets and sulked after being humbled by their girls. Ten-pin bowling is a great leveller.

Outside in the pale spring sunshine, some of Southend's problems of identity began to emerge. Up on the top of the cliff were those Regency terraces round which I'd sauntered earlier, gleaming in immaculate white paint above their sloping front aprons of greenery. Just in front stood the Palace Hotel – or, rather, sailed. Like a great white ocean-liner, the Palace's cheese-wedge prow cut the air majestically. Elaborate ironwork, side turrets and ornamentation encrusted its flanks. Oozing atmosphere, the Palace dominated its corner of the seafront. Adulterous couples should have been entwined on every balcony. But its only inhabitants were homeless families, temporarily housed here. A closer look revealed grimed-over windows, missing chunks of plaster, rusting iron and flaking paint. Nowadays, if anyone could afford a week in the kind of ambience the Palace used to offer, they'd take themselves off to canoodle in Cairo or dally in Darjeeling for the same money.

The entire ground floor of the Palace seemed to be given over to palmists, fortune-tellers, snooker dens and novelty shops packed solid with seashell dollies, copper kettles and Original Willy Exercisers. It was mid-day now, and that early morning solitude was gone as if it had never been. Thousands of people were in view, jostling along the seafront as the amusement arcades shouted for attention. Up amid the elegant architecture of Cliff Town and out on the fire-emasculated pier, I'd completely missed the shift in atmosphere that had overtaken Southend. Now the flash motors had arrived from London and were turning heads as they squealed round corners or pulled up with a snarl and jerk to park half-way across the pavement. Groups of hard lads in shades and soft hats were parading, posturing for the glances of girls like high-heeled blobs of candy-floss. A lot of East London rivalries had been transported unsweetened to Southend for the day, with the inevitable growlings and squarings-up. Suddenly the town seemed full of policemen in twos, strolling along or standing with folded arms on the street corners. Nothing oppressive, but a word to the wise – Old Bill's about, lads, so cool it. Alsatians and police horses underlined the message. Southend has suffered in the past from Mods/Rockers and Mods/Skinheads confrontations. That kind of gang warfare seems to be out of fashion just at the moment, but the tension was still there, though low-key. In and out of the groups of sharp boys and girls ran the toddlers of the family day-trippers, aiming like guided missiles for Southend's narrow strip of sand directly below the promenade railings. The separate worlds of youths and of families rubbed shoulders along Southend's Golden Mile, neither coinciding nor colliding.

The Kursaal was in some ways a sadder sight than the Palace Hotel. This Edwardian dream of a dance hall, down at the eastern end of the seafront, used to be the focus for any evening's entertainment that included fun, live music, drinking, dancing and sex. Here all the bands played, but favourite of all were those who could hammer out gut-bucket rhythm 'n' blues, hard, loud and basic – Southend epitomized. Now the Kursaal stood empty under its wonderful colonial central dome, silent and blank-eyed, waiting for the developers to transform it into a smooth amusements complex, more suited than its old sweaty function to the image that the new Southend is trying so hard to wrap round itself.

'The old Kursaal was fun, sure, but people thought it gave the town a bad name,' said the Southend-born-and-bred barman in the nearby Minerva pub as he chewed slowly on our conversation. 'Too much aggro round about chucking-out time. The trouble is, you've got to admit it, Southend can be dodgy at times, especially late at nights. I say this even though I was born here and like the town. This end of the seafront is as seedy as it ever was. Crowds of young Londoners come down here by the coachload, and get in the Foresters along there and get roaring pissed. Some of them always miss their last train home, and that's when the trouble starts.'

On the beer terrace of the Foresters' Arms ('Night and Day We Are the One for Entertainment – Including Strippers Lunchtime – A Beautiful Pub and Wonderful People – Join Us') three boys in leather jackets, very much on their dignity behind the shades, stared hard at all comers, occasionally passing comments with loud chortles. Three girls in tourniquet-tight skirts and white stiletto shoes watched them and consulted together, giggling behind their hands. It took five minutes for the boys to pick up their pints and slide in beside the girls, ten minutes more for Mister Manners, and then the three couples moved off together towards the arcades, the girls still appraising their catches with sideways glances.

Next door to the Foresters stands the Ship Inn, dating back in part to those eighteenth-century times when Southend was struggling to get established as a respectable resort. There was nothing respectable about the Ship on this Bank Holiday Monday. Its interior, as bare and functional as a Glasgow housing scheme bar, was racked by a disco, manned by a pair of seen-it-all-before lads and so shatteringly loud that it vibrated the spilt beer on the table-tops. The tables in the window were crowded with more unsmiling London boys in soft black hats and dark glasses, drinking lager. You would have needed a resolutely wielded battering-ram to get to the bar. Everybody shouted, everybody smoked, everybody eyed everybody else. The only people in the place who looked over twenty were two men with lank grey locks, wearing shabby suits that might have been sharp when flares were in fashion, drinking shorts and penned into a furious argument. To an outsider, the tension between both the individuals and the groups in the bar felt enormous, but no one except me seemed in any way bothered. This was tribal territory, transplanted entire from the East End for the day. Outside, a police van wailed up and six policemen jumped out to deal with a traffic accident. Someone's motor, a fierce red job with wide tyres parked on a double yellow line, had been lightly thumped by someone else's equally dangerous-looking machine. The policemen smiled wearily as they moved in on the outraged owners, watched with amusement by the young drinkers in the Ship's window. Come on, son – it was just an accident. Don't make a spectacle of yourself, all right? Let's have your name, shall we? Baby-talked off their high horses, the car owners relaxed and began to jibe the youngest of the policemen.

As the seafront pavement steadily filled up and the promenade walls became top-heavy with shouting teenage boys and girls, I walked away from the blare and up those quiet Victorian streets to Southchurch, looking for that sober Southend I wanted to write about. Among the wide, tree-lined avenues where old ladies walked their dogs and track-suited men jogged, everything was quiet. After the raucous excitements of Marine Parade, there was nothing for the mind to bite on. Family cars went north on the roads, carrying the beach-surfeited toddlers home to tea. Cavalcades of scooters went the other way, heading for the evening's fun. Towards opening time I wandered down as well, back to the Minerva where the philosophical barman filled me in on recent attempts to clean up Southend's act.

'There was some plan to build a marina – new concrete jetties off the end of the pier, high-rise des. res., a yacht-basin and God knows what. It fell through, though. I mean, if you had enough money to buy a place in a marina development, you'd want something better to look out at than oil refineries and power stations, right? I know we've got some nice old buildings in the town, but Southend's bread and butter is still your average East Ender. What he wants hasn't changed at all – a few drinks, a bit of you-know-what, some laughs. Southend will never be respectable. People still think of it as good old Sahfend, the place to come and get legless on a Bank Holiday.'

10. Ramsgate

In Harrison's Cafeteria on Ramsgate's Harbour Parade nothing seems to have stirred since the 1950s. The décor is exactly the same: long counter hung with square printed notices, cross-braced frosted internal windows, wooden shelves backed by mirrors, formica-topped tables in ranks, a great gleaming silver espresso-coffee machine. It only needs Dirk Bogarde draped over a chair or James Dean propping up the doorway to complete the time warp. Drinking a cup of 'froffee coffee' in Harrison's as you look out over the harbour is a treat. But Ramsgate nowadays is inclined to blush over places like this. 'We've become a bit shabby, I'm afraid,' and 'Things have stood still here for twenty years,' are phrases that spring to local lips when Ramsgate people talk about their town.

In many ways it's true. Ramsgate forms the bottom portion of the long seaside resort conglomeration that crowds the tip of the Isle of Thanet's snub nose at the north-eastern corner of Kent. The whole area is promoted by the tourist authority under the blanket name of 'Thanet', but the three towns that make up this holiday package don't really have much in common. Margate at the top gets London visitors and London money, and goes bald-headed for the mass market. Broadstairs in the middle relies comfortably on its genteel image and its associations with Charles Dickens to tick along and do very nicely, thank you. Ramsgate, the old-fashioned family resort with its tourist roots starved of nourishment since the growth of private car ownership, has been caught in the middle of the crisis facing such seaside towns. Families no longer come by coach or train for a couple of weeks in a Ramsgate hotel or boarding house. These days they tour the Isle of Thanet, and the rest of Kent, by car. Ramsgate has become one overnight stop among many. And as the long-stay visitors have disappeared, so have many of the town's tourist attractions – the Marine open-air swimming pool under East Cliff, for example, and the narrow-gauge railway that used to take wide-eyed children up through fairy-lit tunnels to the park at Dumpton. The big hotels where the better-off families stayed for their seaside fortnight have felt the pinch, too, increasing costs and inadequate upkeep choking them off one by one. As all the shopkeepers of Ramsgate will tell you, tourist revenue has dropped and keeps on dropping. The High Street has none of the twinkle and glitter you expect from seaside resort shops. Most of the town's pubs are smoky, shabby places where you'll be lucky to find a decent pint or plate of food. The town museum has an exhibition based on Ramsgate's history, but it consists of only a few cabinets of relics and a couple of beautiful models of Ramsgate's famous paddle-steamers. The traditional seafront rides – rollercoaster, dodgems, Ghost Train – are squeezed together miserably under the cliff behind the Pleasure Park on a strip of cracked old tarmac. The whole impression, confirmed by the way Ramsgate people keep apologizing for their town, is of a place very much down in the dumps, seeing itself as the poor relation of its two more confident neighbours. In a word, Ramsgate is feeling sorry for itself just now.

A good place to start the cure for the Ramsgate Blues is at the seaward end of the east pier. Past glories and future opportunities, viewed from here in one of the finest waterfront and cliff panoramas in Britain, soon shunt present gloom out of mind. From Royal Crescent's white Regency bulwark on top of West Cliff, the view leads over the variegated frontages and roof levels of Nelson Crescent, sloping down by way of a run of diminishing red-brick arches shoring up Royal Parade to the flat saucer of land behind the harbour. Here the houses, shops and hotels of central Ramsgate – windows, roofs, chimneys and bellcotes – pack up close in front of the tall tower of St George's Church. Then the Regency reasserts itself as the prospect climbs again through the magnificent tan-and-white bow of Wellington Crescent on East Cliff, and on past handsome Victorian and Edwardian villas to where the cliffs turn north and out of sight. This graceful dip and swell of buildings and cliffs completely fills the inland view. In front of it lies the double Royal Harbour, the inner basin solid with yachts, the outer basin buzzing with activity as fishing boats, orange-topped pilot-boats, filthy old dredgers, motor launches and sailing boats move round the circle of water and in and out of the narrow gap between the east and west piers. Outside the harbour, the big red-and-white cross-Channel ferries of the Sally Line and the Schiaffino freight boats edge between the slimy stone ramparts of breakwaters towards their berths at the western end of the town. If by the time you read this the *camera obscura* has been remounted in its rightful place on the Eagle Café at the end of the pier, you'll be able to enjoy the scene in miniature. Add the active boatyard inside the east pier and the fine beach of good digging sand under East Cliff, and Ramsgate begins to look like a town with quite a few blessings to count.

Even without its thriving harbour, Ramsgate would be well placed to attract tourists with its long history and wealth of lovely and interesting buildings. In 449 Hengist and Horsa brought their pioneer Saxon invasion party ashore just to the south at Pegwell Bay; and St Augustine chose the same spot, a century and a half later. Succeeding waves of marauding Norsemen followed, until the Normans arrived to discourage any further incursions. By that time Ramsgate, site of one of the very few breaks in the chalk wall of Thanet, was well established as a fishing settlement and small harbour. When the Cinque Ports trading confederation was at its height during the Middle Ages, Ramsgate was a satellite port of Sandwich, and built itself a better harbour to cope with the increase in fishing and trade first with the Continent and, later, with the Baltic ports. Its harbour was still a rough and ready affair, though, playing second fiddle to the main refuge at Sandwich.

Then an ill wind blew Ramsgate a lot of good during a violent storm in December 1748. The notorious Goodwin Sands lie a few miles south of the town, separated from the Kentish coast by a strip of comparatively sheltered sea known as the Downs. Here ships had always been able to ride out storms, but the 1748 tempest was too much for them. Every ship at sea that night ran for shelter, many of them to Ramsgate. The little harbour, filled with sheltering ships, proved itself equal to the task of protecting them; within a year Ramsgate had been designated the coast's chief refuge, and a fine new harbour was under construction. It took more than forty years to complete the piers, the inner cross wall dividing the harbour into two basins, the sluices for scouring away silt, the gates, dry dock, harbour buildings and lighthouse. In 1774 the great engineer John Smeaton was brought in to advise on the silting problem, and stayed on to see the end of the long labour in 1791. His sluices are still in operation, and the whole harbour layout hasn't changed much since he oversaw its improvement. It brought Ramsgate greatly increased business; but by those closing years of the eighteenth century the town was already set fair on a new course, as the fine folk of the Regency began to look to the seaside for their health and entertainment.

Albion House stands high above the harbour where the rise of the ground levels out into East Cliff. These days it's a sad sight, a scabby old building patched with blotches of damp, badly in need of a facelift, its first-floor balconies rusting, its gutters leaking down the walls. Ironical Fate now has it playing host to the Environmental Health Department, an inglorious come-down from the great days when Princess Victoria stayed here. Alongside Albion House is Albion Place, built at about the same time in 1789. Mrs Fitzherbert used Albion Place between 1797 and 1799 as one of her homes in exile while she waited patiently for her royal George – at that time being given hell by his contemptuous wife, Caroline of Brunswick – to call her back to Brighton and bliss again. Jane Austen stayed at Albion Place in about 1803, and used her fond memories of Ramsgate in Wickham's elopement scene in *Pride and Prejudice*. At present there are plans to halt the downward slide of these historic houses, smarten them up and convert them into a language school.

Round the corner from Albion House, another clutch of conversion jobs is hatching along the arc of Wellington Crescent, built and named in the decade after Waterloo when Old Nosey was the hero of the land. William Powell Frith, mid-Victorian painter of enormous bustling panoramas such as *The Railway Station* and *Derby Day*, lived here, and had one of his greatest popular successes with his 1854 painting, *Ramsgate Sands*. Like Albion House, Wellington Crescent has slid slowly down in the world to its present state as a row of cheap hotels, with lines of washing flapping between the gossamer-slim ironwork balconies. Many of these places are being sold off for modification into self-catering flats, as are the big hotels that stand beyond, reacting to that trend which is changing the holiday nature of fading family resorts. Families who don't want, or can't afford, to be tied to an all-in hotel bill and timetable for their week at the seaside can pay for a base and use the rest of their time and money as they want, in or out of the town. It's a good, reliable basket for Ramsgate to put some of its eggs into, keeping the splendid old buildings from the demolition crane while giving the tourist public the freedom it currently demands – a sign that the council and the tourist authorities, if not all the townsfolk, are coming to practical terms with the death of the old seaside-holiday tradition.

In the corresponding position across the town on West Cliff stands Ramsgate's grandest legacy from its Victorian years, the splendid Royal Crescent, built in the classic Regency style between 1826 and 1861. No ragtag and bobtail of washing lines and boarding houses here – the smart Regency Hotel occupies the centre of this proud and carefully maintained crescent, the gateway to many other fine Regency terraces and squares in this part of Ramsgate. Infilling of green lawns and gardens with less distinguished building in the late Victorian years makes it quite a journey of exploration to seek out the single graceful curve of Liverpool Lawn tucked away behind Hertford Street, or the right-angle run of Guildford Lawn opposite the public library, its former view down over the sea blocked off by the great red slab of the Edwardian Lawn Villas. Karl Marx is said to have stayed at No. 6 or No. 7 on the curve of the angle of Guildford Lawn; more certain is the presence in Ramsgate in 1876 of Vincent van Gogh, who was turning an honest penny taking classes at Mr Stokes's school at No. 6 Royal Road, just behind Royal Crescent. There's a crazy and fascinating 10p-in-the-slot machine in the town museum at the back of the library where, with a push on the button, you can set Vincent a-jerk, trying to kick off the pot of Dulux in which his foot is stuck. This eccentric device also features a JCB digger emptying earth over St George's dragon, a naked man pedalling a glove-shaped bathing machine, and Mr Charles Dickens seated at a desk pondering his latest masterpiece. After a lot of bad-tempered scratching and poking with a quill pen, the writer lifts up his literary labours to reveal a piece of paper inscribed '✗2 Pints Today Please. C Dickens'.

Ramsgate's waterfront, cradled in the outflung arms of Regency architecture, is a striking collection of varied buildings, each a distinct piece in the jigsaw of the town's history. The Pleasure Park under East Cliff, housed in a great stone barn of a building that looks like one of those 1930s factories on the Great West Road out of London, squats near the site of the London, Chatham & Dover Railway's seafront station which brought the trippers right on to the sands, until it closed in 1926. Next to it is the green-roofed Pavilion, once the scene of holiday shows and concerts, now divided between Peggy Sue's rowdy glitz-and-glitter 'fun pub' and the Ramsgate Casino; opposite this stands the wonderfully overblown Queen's Head pub, by Art Nouveau out of classical Greece in glazed tiles of ochre and turquoise.

The tall and imposing Royal Sailors' Rest Home, Edwardian philanthropic grandeur in every line, faces the centre of the harbour. Opened in 1904, it was equipped rather optimistically with a temperance bar. Ramsgate's famous fleet of smacks or sailing trawlers, venturing across the North Sea in search of flatfish off the coasts of Belgium and Holland, numbered well over 150 in those days. The town's vulnerability to air-raids in the First World War resulted in smack after smack being destroyed; and when the fleet was ordered to move out and base itself in faraway Brixham, Ramsgate's fishing industry received its death blow.

Nowadays a few trawlers and pot-fishing boats operate out of the harbour, while memories of Ramsgate's great fishing days are enshrined in the cluster of buildings at the western end of the waterfront: the Ice House under West Cliff from which the smack skippers would draw a ton of ice apiece before setting out; the Sailors' Home of 1878 which soon meta-morphosed into the Sailors' Church where shipwrecked mariners could be sheltered, fed, clothed and shriven under one roof. Next to it stands the turreted and castellated Ramsgate Home for Smack Boys, its name, emblazoned over the door, guaranteed to bring disobedient young visitors to order. The boys who cooked and skivvied aboard the Ramsgate smacks in Victorian times had a hard time of it, always at the mercy of a bad-tempered skipper or older crew members, sleeping rough on deck or in odd corners of the boat, often bullied and knocked about, badly paid and worked until they dropped. Many of them were orphans or rejects from bottom-of-the-heap families, spending their time ashore shifting from one miserable flop-house to the next. When it opened in 1881, the Home for Smack Boys was a haven for these young scapegraces, the only one of its kind in the country. It closed when the smack fleet decamped during the First World War, by which time engine power was superseding sail and the skippers could do without their cheap slave-labour. Nowadays the Smack Boys' Home houses a couple of shipping agents, a sign of the way in which the wheel of the harbour's fortunes has turned.

In 1821 the harbour was styled the 'Royal Harbour of Ramsgate' by gracious pleasure of King George IV, delighted by the warmth of his send-off when he embarked here. His niece Victoria, arriving ten years later to open a new flight of steps at the east pier, refused to walk up them until the red carpet laid for her had been removed – strong-willed even at twelve years old, she was determined to be seen as an ordinary mortal. During this century's two world wars, the harbour, a few short miles from the French and Belgian coasts, was ideally sited for enemy attack. Zeppelins, torpedo planes and huge Gotha bombers operated over Ramsgate in 1914–18; mine-laying aircraft, naval bombardment and more bombers during the Second World War, which saw an estimated 500 bombs dropped on the town in one three-minute raid at the height of the Battle of Britain. More than 40,000 men were landed at Ramsgate from

Dunkirk in June 1940; and, four years later, the harbour sheltered part of the D-Day landing force.

Just as the First World War evacuation of the town's smack fleet put paid to Ramsgate's fishing heritage, so the regular summertime visits by paddle-steamers from London did not survive the 1939–45 war. The *Eagles* had been part of the holiday tradition of Ramsgate, bringing thousands of day-trippers on jaunts to the Isle of Thanet. Their demise, allied to the ever-growing numbers of private motor cars in the 1950s, helped to push Ramsgate's attractions as a resort down the league table. The Royal Harbour, however, dragged itself out of the slough of despond to run the world's first hovercraft passenger service in 1966 across to Calais. The bigger hovercraft that soon came on the scene couldn't be handled by Ramsgate's harbour, and the operation was shifted around the cliff to Pegwell Bay; but the old, disused hoverpad is still in place on the eastern side of the cross wall.

In recent years the harbour has gone on keeping up with the times, the inner basin being converted into a yacht marina, and a new ferry and freight terminal built on twenty acres of reclaimed land just outside the west pier. These new developments have given the town a tremendous shot in the arm. The Sally boats nip across to Dunkirk in a couple of hours for anything from a day excursion to long weekends or longer. The arches under Royal Parade are full of chandlers, boat repairers and marine engineers, all thriving on trade from the marina. The shops and pubs of Ramsgate get a certain amount of business from the yacht owners, though some of these practical people bring their own stores with them and stay self-contained. Heavy lorries roar along Military Road from the freight terminal, making much of the hairpin turn up on to Royal Parade. The Ramsgate townsfolk may wring their hands over the fading of resort splendour, but most local people say they are proud of their active, well-set-up harbour. There's a cloud on the horizon, however: lined with silver in some opinions, black all through in others.

The museum in Ramsgate's library may be short on interest, but the excellence of the maritime museum in the Clock House on the harbour's cross wall more than makes up for it. Here are ancient cannon, glassware, ship models, cases of gleaming navigation instruments, wreck charts of the Goodwin Sands, a giant ship's copper kettle. There's a full-size ship's wheelhouse where you can spin the wheel to set a 360°-panorama of

Ramsgate harbour revolving past the windows: town, cliffs, sea horizons, ships, buoys and a yacht with a shouting, gesticulating crew about to be run down by your vessel. For my money (donation in the box) this is the best hour's fun in Ramsgate. The chief focus of interest in the museum in 1987, however, was the upstairs room exhibiting plans and scale models of what, if it comes to fruition, will be the most important development of the Royal Harbour since the days of John Smeaton. A London development company is proposing to sink almost £100 million into a radical alteration of the harbour, and the council badly wants the scheme to go ahead. Two new piers will be built out into the outer harbour, and two more along the existing east and west piers. A new, zigzag-shaped cross wall will cut the outer harbour virtually in half. On the new piers will rise 400 smart, expensive and exclusive residences, with their own food shops, wine bars and restaurants. There is to be a new boatyard, a multi-starred hotel, a 300-berth marina and associated boatyard. All this incoming prestige and money, the council hopes, will bring the roses back to Ramsgate's faded cheeks. Pegwell Bay, too – since the hovercraft departed, a quiet stretch of muds and sand given over to wading birds – is in for upheavals under the same plan, which envisages a new development of 390 upmarket houses around the curve of the bay, facing a lagoon enclosed by an archipelago of man-made islands, intended to provide sanctuary for the dispossessed birds of Pegwell Bay.

The developers' exhibition in the maritime museum was a masterpiece of the genre: immaculately presented maps, models and architects' drawings that gave away little in the way of hard facts. What the effects of the Pegwell Bay lagoon and pattern of islands might be on an area constantly threatened by silting problems, or on a bird population cut off from a large slice of its feeding and sheltering grounds, the developers didn't predict. The benefits of the Royal Harbour scheme were presented as new jobs during construction, new service jobs thereafter, new money for the town from the well-lined pockets of the incomers, a major 'people draw' for visitors and a strengthening of links between harbour and town. How the people of Ramsgate viewed this enormous change on their front doorstep emerged as one turned over the pages of the book in which interested parties were invited to write their comments.

Two diametrically opposed camps sprang into being as soon as the proposals were unveiled. On one side were those impatient with

Ramsgate's sad view of itself, its long slide into lower-division tourist status, its preoccupation with its wilting holiday trade and shabby appearance. 'Go for it!' urged these enthusiasts in the comments book: 'A fantastic, far-seeing plan which I hope will not be put off by the "whingers, whiners" etc. who want to live completely in the past.' A recurrent theme was Ramsgate's 20 per cent unemployment problem, made almost insoluble by the Isle of Thanet's isolated position, surrounded by water on three sides. '*We cannot live in the past!* We are an unemployment blackspot for youngsters.' The opponents of the scheme, who included the splendidly named 'Save What Is Left Of Thanet Society' (the SWILOTS?), had several points of focus for their disapproval: the threat to the wildlife of Pegwell Bay, the jarring of modern architecture with Ramsgate's older buildings, the unlikelihood of more than a handful of the promised 1,000 new jobs coming the way of local people. By far the biggest cause for antagonism, however, was the moneyed exclusivity of the development. 'Do we really need all these new houses? The people of Thanet would not really thank you for a millionaire's playground,' stated one opponent, while another raged about what she saw as 'a disgrace to alter yet another part of the environment for rich yuppies to enjoy for two months of the year. What about us residents? A dreadful eyesore.'

The smoothness and the blandness of the well-tailored exhibition got under a number of skins as well. Behind the angry ball-pen splutterings across the pages of the comments book lay a resignation, a feeling that the whole thing had already been cut and dried in city offices and council chambers. The development company had hatched a scheme to attract rich pleasure-seekers, fixed on Ramsgate as a suitably run-down area not too far from London, and held out a carrot of jobs and money that the council couldn't refuse. But how could Ramsgate's shops and pubs compete for the newcomers' custom with the glamorous facilities that were to be on tap inside the golden gates of the new development? Would the townsfolk be reduced to staring through security fences at the frolickings of the rich?

Ramsgate's embarrassment over its current unfashionable image has a lot to do with these resentments. So does a reluctance to see the one part of the town that local people identify with most strongly taken in hand and changed around by outsiders. The eighteenth-century inhabitants of Ramsgate had to come to terms with a far more radical change when the Regency visitors built a whole new town on their patch; but town residents these days expect to have rather more control over what happens to them and their environment. Developments like the Royal Harbour scheme are beginning to put a twinkle in the eye of many another seaside local council – the Brighton marina went ahead in the teeth of vehement opposition, for example, and down in Dorset the same kind of plan has boiled plenty of bile in sleepy Swanage. The inmates of these well-manicured, exclusive mini-townships grafted on to old resorts won't bring back the holiday magic of the days when visitors stayed in and used the towns themselves. Ramsgate, with all its advantages of position, varied architecture, lively waterfront and well-established sailing community, could afford to turn its back on the temptations of the 'millionaire's playground' if it knew where else to look to bring back the old zest of the pre-war years. The professional clown who made his entry in the development exhibition's comments book spoke for both sides in the argument as he wrote: 'Silly situations are part of my stock-in-trade . . . I think this scheme, though well intentional, lacks maturity and foresight. It needs a lot – an awful lot – of amendment. But keep on thinking – Ramsgate *does* need an UPLIFT.'

11. Brighton

I came to Brighton seafront hoping to find a talisman from my student days here in the 1960s. Just up from the Royal Albion Hotel I used to lounge and watch the window display at Louis Tussaud's waxwork exhibition, an action tableau from 'The Pit and the Pendulum'. A recumbent figure in plush knee-breeches raised its upper torso in a series of jerky movements, exuding puffs of dust and a faint creaking that was audible through the window glass, to watch a curved axe-blade swinging towards its nether regions. The whole thing couldn't have been more amateurish, or more appealing.

Alas! Tussaud's has gone, along with Nazir the palm-reader and his shopfront lined with testimonials from the rich and famous. In their place rears the spanking new Ramada Renaissance Hotel, a wonderful confection of green tinted glass, designer girders and latticework. In the great carpeted central square (The Atrium), whole full-sized trees grow under the glass roof. Puffing Havanas, the male guests loll back in their club chairs, in dove-grey suits and white socks, with gold chains on their shoes. The female guests are in superbly tailored business suits. The rich brown voice of money murmurs everywhere. In this hushed, green-shaded, leafy palace, £100 won't be enough to buy you even a single room – with no sea view and no breakfast – for one night. The guests don't worry about silly things like bills, though. In nearly every case it's their companies who are picking up the tabs. The Ramada Renaissance has been placed here on this prime seafront site to cream off delegates to the conferences and exhibitions in the Brighton Centre just along the street. The superb, elegant old Grand – restored to the last curlicue from that IRA bombing in 1984 – owes most of its turnover to delegates, too. So does the florid-faced Metropole. Brighton's seafront simply seethes with money these days, now that the Queen of the South Coast has gone into the conference business. But some things don't change. Ostentatious riches and cheery cheapjackery still live happily elbow to elbow along the front. Jammed in between the swish hotels and luxury penthouse flats is a good sprinkling of tiny shops selling those seaside sweets that are every dentist's dream. It's reassuring to know that prime ministers, trade-union leaders and multinational company chairmen can still slip down the road, when the nibbles strike, for a pound of raisin fudge or a bag of sugar mice.

Adaptability has been the name of Brighton's game all the way through its two and a half centuries as a popular seaside resort. The little fishing village of Brighthelmstone had seen some excitements in its time – notably a burning raid by the French in Tudor times and, a hundred years later, the escape of the future King Charles II from a nearby beach after the Battle of Worcester. But it had stayed a small, insignificant place where life was a round of fishing, making and mending of nets and tackle, selling and bartering of fish and farm produce. During winter storms Brighthelmstone yielded the most shoreward of its flint cottages to the waves. At times during the early eighteenth century it looked as if the whole place was going to fold up. If you didn't mind bugs, cold and damp, you could hire a cottage in the village for five shillings a week and taste at first hand the poverty of a fishing village deep in the doldrums. Then, in 1750, came Dr Richard Russell of Lewes and his tract *De Tabe Glandulari: Sivi Usu Aquae Marinae in Morbis Glandularum Dissertatio* (Glandular Diseases: or a Dissertation on the Use of Sea-Water in Affections of the Glands). Russell soon set up in Brighthelmstone, a spot that exactly suited his requirements of salt water, a flat sandy shore and 'lively cliffs and downs to add to the cheerfulness of the place'. The doctor's tract, recommending sufferers from all kinds of diseases to drink and bathe in seawater, had a tremendous effect in an England where too many well-off people with not enough to do over-ate and over-drank their bodies into breakdown. They were desperate for cures, and mad to find somewhere new to become fashionable. Brighthelmstone filled the bill. Between 1750 and 1780 the fishing village puffed, swelled and burst out into Brighton, the jewel of seaside spas.

What happened in that shallow valley rising gently from sea to downs was happening also at other places round Britain's coastline: Ramsgate, Scarborough, Aberystwyth, Blackpool. Land values soared and specu- lators made enormous profits. Smart villas replaced flint-and-boulder cottages. The fishing industry declined as fishermen looked ashore and spotted a chance of warm, dry, safe and lucrative employment as lodging- house keepers or domestic servants. In Brighton the Steine, the fisher- men's traditional net-drying ground, became a fashionable perambulating area between fine new houses. Today it's hard to see even a shadow of that vanished Brighthelmstone, though the tangled maze of narrow alleyways known as The Lanes, just behind the Old Ship Hotel, gives an idea of its character. Everyone visits The Lanes, inching round the corners and banging elbows in shop doorways. Brighton's antique shops are famous, and twenty years ago most of them were squeezed into The Lanes. You could buy a fake Chinese bowl for a few pennies, or the real thing for a few hundred pounds. Since then these emporia have swung dramatically upmarket and edged their way out of The Lanes to greater respectability and more elbow room in the adjoining streets. The Lanes have become just one elongated jewellery shop – and not a cheap one either. The coffee bar where I used to gloom adolescent evenings away over lemon tea and the juke box is a jewellery shop. So is the junk place that sold Indian scarves, terrible old pottery and elephant's-foot umbrella-stands. These rubbish-filled, enchanting Aladdin's caves still exist in Brighton, but you have to go well inland to find them.

The chief asset of Brighton, though, the carrot that entices holiday-makers, conference delegates and house-buyers with well-lined pockets, is that incredible wealth of Regency architecture dotted along three glorious miles of seafront from the crescents and squares of Hove to the dream-like symmetry, perspective and scale of Kemp Town. Inland, too, all along the old Steine, spreading up the roads towards London and out behind the seafront and clifftop houses and hotels, the Regency – or its flattering imitations of a few years later – rules with a rod of elegance. Even the plainest terraces and individual houses, far back from the seafront show window, have a dignity and unity that makes strolling among them a pleasure. When it comes to the great set-pieces – Royal Crescent, Royal York Buildings, Kemp Town – only Bath can really compete with Brighton; and Bath lacks that harlequin atmosphere of excitement and stimulation produced all over Brighton by the interplay between elegance and raffishness. These two contrasting elements collide and react most vividly in the wild splendours of the Pavilion, conjured up at the very heart of Brighton by the Prince Regent, George IV-to-be, in 1815. Brighton owes to the Prince of Pleasure, more than to any other single person, her ripening into a golden age which lasted until well into the present century. George delighted, scandalized and amused society by his indiscretions, affairs, wild extravagance and sentimental soft-heartedness. He had the reins of power laid in his palm at regular intervals when his father's porphyria-induced mental instability was on an upsurge, but the King kept recovering. Tension and frustration, together with a miserably unhappy marriage, hurled George headlong into folly. The acknowledged leader of fashion, with a different set of shoe-buckles for every day of the year, egged on by sycophantic courtiers who thronged Brighton to flatter and copy him, George found self-expression in tinkering with the plans for the Pavilion. An oriental temple was to be the grand effect; and soon the now familiar onion-domes, slender minarets and fine stone lattice-work overlaid the original villa that had been built thirty years before on the site. The surprising thing to today's visitor to the Pavilion is the extreme lightness of the external design, which anchors the whole fantastic structure solidly to the ground and at the same time calls the eye upwards through the swelling curves of the central onion-dome that tapers away to a point in the sky. Contemporary observers weren't sympathetic. 'Turnips and tulip bulbs', opined Cobbett; 'pumpkins and pepper-boxes', fulminated Hazlitt. Sidney Smith got in with: 'One would think that St Paul's Cathedral had come to Brighton and pupped', while a Byronical rhymer in 1830 dismissed it thus:

> Well, Cockney, may you drawl, 'What's there?'
> It is the Pavilion – see!
> The architecture's worth a stare,
> The order Cherokee!

The interior is full of too many twining dragons, three-dimensional plantain trees, monsters and other fantasies to describe here: you'll have to go and wander round this wonderful, exotic place for yourself. What the Prince Regent did for Brighton – and the spirit in which he did it – is summed up in a painting done in 1944 by Rex Whistler, now hanging upstairs in the Pavilion. It shows George, naked but for Star and Garter, a pair of wings, dancing pumps and a diaphanous piece of material coyly floating across his loins; he is kneeling on the beach in the act of awakening the Spirit of Brighton in the shape of a nude beauty. She stretches, luxuriating, on the sand, arms behind her head, in the moment between sleeping and waking, as yet unaware of the pot-bellied angel above her who, his face suffused and pink with lust and with finger to lips and roguish glance, is enjoining silence on the onlooker as he plucks her flimsy shawl away. The girl Whistler has painted so lovingly, with her rosy cheeks and pink lips, is very definitely a twentieth-century nymph; but the ribbon round her waist carries the name of Brighthelmstone. Whistler painted the picture while the D-Day landings were taking place. He was killed leading his tank troop a couple of weeks later, so the painting turned out to be his last.

Those visitors not intent on architecture still head as if drawn by magnets for the other chief gem in Brighton's crown, the Palace Pier. All through Queen Victoria's long reign Brighton had kept its popularity, but the appeal of 'glittering Brighton' had swung inexorably downmarket since the opening of the London and Brighton Railway in 1841. Now city clerks and manual workers could bring their families down by cheap round-trip tickets for a good day's blow-out at Brighton. The quality were appalled and soon left the centre of Brighton to the many-headed, retreating out to reserves on the clifftops. Thomas Read Kemp sank an entire fortune into building the finest of all of these on the cliffs to the east between Brighton and Black Rock, the unparalleled Kemp Town. If there is one compulsory piece of rubber-necking to do, it's this. You won't see more magical balancing of shape, size, line and curve anywhere in Regency-inspired architecture. Kemp Town was not actually completed until the 1850s, and Kemp himself died abroad, penniless; but his masterpiece still dominates everything around it, effortlessly.

The West Pier opened in 1866, but it was the Palace Pier that really pulled the trippers in. From its opening in 1899 onwards, the Palace Pier became a symbol of the jolly, carefree, rowdy Brighton of the day trip and the naughty weekend. It still is. You still have to pass pavement vendors of unlikely gimmicks and cures to get on to the pier proper, and music still blares down the decking and through the central pagoda – not a quavering brass band these days, of course, but non-stop, inescapable beatbox thump. Each roof ridge is outlined in painted light bulbs, as are the main surfaces of the whole structure: a fine sight at night, when the pier appears to float in a bath of coloured light above phosphorescent waves.

There's plenty of vulgar fun on the Palace Pier, too. In the Royal Wedding year of 1981 the *crêpe* stall did a roaring trade in loyally entitled specialities: the 'Princess Diana' (raspberries, chocolate sauce, cream, two strategically placed peaches) and the 'Prince Charles' (same, minus the peaches, plus a banana). On my last visit the pierhead theatre-cum-bar had been flattened and was awaiting restoration. Here there used to be – and, I trust, will be again – a museum of vintage slot-machines where, in exchange for your entrance fee, you were handed five old-fashioned pennies – warm, heavy and clumsy, stinking of copper – to put in the slots.

The animation of most of these miniature shows was primitive in the extreme. My favourite was 'The Prisoners At Work'. Cell doors opened to reveal two little wood-and-cloth figures of convicts. The mechanism was a standard one, causing each figure to perform the same gestures, all the movements wildly wrong for the supposed trades. The seated convict, sewing mailbags, stabbed his tiny hands spasmodically from side to side over the sacking on his knee as if beating off hornets, while his standing counterpart jerked a sledgehammer to and fro on a horizontal plane at chest level, the pile of stones at his feet never even threatened. Other well-remembered treats were 'The Miracle Man – does he defy Gravity?'; 'Don't Blush – 1d. for 15 of the Best – Saucy'; 'The First Night – Blooming Lovely'; and 'The Seance', with levitating ladies in respectable tea-gowns and flowered hats. There was also a table-football machine with heavily moustachioed teams in knee-length shorts and real woollen jerseys.

Half a mile along the prom, however, the poor old West Pier has had a disastrous time of it, a steady downward path leading to its closure in 1975 in a state of total dilapidation. Since then it has stood empty, gaudy paint peeling off the candy-floss stalls, salt eating into cast-iron dolphins, columns, railings, roof ornamentation. By 1988 great gaps had appeared in its length, coils of rusty barbed wire were sagging from climbable points and the supporting legs tottered and quivered in heavy seas. But the talk was still of rescue for the sad old pier, as it has been every year since closure. A cheque for £8 million was supposed to be on its way from English Heritage. By the end of the summer the restoration would be well under way. It was going to be turned into a casino . . . a nightclub . . . a posh restaurant . . . a refurbished pier to outdo its rival just down the beach. It's rather an embarrassment to the council. They can't get rid of it, because it's such an obvious potential asset, because there would be an outcry from conservationists, because it would cost an enormous amount to pull it down, because Brighton is trading harder than ever before on nostalgia and traditional resort atmosphere. They can't restore it because they are rate-capped and haven't got the money. They can't leave it the way it is, because it looks so awful. A sugar daddy is the only solution anyone can think of, but he would have to be a sugar daddy with an awful lot of sugar to throw away.

If the crumbling West Pier stands for the demise of Brighton as day-trippers' Heaven, then the blank-faced modernity of the Brighton

Centre just above it represents hope for a new direction in the future. At the turn of this century the critic Lewis Melville noted with disgust that 'Brighton has developed into the Cockney's paradise, the Mecca of the stockbroker and the chorus-girl. The glory is indeed departed.' But two world wars, and the social upheavals they brought, changed the face of the seaside town beyond recall. Brighton could still flash out in violence from time to time – the racecourse gang slashings and kickings of the 1930s, the world of Pinkie and his mob from Graham Greene's *Brighton Rock*; the Mods and Rockers' seafront and beach battles of the 1960s; Mods and Skinheads in the 1980s. There were – and still are – Ghost Trains, candy-floss, knotted hankies and ice-creams. The dolphins at the Aquarium still squeal 'Happy Birthday To You' while walking on water. But money has begun to flow like champagne here. It has been boom time in the south of England for years, the south-east in particular. Brighton has a Festival, a University, theatres, restaurants, foreign students from early spring to late autumn bringing in extra trade for the shopkeepers, sea breezes, glorious buildings, glamour, superb downland and cliff scenery. Big money has already built an enormous marina, covering 126 acres, out to the east at Black Rock, and has studded the cliffs above with unlovely but extraordinarily expensive penthouse apartments. It's no wonder that in 1977 the council dipped into its pocket for £9 million to build the Brighton Centre. Nearly 6,000 delegates can sit down together. Conferences and exhibitions follow each other in a succession booked almost into the twenty-first century: International Fish Farming, Southern Flower Show, International Congress and Exhibition of Emergency Surgery, Drag Racing and Custom Car Show, Society of Clean Air, Church of God of Prophecy. Religious-testimony conferences are enormously popular. I saw a minister and a sufferer engaged in hands-on-head, fervently prayerful healing on the pavement outside the Centre during one such conference's lunch break, while on the other side of the tinted windows scores of delegates jostled round tables laden with expensively packaged tapes of advice and admonition from the charismatic American preacher they'd all come to hear.

Conferences and exhibitions make up only half of the Brighton Centre's usage, though – the week after the religious get-together (free use of facilities), rock heroes Status Quo were at the Centre (exceedingly costly use of facilities). The conferences get the Centre free, simply to draw people into town. Most delegates treat these events as a chance for a damn good holiday mixed with a little work. People are generally in free-spending mood. Brighton's restaurants, pubs, shops and entertainment venues all benefit. So do the Grand, the Metropole and the Ramada Renaissance, as well as all the less expensive hotels. It's become all too much for some organizations such as the TUC, which is no longer to hold its annual conference here. The TUC leaders think Brighton has become too pricey, snobbish and yuppified. They may have a point. But when was it anything else, in part at any rate? The fashionable focus has simply shifted back to where it was a couple of hundred years ago, slap in the middle and bang on the front. Struggling life goes on meanwhile out in the dull, concrete-laden streets of the Moulsecoomb and Whitehawk housing estates, pushed under the edge of the Downs to the east. Walk out here up the Lewes road from the splendours of the seafront to find out how widely that incoming money really circulates.

The balance of Brighton's inner life, the life that goes on summer and winter in and out of tourist and conference seasons, is probably best struck in those hinterland streets, all sloping, all different, that snake around, inland of and above the seafront. Here are the inexpensive eating-places, shops where you can haggle over old curiosities that set you back pence instead of pounds, pubs serving local beer and cheap food. Ten minutes' walk going north from anywhere along the promenade, and you'll find yourself in streets where it's easy to moon about all morning, spend almost nothing and soak up an atmosphere that's varied, stimulating and relaxed. At Queen's Park, up a side road at the top of Edward Street, an imposing arched gateway, decorated with lions sticking their tongues out, leads you into a few acres of trees and grass centred on a duck pond, unvandalized and quiet, a favourite haunt of granny-and-toddler duos, all tucked away in a little tongue of slanting ground. Kemp Town, the Pavilion, piers, hotels and the Brighton Centre are only a short stroll away, but you'd never know it. Contrasts like this make Brighton special, still the Queen of the South Coast for my money.

SOUTH COAST

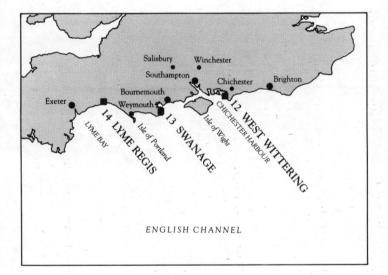

12. West Wittering

Seekers after English village charm can cease their search. West Wittering has it. A bench on the green under a horse-chestnut tree looks out on to colour-washed cottages behind brick and flint garden walls. The well-clipped green runs back to the playing field of West Wittering Parochial School. Squeals of children playing tag compete in a drowsy sort of way with that seductive, summery flutter of lawn-mowers in cottage gardens. The pointed tower of the church looks benevolently from its trees over school, children and village green. At West Wittering, God's in His heaven; usually a warm blue one along this stretch of low-lying land south of the Sussex Downs.

The broad arrow-head of the Selsey peninsula, hanging from the underside of West Sussex, has somehow escaped the massive over-development that has filled the rest of the county's coastline with an almost unbroken string of building. For forty miles, from Bognor Regis all the way to Peacehaven, you'll be lucky to find any gap where countryside meets shoreline. Sunshine and sandy beaches have seen to that. But the peninsula is different. The little railway that once threaded its way across the flat landscape to Selsey Bill has long since closed. B-roads and country lanes connect a scattering of small villages dependent in about equal measure on farming and commuters for their survival. Selsey Bill itself is a solid block of holiday houses and caravans; three miles to the west, East Wittering and Bracklesham have blurred and run together along the shore. Green, fertile farmland still stands between and behind, however. West Wittering, a mile or so west of East Wittering and tucked into the tip of the peninsula, is completely surrounded by fields lined with hedges and freckled with copses. The direct road to the broad beach at Bracklesham Bay passes the village by. It lies half a mile inland, too, flavoured only indirectly by the sea. You'd have to go almost to Eastbourne at the other end of the county to find another spot so near the coast with such a feeling of remoteness.

Not that West Wittering hasn't changed, enormously, since the turn of the century. In Rookwood Newsagent's shop on Rookwood Road you can buy a marvellous record of West Wittering as was, written by a local couple, Keith and Janet Smith, entitled *Witterings Then & Now*. Here, caught in foggy, tattered old snapshots, is the vanished village whose life flowed entirely round its shops and farms: ancient brass-snouted lorries in the village street, schoolchildren in pinafores and nailed boots, delivery boys on laden bicycles. The old flint cottages and farmhouses still stand along West Wittering's lanes under different hats and coats, but the green spaces between them have been infilled with smart, beautifully kept houses and spotlessly laundered gardens. Some of these form private estates; others represent the one-off efforts of local builders. The expansion of the village has been kept, somehow or other, within rigid bounds. It's as if West Wittering's houses have been poured into a mould. Leaving the village by lane or footpath, the houses simply stop. There's no straggle or sideways creep. It's a tidy arrangement, a status quo jealously guarded by the inhabitants. They even fought off the seemingly irresistible challenge of Billy Butlin in 1952 when the holiday camp supremo was making eyes at the beach below the village. The West Wittering Estate Company came into being, dished Butlin's plans and stayed on to see off other would-be developers of those precious acres of rural lifebelt around West Wittering.

The village green is flanked, as any perfect green should be, by the pub on one side and the church on the other. 'Good afternoon,' beams the cheery man behind the bar of the Old House At Home. A farm labourers' alehouse until its chance arrived with the closure, early this century, of the Dog and Duck Inn across the green, the Old House At Home has interior decorations unlike any other pub: toy rabbits in wedding dresses and vicar's garb, original cartoons, nice watercolours of local churches, silly joke notices, china dogs and horses. Immaculately dressed elderly ladies, high-heeled pumps agleam, gather under the plaster flower baskets for their mid-day glass of Riesling or gin-and-it. The chaff flies thick and fast. Max the boxer dog, ferocious after closing time, turns into a wriggling hand-licker as his acquaintances offer him surreptitious crisps and chunks of sandwich. Opposite the pub stands one of the tidiest garages in creation – no pools of oil, filthy old rags or piles of swarf. It doubles as the village grocery: 'Two gallons of 3-star and a tin of baked beans, please.'

On the far side of the green a short, square bell-tower juts out of the north wall of the Church of St Peter and St Paul. An unevenly flagged path winds between the gravestones to the door of the flint-built Norman church, standing where a Saxon monastery was founded, back in about AD 730. The Danes, raiding here half a century before the Conquest, reduced the monastery to rubble. A fragment of stone from the original building, deeply scored with a cross, is displayed inside the church, along with more crosses gouged into one of the nave's pillars by thirteenth-century pilgrims visiting a shrine to St Richard of Chichester. Outside in the graveyard under the south wall of the church are ranked the graves of West Wittering inhabitants down the years, among them a beautifully restored one to Daniel Hack, Mariner, A faithful Servant. Daniel died at the age of thirty, along with his shipmates, in a sea disaster in February 1770, depicted at the top of his tombstone by a dismasted, wave-torn vessel rolling under lowering clouds, the sun just breaking through. His poetical epitaph reads:

> The Boras' Stormes and Neptun's Waves
> Have tosfed me too and fro
> In fpite of both by God's Decree
> I'm harbour'd fafe below,
> Where I do now at Anchor lie
> With many of our Fleet,
> But once again I muft fet fail
> Our Sav'our Chrift to meet.

West Wittering remained virtually undiscovered by the holidaymaking outside world until well into this century. One eminent incomer was Henry Royce, who came here in 1917, worn out by his high-pressure car-building business in Derby. The Hon. C. S. Rolls may have sold 'em, but it was Royce who built 'em. The solitude of the little Selsey village obviously did the exhausted engineer a power of good, for it was in the converted barn known as The Studio on the corner of the village green that he came up with some of his best designs. The 'R' engine that powered the Supermarine seaplane to victory in the 1929 Schneider Trophy races first went on to the drawing board here. The races took place between Gosport and the beach below West Wittering, and most of the village turned out to see the brainchild of their adoptive squire come good. Royce's house, Elmstead, stands behind its neat garden and high limestone wall in Elms Lane, a long, handsome building with shuttered windows. Plaques here and in the wall of The Studio keep Henry Royce's memory fresh in today's village.

Footpaths leave West Wittering for most points of the compass. Walking north up Ellanore Lane from the village green, you pass a couple of houses, then are immediately among the fields. Trees lean inland, bent by the constant sea-wind, and across the ploughland comes a low roar from the waves beating on the beach, a few hundred yards to the west. Soon you

97

can see sails crossing the end of the lane, where a rickety stile gives a view through a thicket of bushy-headed alexanders on to the enormous panorama of Chichester Harbour. The path bends round on itself to run south above the marshy tideline of this great inshore expanse of water whose branches push miles inland past little waterside sailing villages. It's a huge view through half a circle: green water and low green islands, white sails scudding after each other from end to end of the harbour. Sailing enthusiasts flock to Chichester Harbour, its creeks and saltings, boatyards and waterside pubs. In any of these you'll get a good dash of salty chatter with your beer.

West Wittering stands aside from this sailing world, too land-bound to take part. Bird watchers and botanists come to the village, however, intent on the waders, geese and sea plants of East Head, whose sand dunes form one side of the narrow entrance to Chichester Harbour. Gradually but constantly reshaped by the force of waves pushing through that constricted opening, surrounded by sea and saltings, East Head is a lonely, windy place to linger, face down in the sand with a hand lens, or head up with a pair of binoculars. Or you can turn east along the wide, unfrequented beach below the village. Here, as in few other places on the south coast, small children can slip into that delicious private world that spins out for hours of wandering along a deserted tideline, picking up shells, stones and bits of driftwood. Strolling on the greensward footpath above the sand that leads towards Bracklesham Bay, you walk by the gardens of houses that have given full rein to architectural fantasies not seen in neatly maintained West Wittering. Great, grand agglomerations of chimney-stacks and roof angles stand side by side with round-ended 1930s extravaganzas that are already fading away under the attacks of wind and salt spray. The strip of coastal building ends at Cakeham Manor, a fine brick farmhouse with a tall tower, built to his greater glory by Bishop Sherburne of Chichester in Tudor times. From here it's a short half-mile back to West Wittering.

With such a splendid, uncrowded beach, such vast views over Chichester Harbour and such a protective girdle of fields and trees, West Wittering ought to be marked down by a demanding tourist trade just crazy for this kind of 'find'. That it isn't is due to the vigilance of the villagers and of the Cakeham Manor and West Wittering Estate Companies. Living on one of the most popular stretches of coastline in Britain, in a place where children can bike round the lanes and dawdle along the beach in safety, where no one squirts graffiti from an aerosol or leaves chip papers on the pavement, is a rare enough blessing to be worth fighting for. It sounds like Heaven – and, to a stranger, that's how it feels. But not everyone sees things this way. Those private estates, the neat lawns and tidied-up old farm workers' cottages stick painfully in the gullets of those whose roots in West Wittering go back to the days before commuters and retired incomers smartened up the village.

In their book, *Witterings Then & Now*, Keith and Janet Smith include among the old photos a poem, 'Weep for Wittering', written by a member of one such long-established village family. Albert Cate addresses his great-grandmother Amy, who lived through all but a few years of the last century. In these verses Mr Cate voices all the bitterness of village people all over the country who have stood helplessly by while their villages have been smoothed, tidied and revamped beyond recognition by outsiders well-heeled enough to have their way. West Wittering's new population may have contrived to put the village beyond the reach of the cruel world, but it's no longer the working community that Amy Cate knew:

> The village bakehouse closed, Gran,
> No more the faggots burn,
> And if you wanted Sussex bread,
> I'd know not where to turn.
>
> The village street is changed, Gran,
> Old names they no longer keep,
> Shall I tell you more, Gran,
> Or does it make you weep?
>
> The people too are different,
> They do not plough and sow,
> For they get up in the morning
> And it's off to town they go.
>
> They care not for the village,
> It's just a place to sleep,
> If you were only here now,
> Oh, how you'd want to weep.

13. Swanage

'Unashamedly up-market Swanage Yacht Haven combines its own interesting character with an atmosphere of tranquillity . . . imaginatively designed waterside homes, each with its own mooring and enjoying outstanding panoramic views over land and sea. A real village community in every sense of the word . . . just a 2½ hour road journey from Central London . . .'

The development company's glossy brochure couldn't be more seductively – or revealingly – phrased. Rising from the rubble of the old Grosvenor Hotel on the southern side of Swanage Bay, the dream 'homes' (car-ports, sun lounges, roof gardens) have everything in common with some rapaciously developed stretch of the Costa del Sol, nothing at all with the fading, settled, dove-grey gentility of the little resort at their elbow. A two-bedroomed version down by the water could set you back more than £250,000. Very few people in this part of the world could even dream of footing such a bill. The prosperity that Purbeck stone and Purbeck holidays brought to Swanage over the years has long since slid away. The developers may be locally based, but that brochure was not intended to be read much outside London and the well-heeled South-East. The quarter-million-pound price-tags make that clear, as does the description of the attached facilities: marina, wine bar, residential club and craft shops. Not even the richest and most carefree city slicker would embark on a daily commuting trip from Dorset to London and back. So these are weekend fun houses for rich Londoners, or summer homes for yacht owners. Resentment against such incomers, and against the whole out-of-keeping, sore-thumb development, bubbled merrily away in Swanage from the day in the mid-1980s when the Yacht Haven plans were first revealed. Resistance to the scheme began with mutterings in pubs and front rooms, and swelled into a full-blown row that split the town into two bitterly opposed factions. Tempers were lost, in private and in public; accusations of libel and sharp practice flew about. The argument went all the way to the House of Lords. Swanage, the run-down resort that had seemed to be supinely accepting what was in store for it, was up on its hind legs and barking furiously at the intruder.

The Isle of Purbeck has always been an independent-minded sort of place, isolated from both the rest of the world and the county of Dorset, a hard pimple of practicality on the smooth underbelly of the south coast. The Purbeck Hills run east and west across the middle of the peninsula, dividing the northern heaths and marshes from the southern cliffs and stony downlands. The spectacular ruins of Corfe Castle plug the gap in the Purbeck Hills behind Swanage, sealing off the town into isolation. As recently as the eighteenth century there was no effective communication by road between Swanage and the outside world. Everything came and went by sea. Purbeck marble had gone into just about every medieval cathedral in the land, and the workable, durable Purbeck freestone into houses, walls, harbours, streets and roads; but roadless, isolated Swanage missed out on the profits until new quarries by the town were opened at about the same time as old London was burning in the Great Fire. Swanage acquired quays and jetties, great mounds of stone along its sea frontage, crowds of sweating quarrymen and stone-shifters, stone-dust in the summer, mud in the winter. None of this added to the scenic attractions of the area. Quarrying doesn't do the landscape any favours at the best of times, and the dusty little stone port shipping out tens of thousands of tons a year was more concerned with business than appearance. Rebuilding London gobbled up whatever the Purbeck quarries could supply. So did the turnpikes and sea defences of Georgian England and, in their turn, the Victorian new towns and new roads. It wasn't until the enormous Townsend quarries above Swanage at last began to give out towards the end of the nineteenth century that the town relinquished its long grip on stone, cleaned up, broadened out and put on a well-scrubbed smile for the holidaymakers.

I first knew Swanage when, at boarding school nearby in the 1950s, it was the place my parents stayed during their weekend visits. Swanage meant lunch at the Wolferton Hotel, with brown soup and Dorset Knobs (crunchy little balls of biscuit that went with cheese), followed by a bracing walk along the sand which evaporated the precious day more quickly than it could be savoured. Boys with a different brand of parent brought back to the dormitory thrilling snippets from their own outings: lobster and lager in the Trocadero's swanky dining room, with a present beside every youngster's place; an afternoon on the one-arm bandits and sideshows in Playland; tea at the enormously kudos-laden Grosvenor high above the pier and harbour; *Blue Murder at St Trinian's* bringing the sated day to a close in the Swanage fleapit cinema. There was no shortage of fun and frolics at Swanage in the undemanding '50s. Going back to the town recently, thirty years on, was a poignant business. Somehow the grey of the building stone seemed to have insinuated itself into the atmosphere. The high and mighty Grosvenor was a shuttered, blistered hulk, its shabby old body in the throes of being smashed down to make way for the Swanage Yacht Haven, Phase One. Other well-remembered hotels had changed their status, too – the seafront Royal Victoria's late Georgian splendour now encased holiday flats. So did the Wolferton. The Trocadero was a mini-mart. The Corrie was about to be pulled down. Of all Swanage's hotels, only the Grand and the Pines were still in business. More and more fine old buildings in the town were being demolished to make way for retirement flatlets or weekend homes. Over those three decades Swanage had become a lot less remote from London, improved roads making light of what had been the best part of a whole day's journey. Now you could leave your city desk at five o'clock and be opening your other front door before nine. Local people seemed resigned to the switch-over from holiday resort to weekend town and retirement haven. At least outside money was still coming into Swanage, as the bookshop owner pointed out to me, and there were even one or two benefits: a better, quieter class of visitor, and one or two unfamiliar faces in the winter months when Swanage residents were grateful for anything new to look at and talk about.

At first glance the town might appear to be just another tattered, hangdog resort whose day has long gone. That impression is reinforced by the sparseness of the summertime crowd on the pier, hanging over the cast-iron-rope railings to watch wind-bitten sailors hunching their way around their small boats in the Sailing Club's yard; also by the yawning knots of teenagers kicking their heels in and around Playland, still limping on as an amusement centre. The shopping streets of Swanage are a curious mixture of smart boutiques and delicatessens alongside old-fashioned ironmongers', dingy electrical shops and dry cleaners'. There's a water-sports hall near the pier and the Mowlem Theatre on the seafront: the basic equipment of a seaside holiday town.

It takes time for the stranger sights of Swanage to creep up on you. The streets, corners and crannies of this modest little town are packed with curiosities in stone and ironwork, all eccentric in design or out of place, grandly over scale or chiming oddly with their neighbouring buildings. Once tuned in, you soon become adept at picking out these curiosities. A stroll around Swanage becomes a treasure hunt, unearthing more and more obelisks, elaborate frontages, towers, archways, statues. Almost all were brought here from London, giving Swanage its nickname of 'London by the Sea'. This wonderful diversity of objects was dispersed all over the town in the late nineteenth century by George Burt, a local stonemason. Burt's uncle, John Mowlem, had founded a firm which secured a large number of contracts for rebuilding in London at a time when zealous Victorian improvers were replacing old with new all over the capital. George Burt, holding the reins at Mowlem's after his uncle retired in 1844, didn't see why so much fine workmanship should be allowed to go to waste, and he saved some of the best pieces of demolished London to glorify, if not always to beautify, his birthplace down in the Isle of Purbeck. Many splendid bits went into his own High Street residence, Purbeck House – now a convent, but built in 1875 as a great granite statement of permanence and pride. Crow steps adorn the gables and granite crazy-paving the walls; there are towers, battlements, cupolas and columns. The whole building looks more like a grand Scottish hotel than the retirement house of a Purbeck stonemason. Built into the walls, angles, stable block and gardens are parts of London's old Billingsgate Fish Market (columns and balustrades), the Albert Memorial (walls), Hyde Park Corner (archway), Westminster Hall (gargoyle), the medieval Houses of Parliament (carving), Waterloo Bridge (columns) and the Royal Exchange (statues) – these among many others. The mish-mash should look cheap and pretentious, but it doesn't. Perhaps it's the intervening century that has invested George Burt's grotesque, lavish residence and grounds with dignity.

Just down the High Street from Purbeck House is Swanage's Town Hall, its entire façade lifted complete by Burt from the Mercers' Hall, Cheapside, in the early 1880s. The small, square Town Hall building reels under the weight and opulence of its splendiferous front, where chubby cherubs are draping the Virgin Mary's shoulders in a shawl, all enclosed in a smother of folds, foliage and chevron zigzags. Burt acquired this masterpiece, designed by a pupil of Sir Christopher Wren in the 1670s to replace a frontage destroyed in the Great Fire of London, when it was condemned as being too dirty. He also sprinkled Swanage generously with lamp standards, bollards, gates, obelisks and towers from various corners of London. But Burt was no mere snapper-up of unconsidered trifles. Purbeck House was not his sole original contribution to Swanage. He also spent thirty years laying out a complete country gentleman's estate on Durlston Head, a section of quarried-out rough ground on the clifftops above the famous quarry-holes of Tilly Whim Caves. Here, in what these days is the Durlston Country Park, stands Durlston Head Castle, built in the 1880s in turreted and crenellated magnificence on a peerless site overlooking Swanage and Durlston Bay. 'The architectural features of a refreshment buffet, a tram terminus and a Norman keep' is one accurate though not too flattering 19th-century description. Below the castle stands another Burt extravaganza, his 40-ton, 10-foot Great Globe, made of Portland stone with a world map cut into its surface. Burt thoughtfully provided a slab nearby for graffiti-merchants to unload their burdens on. He also filled his clifftop estate with maps, information blocks, direction posts, pathways and shrubbery – and opened the whole place to the public, as well as the old quarry caves of Tilly Whim, where his uncle, John Mowlem, had been one of the last workers before Tilly Whim closed, shortly before Burt was born.

John Mowlem was a great benefactor to Swanage, though he, too, had his little fads. It was he who had the Alfred Memorial put up in 1862 on the Swanage seafront, topped with a garland of Crimean cannon-balls, to commemorate a sea-battle between King Alfred and the Danes that never actually happened. Swanage residents and visitors alike have spent a century debating the merits or otherwise of the legacy of Mowlem and Burt. Between them they certainly had more influence on the appearance of Swanage than any of the town's other sons. There's a tendency in Swanage to view their legacy as ostentation of the kind you might expect from local boys made good – probably justified in the case of Purbeck House with its riot of elbowing bits and pieces. But uncle and nephew obviously both adored Swanage and couldn't wait to get back and retire here. They gave open-handedly to the citizens of their town in land, endowments and buildings. Who can blame them if they let themselves go over the top on occasion?

There are attractions other than the Burt and Mowlem relics to be found inland – chief among them the little Tithe Barn museum beside St Mary's Church in the oldest part of Swanage. Here you can learn of the rough, dangerous and health-sapping toil of the Purbeck quarrymen, who were delving deep by candlelight well into this century. On the other side of St Mary's is a group of cottages, several centuries old, admiring their reflections along with the black-faced swans in the old millpond and leat, fed by a spring, the ancient centre from which Swanage grew outward. Here also stood (before it was removed to its present site at the back of the

Town Hall) the town's lock-up, erected 'for the Prevention of Vice & Immorality By the Friends of Religion & good Order A.D. 1803'. The size of a garden shed, there was standing room only on quarrymen's pay nights. Such delights are to be picked out as you ramble along the roadways down which for centuries the cartloads of Purbeck stone jolted to the ketches in Swanage Bay.

Now, as then, most of the liveliness that is left to Swanage is concentrated along its sea frontage: the water-sports hall, Playland amusement arcade, Mowlem Theatre, beach. Around the curve of the bay between the Royal Victoria Hotel and the Mowlem Theatre are old, massively sturdy quays and loading ledges in an area known as the Bankers, where the stone piled high in pre-resort days. Carts full of stone were pulled by horses into the sea and emptied into lighters which ferried the precious stuff out to the ketches anchored in deeper water. These days, the good building stone is so far down that it's uneconomic to get it out. The stone nearer the surface can earn a quarrying company a reasonable return, but it's all weak, flaky, fractured stuff, really only good enough for roadstone. That's why locals were sceptical of the Swanage Yacht Haven company's promise to 'make good use of the attractive Purbeck stone', and why they weren't surprised to see the local stone used for cosmetic purposes in a very limited way.

The development that has caused all the fuss lies just to the east of the pier. It's not the intrusive brashness of the architectural style that really upset the objectors, nor the demolition of the Grosvenor Hotel. What stuck in people's gullets was the proposed marina which was to form the heart of the Yacht Haven development. Each prestigious waterside home was to have its own stake in a herringbone lattice of 250 berths directly in front of the new 'village'. A breakwater of Spanish stone – not of Purbeck – would curve out to form a sheltered mouth with the end of the pier. Swanage's small fleet of less than a dozen pot-fishing boats, at present using moorings out in the bay that are free (though the fishermen have to maintain them), would be accommodated inside the new breakwater in their own corner – but at a price. What the fishermen think about these proposed arrangements was relayed to me, full strength, by the owner of a nearby tackle shop.

'What sort of people are going to buy up these houses? Let me tell you – people who can afford a quarter of a million. Are they going to bring anything to a small-town community like this? They won't bring any of their money into Swanage, what with all those dinky little shops and boutiques in the marina. For God's sake!' He could hardly bite back on his anger. 'Oh, yes. They promised us a lot of jobs for the locals. But have we seen any of them yet? Have we hell. And have they thought about what's going to happen to Swanage Bay when they build that breakwater? The tide sets in from the east here, and comes back again from the west. That great thing will stop the sand getting back to the beach. I reckon in fifteen years Swanage Bay will be just one great sandbank. Not that the Swanage fishermen will mind – they'll all have given up by then. Have you seen the "Say NO to Marina" stickers in their car windows? That'll tell you what they think about being shoved behind that breakwater. And as for that so-called village – how many people who buy one of those things is going to be here in the middle of February when it's been raining for a week and everyone's fed up? Is that a real community?'

The bad feelings went on pouring out. The marine development had whipped up far more resentment in the town than the developer had bargained for. 'Open-door' meetings of the council were humming with rage. You could get hold of the developers' glossy brochure only if you had a posh accent and weren't a local. All this didn't sound like a spontaneous outburst – more like the objectors' public manifesto, obsessively hatched and served with bitterness to any stranger willing to lend an ear. What the marina development had tapped into was a deep pool of shame – shame at the down-at-heel shabbiness that has crept up on Swanage, and shame at the common feeling of helplessness at the hands of moneyed, powerful outsiders. Deep contempt, too, for the 'real village community' adumbrated in that inaccessible brochure, here in a part of the world where real villages really do exist, and spend a good deal of their time struggling against depopulation, poor services and rural poverty. The tackle-shop owner wasn't at all impressed by the arguments of fellow shopkeepers in Swanage who were all for the marina and the new life they hoped it would spark into the town.

'New life? Nonsense. Yes, we've become a bit tatty as a town since the visitors dried up – I wouldn't deny that. But what difference are a lot of yuppies going to make? Still, it looks like it's going to happen whether we want it or not. We took them to the House of Lords over the marina, but we got beat 3 to 2. That's it.'

As things turned out, he was wrong. Some time after our conversation, the council held a consultative referendum over the affair. Twice as many people voted against the marina as opted for it. The council pointed to the phrase 'consultative' and went on backing the scheme, to the fury and outrage of all the objectors. Then the House of Lords stepped in again, to trip up the developers' private bill as it seemed to be clearing its final hurdle. There would be no great concrete arm off Peveril Point, and no private berths for the lucky residents of Swanage Yacht Haven.

The waterside 'village' goes on going up, however. Perhaps there's sufficient compensation for the lost marina in the wonderful view round the curve of Swanage Bay and out towards Old Harry Rocks. Cradled in these gorgeous chalk arms, small-scale, gentle-mannered, full of the eccentric chippings of history, Swanage ought to be prouder of itself than it is. Any town that could swallow George Burt's two palaces and Great Globe ought not to strain too much at the Yacht Haven, extravagant enough to take its place as just another of Swanage's agreeable follies. The best-known of these stands right beside the Haven, the Wellington memorial clock tower, removed from London Bridge by Mowlem's in 1867 and re-erected here the following year. George Burt and John Mowlem would certainly have been in favour of any scheme with a chance of rolling back some of Swanage's present-day pall of lethargy and pessimism. No one would have dared to say no if Burt had come up with the marina scheme in the days when he ruled the roost in Swanage.

14. Lyme Regis

Lyme Regis lies at the meeting point of Somerset, Dorset and Devon. There's only a slip of a sandy beach, and the harbour end of it occasionally plays host to mechanical diggers and caterpillar tractors. If that's the case when you arrive, take your cue from the local sunbathers and sandcastle builders, and don't bat an eyelid. They've seen it all before, and are happy to squeeze up a little more tightly and yield another few tons of sand to the diggers. It's all in the good cause of shoring up for another year Lyme's battered old sea-defences, at the centre of which lies the curving stone Cobb, safeguard and totem of the town between the cliffs. Without the sheltering arm of the Cobb, Lyme's little beach would be pounded to pieces in short order. As it is, each winter's seas get round (and over) the Cobb as Lyme Bay produces its spectacular storms, to bite chunks out of the other breakwaters and jetties of the harbour.

The central part of Lyme Regis stands half a mile to the east of the Cobb, but it's the crooked old jetty that is the proper heart of the place. It curves out into the bay, forked like a snake's tongue, massively built of plain stone blocks whose variety of size and composition shows how many times the Cobb has been battered, breached and rebuilt during its seven centuries of existence. Those storm waves that in years past have broken through the Cobb have gone straight on to tear down or wreck the seafront buildings of Lyme – nearly 150 of them in the terrific gale of 1377. No wonder the medieval townsfolk were glad to subscribe to the 'Cobb Ales' or fund-raising feasts that kept their sole defence in working order. The Cobb was not just a shield against the sea, however: it was also Lyme's only effective means of contact with the outside world until the seaside boom of the late eighteenth century at last forced the town to do something about its appallingly bad approach-roads. Before 1759 nothing on wheels could get near the town centre – everything had to be brought in by packhorse. Standing at the seaward end of the Cobb, you can appreciate the problems of getting wheeled traffic into and out of a place boxed in behind and on each side by such steep hills. Try leaving Lyme on a push-bike and you'll soon get the picture!

Transatlantic and Mediterranean trade by way of the Cobb had made Lyme one of England's foremost ports by Tudor times; and even when the Duke of Monmouth landed here in 1685 on his losing gambler's throw, the town was getting more profit out of its sea trade than was Liverpool. At about the same time Celia Fiennes arrived in Lyme to find 'a seaport place open to the main ocean, and so high a bleake sea that to secure the Harbour for shipps they have been at a great charge to build a Mold from the town with stone, like a halfe moon, which they call the Cobb, its raised with a high wall and this runns into the sea a good compass, that the Shipps rides safely within it'. There was a gap between the shore and the Cobb of those days through which shingle was carried by the sea, to pile up against groynes on the beach as a stiffener for the unstable land on which Lyme is built. The closing of this gap in 1756 made the Cobb more than ever a solid, reassuring sight and symbol for Lyme residents, and for the new visitors beginning to arrive to recruit themselves with fashionable sea-bathing and sea breezes. The sloping, wave-pounded old jetty fascinated them. Jane Austen gave headstrong Louisa Musgrove a nasty tumble here in *Persuasion*. A century and a half later, John Fowles did the same in *The French Lieutenant's Woman* for Charles Smithson, though the fall of that quizzical bachelor was to last half a lifetime. There's something about the Cobb – perhaps its great age, or its combination of sinuosity and solidity – that continues to work on the imagination of its beholders.

The Cobb is a magnet for sunbathers, leaners on railings, strollers through sheets of spray, shelterers from keen breezes and spenders of an idle hour. It does for Lyme what a market square does for other towns. You go down to the Cobb for a chat or to watch the world go by. In the old Customs shed at the fork of the jetty there's a small aquarium whose long seawater tanks hold six-foot conger eels lying placidly on top of barnacle-encrusted lobsters, and dogfish stacked four or five deep in the corners. On the sheltered eastern side of the Cobb are the small yachts and sailing dinghies, on their sides at low water or upright at high tide. Other, more business-like boats lie ready to take parties out on sea-fishing trips, or to go out on their own account after crabs and whitefish. All the fishing in Lyme nowadays is done by the Wason family, who sell their catch salty-fresh in their shop in town or from their whelk barrow at the foot of the Cobb.

From the Cobb's far end there's a superb view inland of the tottery cliffs each side of Lyme, cliffs that crumble and quake more than almost any others in Britain thanks to the thin horizontal band of greasy black Gault that runs half-way up them the whole length of the bay. Their chalk and Greensand tops have the most precarious of grips on this slippery underpinning, a geological conveyor-belt that inches them remorselessly towards their destination down on the beach below. Falls occur steadily year by year, most of them confined to a shower of doughy mud. From time to time, though, enormous areas go tumbling. To your right as you look towards land from the Cobb are three yellow hilltops, rising from Black Ven (450 feet) through Stonebarrow (480 feet) to the 617-foot peak of Golden Cap. Greensand is not green when newly exposed, but yellow, and fresh falls keep the colours bright on these three summits. It was under Black Ven in 1811 that a young local girl named Mary Anning helped her brother Joseph to dig out the fossil ichthyosaurus that set her on the path to international fame as a finder of and self-taught expert on fossils. The beds of Blue Lias that underlie the Gault here are literally lined with fossils of all kinds: ammonites, belemnites, trilobites, crinoids, oysters, brittle stars, the bones, teeth and scales of fish, as well as the rarer and more dramatic relics of ichthyosaur and pterosaur. Amateur and professional palaeontologists had been coming to Lyme since well before Mary Anning's time, but she was the prime mover in putting the town on every fossil-hunter's map. True to the form of small rural communities, many locals thought her too big for her boots. Geologists throughout Europe, however, who had been groping through a fog of ignorance about the origins of life on earth, recognized the importance of her discoveries. By the time she died of cancer in 1847, the extremely exclusive Royal Geological Society had accepted her into its sacred circle to the extent of including an obituary in its annual address (a unique honour for a non-member), and contributing towards a stained-glass window to her memory in St Michael's Church in Lyme.

On the other side of the town the cliffs continue their shaky march under Ware Cleeves towards the green clifftop belt of woodland known as the Undercliff, setting for many a meeting and heart-wrenching revelation in *The French Lieutenant's Woman*. Here the cliffs have slipped, rather than fallen headlong, to create a series of gigantic, uneven steps of ground interspersed with deep fissures. The farms and cottages that once dotted the Undercliff have lain empty for many generations; no one could live among fields and woods that were apt to disappear overnight. At Dowlands, five miles to the west of Lyme, twenty acres of land subsided together in one almighty slip on Christmas Eve, 1839. The inhabitants of this strip of coastline trickled away to safer abodes during the last century, leaving the Undercliff to local lovers and to the birds, foxes, badgers, insects and plants that crept back to take over the place. To walk the five miles of undulating pathway that thread the Undercliff today is to immerse yourself in a green bath for the senses – no noise, no people, no intrusion of any kind by the outside world on nature rampant and triumphant. There's nowhere else like it this side of heaven.

This extraordinary geography in which Lyme Regis is enfolded gives the town an air of seclusion which clings to it even on the most crowded summer weekend. In spite of a recent influx of tourists from further afield, many of them attracted by the making here of the film of *The French Lieutenant's Woman*, Lyme is still a local resort. In Charles Smithson's day it was a fashionable watering-place for the middle classes, and nowadays has its share of second-home owners who bring their town friends to the pretty early-nineteenth-century seafront cottages along The Walk. But on the beach, and above in the Seaventurer Restaurant and small video arcade under Langmoor Gardens, most accents are West Country. Lyme is the great place for a day out in this part of the world, and these day-visitors don't demand more of the town than they know they'll find: pleasant gardens to stroll through, a nice long view on either side, an ammonite picked up on the shore, a dose of wind and spray on the Cobb, the red-shirted, enthusiastic self-styled Uncles and Aunties of the United Beach Missions. (Uncle Frank: 'A prize for the first child to bring me a hair out of Uncle Keith's head – if you can find one!' Uncle Keith: 'What? Oh, *no!*') You can walk straight off the beach into the bar of the Royal Standard. The crab in the sandwiches comes from the freezer – the staff say they're kept so busy that they just don't have the time to go and select from John Wason's fresh-caught goodies – but the beer is the real thing, strong and tasty, brewed just along the coast by Palmers of Bridport.

Beyond the beach, Broad Street runs steeply from Top of Town downhill, to turn sharply into Bridge Street. Broad Street is as broad as any Cotswold town's sheep-straggle, its Victorian and Edwardian shopfronts the public faces of much older buildings behind. There are many solid, comfortable old hotels in Broad Street, a good example being the Royal Lion with its Prince of Wales feathers and *Ich Dien* motto on top, three times for good measure. During the filming of *The French Lieutenant's Woman*, a lot of time, thought and money went into pushing Broad Street's appearance back into the last century – Serendip Bookshop hasn't yet re-emerged – but the atmosphere here didn't need much adjusting.

There's little of the late twentieth century about such establishments as Collins's provisions store, Baker's Hair Stylists or Ford's electrical shop, or in the cramped old solicitors' offices in large, dark houses where the flies on the windowsills look as if they are very senior partners indeed.

Down at the bottom of the hill, where Bridge Street crosses the walled-in River Lim over the 600-year-old Buddle Bridge, two famous attractions of Lyme stand opposite each other: the Fossil Shop and the Philpot Museum. Customers squeeze their way past one another round the jam-packed tables and shelves of the Fossil Shop. You don't have to buy anything, but your will must be of iron if you can leave this treasure cave empty-handed. Apart from the fossils and lumps of deeply coloured crystalline rock on sale for any sum between £1 and upwards of £100, there's a large display of unsaleable items – too big, too rare – such as ammonites three feet across, split in half and polished, their internal segments filled with sparkling crystallized sand. There are enormous towers of amethyst; ordinary-looking pebbles known as geodes whose hollow hearts are encrusted with gem-like crystals; tiny trilobites like marine woodlice, smaller than your little fingernail. Here Lyme cheerfully, but not aggressively, sets about cashing in on the good fortune lying under its cliffs.

The Philpot Museum on the other side of the road hoards and judiciously displays the town's history with a care and attention to detail rare in such a small-town setting. From the ancient pump-handle fire-engine on the ground floor to the watercolours and prints of old Lyme high up on the second floor at the top of the spiral staircase, the museum is a storehouse where town residents bring their treasures to be puzzled over, pronounced upon and perhaps borrowed for display. There are old paintings of storm waves pounding at the Cobb, old photographs of turn-of-the-century scenes, cannon-balls from the Civil War siege in 1644 (Lyme held out for Parliament for two months, and sent the King's men away empty-handed). A letter dated 11 June 1685 from Gregory Alford, the Mayor of Lyme, to King James II describes how 'This Evening betwixt 7 & 8 of ẙ Clock there came in a great Shipp into ẙ Rode of Lyme not showing any Cullors . . . She filled five great Boats full of men, & they speeded behinde ẙ Cobb, and soe Landed them to the Weftward of ẙ Towne . . . at leaft three hundred men, the Duke of Monmouth in ẙ head of them, soe ẙ they became Maſters of ẙ Towne . . .' Alford rode frantically to Honiton to send this letter even as Monmouth was entering Lyme, and received £20 for his enterprise after the rebels had come to a bloody end, three weeks later at Sedgemoor. Most of the first floor of the museum is given over to relief models and maps explaining the peculiarities of Lyme's coastline and, of course, to cases and cases of fossils. In the centre of all, above the staircase well, hangs the town's old alarm-bell which rang out warnings 'at fire and flood, all foreign sail', inscribed with a caution to practical jokers: 'Strike me in vain, ill luck thy pain'.

The meticulous care with which the Philpot Museum is administered shows to good effect in the pages of its 'Queries' book. Here people write their enquiries when the curator is away – can he give them any information about their great-great-grandfather, believed to have been a ship's captain in Lyme in about 1850? Could he confirm that such-and-such a cottage is built not on Greensand but on clay? Neat notes recording the action taken over the query, initialled by the curator, are inserted in the margin opposite each entry. Until 1988 these initials were J.F.; before illness forced him to give up the curatorship, John Fowles chose this way to give a great deal back to the town where he still lives.

Lyme Regis is the perfect town for strolling around, poking your nose into odd corners. John Fowles's own booklet, *Three Town Walks*, and another published by Serendip Books, *Lyme Regis Walkabout*, make excellent guides to the maze of little streets and lanes that climb the hillsides each side of Broad Street. These are narrow roadways which see only a trickle of tourists. Side-cuts lead off, generally in the direction of the river, to enter courtyards where ramshackle old barns and sheds, piled with someone's obsolete farm machinery or ancient lorries and cars, stand half-smothered in ivy and buddleia bushes. New outlooks constantly open up over walls, gardens or water. From the path along the Town Mill leat, for instance, there's a memorable view over the bright flowerbeds and small trees of Lepers' Well Garden to a group of cottages, each at odds with the next in style, colour and position, rising up Sherborne Lane from the fifteenth-century Gosling Bridge. Sherborne Lane is too steep and narrow for cars (and for many pedestrians, too), a sharply climbing alley which has run in its curving course since before the Norman Conquest. The loudest sounds that residents of Sherborne Lane hear are the slap of children's feet as they dash down the lane, and the scuff of shoes slowly hauling up beside the handrail, polished by the palms of upwardly mobile climbers. Between the old houses you come upon glimpses over the roofs and gardens below and, beyond them, the sea.

These are wonderful views that cost you only a couple of minutes and a certain amount of breathlessness to enjoy, but surprisingly few visitors track them down. With energy and time to spare, you could spend a week following the town trails and your own nose, and still have only begun to delve into the hidden corners of the town. You can lounge between the Cobb and the museum, Langmoor Gardens and The Walk, and take all day over it. Or you can happily give the whole town a miss and hike over the clifftop footpaths to Golden Cap and beyond for the high-level views, or dive into the Undercliff and leave the world behind. These are just a few of the bites to be savoured from the little, sweet apple of Lyme.

WEST COUNTRY

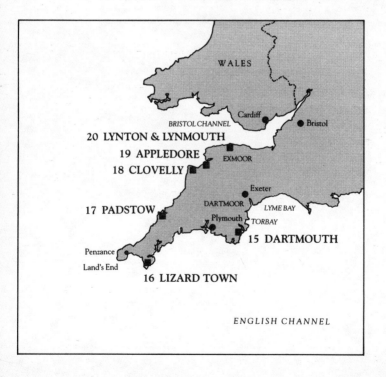

15. Dartmouth

It's quite a business, getting to Dartmouth. The fast dual carriageway of the A38 brings you sweeping down into South Devon from Exeter, full of the joys of summer. But your ardour is likely to be cooled during the hour or more of nose-to-tail crawling once you leave the A38, through Totnes and down miles of minor roads. If, alternatively, you leave Torquay or Paignton and head south for a sunny day's outing to Dartmouth at the height of the tourist season, it won't be long before you're clamped to the end of an interminable queue for the ferries, a mile north of Kingswear on the east bank of the River Dart. Crossing the river to Dartmouth takes barely a couple of minutes, but first you have to get yourself on board those damned ferries. Most of the small towns in this beautiful part of Devon are bursting at the seams with visitors from spring until late summer. Dartmouth is different, thanks to those few hundred yards of unbridged river that lie between town and tourists. It's a curious situation, blessed by locals and cursed by tourist officers, for a place so full of striking old buildings and steep little streets, and so rich in history.

For those whose pleasure lies in these things, and in gazing at water, wooded hills and the changing views of a busy river, it's well worth an early start and a struggle for a parking slot. Dartmouth's parking problem is chronic. There just aren't enough spaces down in the narrow streets. Frustrated drivers circle round, round and round again before snarling away to multi-storeys elsewhere along the coast. But you don't really need a car to explore Dartmouth. An excellent park-and-ride scheme operates from the large car park at the top of the town, bringing you by bus down to the river front and one of the loveliest views anywhere in South Devon. Dartmouth has no beach – it sits nearly two miles inland of the Dart's curving, rocky mouth – but the influence of the sea is strong. The river bulges out into a wide basin between Dartmouth and Kingswear, spreading below rounded hills whose cultivated tops rise from collars of trees. Large houses look down from these woods on to the river, a mass of yacht masts threaded across by the ferries and up and down by excursion boats and big timber vessels making their careful way through the small fry to their quay at Totnes, eight miles inland. The Higher Ferry churns across the river laden with cars, its paddles throwing up foam; while the Lower Ferries slide to and fro like crocodiles, utilitarian rubber tyres round their waists, carrying the foot passengers. Above this activity of the river stand Kingswear's lines of terraces, one above another up their hill, the pastel yellows and greens of the houses contrasting with the darker green of the trees and bushes between them. Behind you as you look out from the North Embankment is the rabbit warren of Dartmouth's streets, and to the north the great red-and-white citadel of the Royal Naval College above the town on its smooth lawns – a mast crossed with two yards in front of lines of windows, domes and towers – British imperial architecture at its most dominating.

Everything in this wide view round the river basin has a watery, nautical tang to it. Plunging in among those narrow, climbing lanes, you catch the atmosphere of a town whose fortunes have been shaped entirely by its position right over a deep-water anchorage, within easy reach of the sea and sheltered by the height, narrowness and curvature of the river-mouth approach. Dartmouth came into being 800 years ago as a port of embarkation for the Crusades. Once established, the town throve on trade – wool and cloth out, wine and all kinds of luxury goods in – with the English provinces in the south-west of France and with the other continental countries. Dartmouth shipowners were mighty men in the prosperous years of the fourteenth century, the greatest among them John Hawley, on whom Chaucer based his Shipman in the *Canterbury Tales*. Hawley owned a large fleet, and he built the first fortifications, a ditch and wall, at the mouth of the Dart against the French marauders who were plaguing England's coastal trading towns. Hawley was a man of blood and iron, a natural leader (seven times elected Mayor of Dartmouth) who on one occasion took a force of ships across the Channel and up the Seine to settle the hash of an invasion fleet assembling there. One notable building still survives in Dartmouth from that exciting time, The Cherub in Higher Street. This small building, all black timbers, tiny windows and low doorways, has two 'oversailing' upper storeys, the top one jutting out a good four feet over the pavement. Built originally as a wool merchant's house and nowadays a beamy, horse-brassy inn, it has stood here, crookedly yet solidly, for more than six centuries.

Dartmouth was secured from the threat of French attack by its twin castles, built towards the end of the fifteenth century on opposite sides of the river mouth. Its sheltered anchorage continued to make the town an important jumping-off place for explorers and adventurers, among them Raleigh, John Davis and Sir Humphrey Gilbert. In 1620 the Pilgrim Fathers made one in their series of false starts for the New World from

Dartmouth, setting out after repairing storm damage in the *Mayflower* and the leaky little *Speedwell* (soon to be abandoned in Plymouth). By this time Dartmouth brigs, each with crews of a hundred hardy men – and a small catering corps of women and boys – were making the long, dangerous voyage in early spring across the Atlantic to the teeming cod fisheries off Newfoundland. Fishermen from the other Atlantic seaboards of Europe joined them in camps ashore, catching cod from small rowing boats, gutting and salting the fish, braving storms, hunger, isolation and exposure in an atmosphere, according to contemporary accounts, of international friendship in adversity. The hazards were tremendous, and so were the profits.

The Newfoundland cod fisheries were worked right up until 1907, by which time the young gentlemen cadets of the Royal Navy had been settled for two years in their new quarters up the hill from the mid-river miseries of HMS *Britannia*. This floating training college, established here in 1863, put its inmates through a hell of bullying, bad food and savage discipline, while turning out a stream of some of the most effective naval officers in England's history. Today's Royal Naval College gets much the same results under a rather more civilized regime. The young men are well thought of by Dartmouth people, though cross-currents between cadets and local boys occasionally lead to black eyes in dance halls, the trouble usually centring round rivalry over girls: another link in the chain of nautical traditions that still anchors Dartmouth firmly to its seafaring past.

It's hard to know how to spread your time so as to take in enough of the splendid items that this long tide of history has sprinkled all over the town. The Butterwalk at the bottom of Duke Street in the heart of Dartmouth is most visitors' prime capture for the camera – four merchants' houses of the 1630s and '40s, with an arcade of granite pillars propping up a lowering frontage of heavily carved dark wood where winged angels, bunches of grapes, grotesque devil figures, full-breasted viragos, dragons, fish and funny faces jostle for attention. The bank next door has carefully continued the theme with its own arcade, albeit in concrete. Just along the road is the tiny building which houses one of the inventions of Thomas Newcomen (a Dartmouth boy, born here in 1663), a great timber-beamed steam pumping engine that nods up and down, hissing and clacking with a well-greased, thick sound at the end of each stroke. A fulsome plaque on the wall from the American Society of Mechanical Engineers lauds 'indeed one of the strategic innovations in world history and the single greatest act of synthesis in the ensuing history of the steam engine'. There are the ship models in the Butterwalk's Borough Museum – beware! you can easily dream the whole day away in front of these – and the jumble of personal possessions giving the flavour of one individual Dartmouth life in the Henley Museum in Anzac Street.

Perhaps the best way to taste the town is to climb one of the narrow lanes, half roadway and half steps, leading up into the twisting streets behind the shops and hotels that fill the flat apron of ground at river level. Clarence Street, reached by steps from the car park on King's Quay, is a good example. At the bottom of the street is the Ship-in-Dock pub, proud of its naval atmosphere with ships' badges over the bar, ship photographs on the walls and ship models on the windowsills. Clarence Street's fine houses, some Georgian, others older, are set ten or twelve feet apart along a curving roadway that runs up to even narrower, steeper and twistier Clarence Hill. From this perch there's a remarkable view, down over slate roofs, angled in all directions below you, into the canyon-like Foss Street and Market Street with their strolling shoppers foreshortened into blobs of heads and feet, then up and over the tower of St Saviour's Church to the green hills rising on the south side of the town and the yacht masts in thickets under Kingswear's ranks of houses across the river. Brown's Hill above the Market Square is another stepped alleyway which in Clovelly or Robin Hood's Bay would be crammed with clicking cameras, its inhabitants barricaded away behind the snow-white shutters and geranium baskets. But here in Dartmouth there's somehow enough space for both locals and visitors to operate comfortably.

St Saviour's Church houses what must be one of the finest collections of church treasures in Britain. Up to the end of Tudor times, the town consisted of two villages, Hardness and Clifton, separated by the mill pool where the Quay now runs. Some vessels came as far inland as St Saviour's and tied up to the church wall itself. The building, thoroughly restored in the 1890s, was opened for worship back in 1372, and is a box of delights spanning six centuries. There's a densely carved rood-screen of about 1480, a riot of intertwined vaulting, tracery, leaves and flowers that shows off medieval craftsmanship at its very best. The dark wood gallery at the west end, with its carved and painted coats-of-arms, dates from 1633. The old south door, now unhinged and standing inside the church, is about the same age; its ironwork tree of life with jagged-edged leaves shelters two low-slung, elegant leopards doing high kicks. The Elizabethan altar, dramatically painted, has the four Evangelists carved into its front legs. Under the chancel carpet (which needs at least two pairs of hands to roll it back) lies the brass to Sir John Hawley, Chaucer's 'Dertemouthe' Ship-man, in full knight's armour, with his feet resting on a lion. He holds the hand of his first wife, Joan, while Alice, his second spouse, stands rather sadly by. In front of the rood-screen is a superb fifteenth-century 'wine-glass' pulpit, its heavily carved stonework of foliage and pinnacles still carrying the original faded reds, blues and golds. During recent filming for television inside St Saviour's, a clumsily wheeled camera bumped the pulpit and cracked it, necessitating a stone-by-stone dismantling and removal to a new position a few feet away. The excavations on the new site brought to light something special: a medieval slate memorial to a bishop or priest, fully robed and holding a chalice. He now lies on show under reinforced glass. Over all these treasures, and many others, curves a lovely dark wagon roof embossed with stars.

Those tourists who do brave ferry queues and roundabout lanes to get to Dartmouth can fix their whole attention on such historic features as St Saviour's, the Buttermarket, The Cherub and, of course, Bayard's Cove on the south waterfront, all cobbles, Tudor buildings and photogenic views – Dartmouth at its most picturesque, and most crowded. There are many other corners of the town to discover, architecturally less distinguished but just as enjoyable – York House on the waterfront, for example, with its rows of fish-tail wall slates in alternating dark and light grey, and its balconies of what seem to be beautifully turned chair legs; or the Station Restaurant on the other side of the Embankment. It was built by the Great Western Railway early this century as a kind of waiting-room for the crowds at the annual regatta wanting to catch the ferries across the Dart which connected with the GWR's station at Kingswear. The building was designated a station, and tricked out like one with chocolate-and-cream paint and toothed awning. In today's restaurant you can look out from your table over the Dart and watch the Dart Valley Railway's green steam locomotives puffing off with their trains along the riverbank towards Paignton, the passenger ferries on their short, straight runs and the excursion boats making upriver for Totnes.

The crowds still come in August to enjoy the Royal Regatta, for

Dartmouth is above all else a sailing town. Many retired naval officers have settled here, a powerful force in keeping up the standards of the sailing clubs and in voting down such suggestions as a bridge across the Dart and an amusement arcade for the teenagers. The notice in the Royal Avenue Gardens, a brisk exhortation, sums up their position: 'THINK OF OTHERS – do not spoil the pleasure of others by damage, litter or unruly conduct.' The tennis courts below the Royal Naval College are pounded early in the morning by these athletic elderly men in crisp white shirts and navy-blue shorts, exchanging efficient rallies with their wives in pleated knee-length skirts and formidable hair-dos. Later in the day they spend long hours checking over their yachts and sailing dinghies moored by the Embankment. Aertex and flannel are the order of the day, along with Second World War centre partings and clipped moustaches, or the side-whiskers and cheekbone tufts of an earlier tradition. Most belong to the Royal Dart Yacht Club, seen as rather snootier and more exclusive than its rival, the Dartmouth Yacht Club. This latter opens its list to a wide range of amateur sailors, or 'yachties' as the locals call them, many without a naval background but still part of that community of boat-owners who count every moment not spent near their prized possessions as wasted. The Dartmouth Yacht Club will happily accept anyone with anything from a large yacht to a small wooden dinghy. There are three marinas to accommodate the 'yachties', a repair barge, a floating dock and any number of chandlers, boatyards and mast-makers to cater for their needs. Some companies keep enormous 'courtesy yachts' here, gleaming gin-palaces for impressing their clients. Scandinavian, Dutch, Belgian and French boat-owners sail over for the summer and base themselves in Dartmouth, using the club houses and other facilities of the yacht clubs. The regatta is the high spot of the year, with sailing all day and drinking, dancing and yarning all night. The social lives of a large number of Dartmouth's retired people revolve around the yacht clubs, which provide them with sport, comfortable drinking perches, friends, security and, from time to time, husbands and wives or some looser arrangement. The two clubs like to get in digs at each other's style, but they are each the bitters in the other's gin. Life would be too bland without the bite provided by that lot over the river.

If the dreaded bridge over the Dart ever gets built, apoplexy will scythe through the yacht-club bars and the tennis courts. Dartmouth will be less than half an hour's drive from Torquay, even at the peak of the summer season. The town will finally get its multi-storeys, arcades and fun parks, and slide gracefully into the modern tourist world. It may yet happen. Meanwhile the 'yachties', the retired folk and the locals, determined that it won't, combine to keep their precious river frontier unspanned and their town as they think it should be: modest, old-fashioned and with elbow room for everyone.

16. Lizard Town

There's a time-honoured tradition among travellers writing about the villages of Cornwall: if it's Lizard Town, abuse it.

'A miserable village on a rotten moor', sneered an eighteenth-century Dean of Exeter. 'A poor scattered village', opined Walter White in 1854. Other more recent passers-by have not been slow to stick their nibs in as well: 'bleak . . . gaunt . . . disappointing . . . a dreary place on the sunniest day, even the houses seem aloof and shun each other's company'.

Good God! What on earth is it about Lizard Town that summons forth such bile? Even Sir John Betjeman, with his vivacious eye for an unlikely place and his passion for all things Cornish, could only manage 'an army housing scheme given over to visitors'; while the like-minded Charles Harper, writing in 1910, saw the houses as 'a flock of sheep huddled together, facing all ways, to escape a tempest raging from all quarters at once'.

Whisk these same writers past the village, and put them down beside the lighthouse or on the cliffs round Kynance Cove or at the door of St Winwalaus's Church down the hill in Landewednack, and their nibs are withdrawn from the vitriol bottle and dipped into the honey pot. Perhaps it's by comparison with the attractions all round it that Lizard Town suffers; or perhaps it's the long and windy journey along the moor road from Helston that has jaundiced the eye of so many beholders down the years. And the sight at the road's end that greets you today, a large car park flanked by gift shops and cafés with a public lavatory as its focal point, certainly doesn't do much to tickle a palate sated with the picture-postcard fishing villages and golden, cliff-encircled bays of the tourist's Cornish coast. Lizard Town is a village still working the surrounding land and sea for its existence; and, as in all such places, you have to step out of the car park and down the road a little to begin to enjoy it for what it is.

Lizard Town found one visitor, at least, to champion it in print. The Reverend C. A. Johns means to Lizard Town what Kilvert means to Clyro or Laurie Lee to Slad: mention his name in the pub and you'll draw out a smile of recognition and pleasure, probably followed by a quote. His little red-covered book about his stay here in the 1840s, *A Week At The Lizard*, is an enjoyable read, lively and informative, full of details that record how day-to-day life went on. There are long lists and descriptions of the rare flowers of the district, the birds in the cliffs, shipwrecks in the bays. You can read of Lizard fishermen catching bass and pollack using a tuft of goat's beard as bait, of the 'foggin' or currant cake they took on their sea trips, of Mr Johns himself finding twelve species of Leguminosae growing so close together that he could cover them with his hat. He found the inhabitants of Lizard Town 'in general quiet, industrious and orderly', and obviously got on well enough with them to be invited out on a fishing expedition – though the 'young friend' who accompanied him became so seasick that he had to be landed in Kynance Cove.

But even the well-disposed Mr Johns could not find much to praise in the road from Helston, 'a long, weary road, skirted by commons or lined by treeless hedges, and on either side a flat, tame country, with but rarely a distant peep at the sea, and no indication of a bold coast'. Those are still the characteristics of the Lizard peninsula: flat, treeless and scoured by sea-winds. The geography of the place is another scenic disadvantage to Lizard Town. Most of Cornwall's coastal settlements tumble prettily down clefts in the cliffs, their approach-roads descending to give that first thrilling view down onto clustering roofs. The houses of Lizard Town, in contrast, run up, over and along the ridge at the end of the Helston road. You can't get an overview of the place from the middle of that drab car park. Your first instinct is to rush straight through the village and down to the splendours of the incomparable coast that lies just beyond. But stand at the lower end of the car park facing the Lizard Hotel and the layout of Lizard Town begins to make sense. The two hotels, the long Lizard Hotel and the tall Caerthilian, form the centrepiece of the village, standing white and solid at right angles to each other. The Rev. Johns enjoyed his stay at the Lizard Hotel, though he warned his readers that it was the only such place of any size in Lizard Town: 'Strangers, therefore, are recommended to telegraph for rooms, when they will be sure of civility, comfortable lodgings, and a good table, beer and wine included.'

From the Lizard Hotel run the narrow streets of the village, winding between bungalows, turn-of-the-century large houses and the massive granite blocks of farmhouses, barns and farmyard walls. Cowpats splash the roads, and foxgloves and buttercups line the lanes. To the right of the Lizard Hotel the Victorian Kynance Terrace, a snippet transplanted from some South Coast resort, leads down to the lane where the post office stands like a French railway station with its corner blocks and window frames in raised stone. Its dark interior contains an ancient wooden counter and shelves crammed with oddments. Just along the lane is the little village museum, open during the summer, housing its collection of Lizard tradition and natural history in an old barn. From here you can walk past a court of knobbly stone farm-buildings to reach the hedgebank path across the downs to Kynance Cove's enchanted circle of serpentine cliffs, caves and offshore rocks, the goal of most visitors on a summer's day.

Another magnet that draws the tourists away from the village is the church of St Winwalaus at Landewednack, reached by way of Beacon Terrace to the left on the opposite side of the road from the Lizard Hotel. You drop down the hill past Churchtown Farm, where nothing seems to have stirred for a century, to come to the beautiful Norman church with its chequered tower of serpentine and granite, and Church Cove below where the lifeboat is stationed. These are treats not to be missed. But to see a little more of Lizard Town's own delights, walk down the lane that skirts the left side of the Lizard Hotel, past Peter Skerten's stained-glass works in a tiny wooden hut, the Caerthilian Hotel and the post office, to reach Penmenner Road. A line of small hotels and boarding houses brings you to a secluded spot where the tarmac gives way to a stony lane descending the field slopes between flowery banks of granite. On the left stands Parc-an-Castle, a fine Edwardian house built in 1904 to echo St Winwalaus's Church in the light and dark stone of granite and serpentine. One story says that the house was put up on the site of a prehistoric fortification; another, that it was built by the present occupant's grandfather to out-dignify Wartha Manor, the house that stands just below. This splendid place, rich in tall chimneys and ironwork on the roof, was built by a Lizard Town silk-merchant, John Roberts, a few years before Parc-an-Castle. Mr Roberts's third wife was a Frenchwoman, and he imported craftsmen from her native land to decorate the interior of Wartha Manor in suitable style with carved bunches of grapes.

The land descends from Wartha Manor to a grassy valley just west of Polpeor Cove, known as Pistol Meadow, supposed to be haunted by the spirits of the several hundred victims buried here after the wreck of a transport ship. The coastal path gives an easy walk eastwards above the disused lifeboat station, still standing over its slipway in Polpeor Cove. Fishermen use it these days to store their equipment and dry their nets over the slipway railings, but it has seen desperate times. From the tip of the Lizard peninsula a reef of rocks, some submerged and others half exposed, runs for nearly a mile out into the sea. These hidden teeth have chewed up hundreds of ships and thousands of lives. The lifeboat has occupied a central position in the life of Lizard Town ever since the first one was stationed on the cliffs below the lighthouse in 1859. Stations have been opened, closed and re-sited since then; but the dangers of this coast bind the villagers to their lifeboat as fast as they have done for over a century. The Rev. C. A. Johns included in the second edition of *A Week At The Lizard* the story of two barques, the *Marianna* and the *Rafflino*, which set sail with cargoes of rice from the East Indies on the same day in 1872. They ended their voyages together, too, piling up within hours of each other in thick fog on the Stag Rocks under the lighthouse.

If the lighthouse had been equipped with the foghorn it has now, the two barques would never have got so close inshore. Today's fogbound sailors more than eight miles from land can hear that great mechanical double-groan, blasting over the water every minute. On clear nights the flashes from the Lizard light reach out nearly four times as far. The Lizard Town folk of the early seventeenth century would not have been amused. They were notorious wreckers and plunderers, stripping wrecks of their goods and using the timbers to build their houses – in its opportunism and profit-motivation, a kind of extension of the smuggling that most of them were engaged in. When Sir John Killigrew, a former buccaneer trying to turn an honest penny, put up a coal-burning beacon in 1619, Lizard men were not impressed. 'They have been so long used to repe profite by the calamyties of the ruin of shipping,' he wrote in a letter, 'that they clayme it heredytarye, and heavely complayne on me.' The locals called the wrecks 'God's Grace', and they bitterly resented Killigrew's interference. His light didn't last long, but in 1751 the present structure of two towers was built above Lizard Point and the Lizard inhabitants turned resignedly away to their smuggling.

Along with Kynance Cove and Landewednack, the Lizard lighthouse pulls in the crowds year by year. The four keepers who live with their families in the barrack-like houses between the towers have just about the heaviest workload of all their calling. They work an eight-hour shift turn and turn about, switching on the light and foghorn by hand, seeing to the smooth running of the old oil-burning engines and cleaning their brass-work, cutting the grass round the station, cleaning the lens of the light, checking and repairing, dealing with visitors (courteously and at length) and operating the recently installed computers which, ironically, will one day do them out of a job. Lighthouse keepers are a threatened species. Full automation of all Britain's lighthouses and light-vessels is scheduled for the end of the century. Several in the area, including the Seven Stones, Wolf Rock and Bishop Rock, are already controlled from the Lizard. When all have been brought under the electronic umbrella, a very individualistic, strongly independent breed of men will lay their burden of vigilance down for good. The job demands opposing qualities that very few possess.

'I've shed tears over this job,' says Philip Griffiths, one of the assistant keepers at the Lizard lighthouse, remembering the misery of being incarcerated for two months at a time at the age of seventeen in a tower miles from land with two older men. 'Some men can be right bastards, others you think would make a good dad. One man had been a monk in some monastery in Afghanistan. A lot of them are running away from things, wanting to be on their own. It took me ten years to learn how to deal with the minds of different men.'

Wolf Rock and Bishop Rock were the worst: towers rising straight out of the sea, with no room round them to exercise and get away from the other men. A smoker can make the lives of his non-smoking colleagues absolute hell. So can a man with no hobbies, constantly distracting his companions from their time-absorbing pastimes. Philip whiled away the barren weeks reading and painstakingly making miniature sheds and houses for his model railway. He had joined Trinity House as a teenager, partly because of the long holidays (eight weeks on, two weeks off) and partly in response to teasing from his friends over the wetness of his employment in the greengrocery trade. 'You mustn't be too much of a wimp, and you mustn't be too macho – able to grin and bear it, but flexible above all.'

He's well aware of – and making plans to soften – what will happen to him sooner or later: the golden handshake, early retirement and the cutting of a plait of pride and stoicism that will have tied him uncomplainingly to his demanding job for thirty years.

'I stand by the light and think to myself: tower 1751 – lens 1903 – electricity 1924 – diesel engines from the 1950s – computers 1987. What a wonderful range of old and new equipment to work with. What other job could you do that in? I think of all the keepers who have stood here for the past two hundred years, and what some of them would think if they could see those computers, or look out to see a ship going full astern.'

Unlike their ancestors, the present-day inhabitants of Lizard Town are proud – and fond – of their lighthouse. Selling ice-creams and postcards to its visitors is one strand in the village's economy. Others are the farming and fishing that have always gone on in the area. A few boats still go out for crab and lobster from the coves round Lizard Town, but several village men work bigger boats out of Newlyn and other larger ports. It's the serpentine industry, however, round which the identity of Lizard Town revolves, like a cathedral city round its church. The serpentine rock, a fusion under intense heat and pressure of the minerals olivine, augite and hornblende, lies in bands along the tip of the Lizard peninsula. The feeling of serpentine under the fingers has been well described as 'waxy or greasy; fibrous varieties silky; massive varieties earthy'. Francis Kilvert of Clyro, examining the cliffs at Kynance Cove in 1870, went into characteristic raptures over their colours: 'I never saw anything like the wonderful colour of the serpentine rocks, rich, deep, warm, variegated, mottled and streaked and veined with red, green and white, huge blocks and masses of precious stone marble on every side, an enchanted cove, the palace of the Nereids.' It's when serpentine is polished that the best of its colour is brought to the surface, a warm glow shot through with snaking lines of white – hence the name. Prehistoric people knew its attractions and made it into rings and necklaces. Serpentine was used in building, as in St Winwalaus's Church. It didn't become an industry, however, until Queen Victoria and Prince Albert took an interest. Then, like Whitby jet, serpentine became big business in Lizard Town. Local workers sent 'handsome vases, candelabra and other ornaments' to the Great Exhibition of 1851. The Poltesco factory was opened at Carleon Cove in the 1860s and turned out serpentine knick-knacks for thirty years, employing nearly 100 people, until competition from cheap foreign marble forced it to close. But Lizard Town knew it was on to a good thing, and small serpentine works were set up all over the village. Nine or ten businesses operate in Lizard Town today, the small hut-like buildings containing their workshops standing between the houses and general shops on the streets. Buying a serpentine ashtray, egg or barometer case is as much a part of a day on the Lizard as visiting Kynance Cove and the lighthouse.

David Hill, a youngish, quietly spoken man born and bred in the village, spends each October with the other serpentine workers quarrying the rock from pits in the downs to the west of Lizard Town. They find the quarries filled with flood water which has to be pumped out before work can begin.

In the old days, before modern pumping machinery made it possible to work the same digging year after year, the workers would prospect for a new site, looking for the light fingers of stone on the surface that told of good stone underneath. Prospecting still goes on, as the old veins are worked out, with the blessing of the owner of most of the land hereabouts, Lord Falmouth.

Those old workers did the whole thing with pick and shovel, but nowadays the men club together to hire a digger and work the same quarry. The best serpentine, known as mild stone, lies in light-coloured plates in the clay. The darker the colour, the harder and more awkward to work the stone. You insert the single claw of the digger into one of the joints between the plates of serpentine, and up she comes. Then the great block of stone is knocked into convenient sizes at the quarry.

'The worst thing is the quarrying,' David Hill says. 'You get a big lump of stone, maybe sixty or seventy tons, and you've got to knock it down to size. Every single piece has to be knocked out by hand. It's a bit depressing standing there and looking at all that hard work in front of you.'

The stone which David brings back to his workshop by the car park represents his whole winter's employment. The workshop is a tiny, dusty room behind the shop where his wife sells the products throughout the summer. An electric lathe sits on the bench, its chucks with their tungsten-carbide tips lying in heaps beside it – a far cry from the old lathes driven by foot treadles at which the serpentine workers would smooth out the stone with tools made out of discarded mining equipment. The workshop floor is thick with stone dust and piled with roughly rounded chunks of serpentine scored with white chisel cuts from the quarrying. Small pieces go to make the bowls, ashtrays and eggs, larger ones the barometer cases and urns. The largest are turned into the four-foot-high lighthouses topped with brass electric lamps that only tourists with money to burn can afford.

David picked up a medium-sized piece and showed it to me. 'You can tell what you're going to get out of a piece of serpentine as soon as you've got it. This one here will be for a barometer case.'

He dipped the greyish lump of serpentine into a bucket of water. Instantly the deep red of the stone shone through, glowing in the bucket. Red was the most popular stone in the old days and consequently the hardest to find today, though David knows likely sites where he might pick up a piece thrown away a century or more ago. A red serpentine egg from his shop will set you back three times as much as a green or grey one.

The chisel chinked as David hammered away at the serpentine lump, levelling it off flat enough for the lathe. He wore goggles to protect his eyes from the flying chips, but his lungs must absorb as much dust as a coal-miner's. When it's roughly shaped, the stone is heated over the gas and smeared with 'glue', a home-concocted lubricant, before being cooled and turned on the lathe. Then comes the elbow-grease as the serpentine is rubbed with increasingly fine grades of emery-paper, polished with 'flour emery' on a cloth or piece of corduroy, and finished off with jeweller's rouge and a drop of olive oil. All these grits and powders are kept in battered old tin boxes on the workshop shelves. From a rough piece of serpentine off the lathe to the smoothly gleaming end-product might take an hour of hard rubbing.

David took over the business from his father, but he doesn't see young school-leavers wanting to keep the tradition up. 'It's too hard and dusty. In a few years' time the one or two old boys who are doing it now'll be dead, and then it'll just be folk of my age.'

Other village people don't agree. They don't want to see the serpentine trade taken over by outsiders, or run as a kind of protected curiosity, kept alive by handouts from the tourist industry; but they are well aware how closely Lizard Town and its serpentine are linked in the visitors' expectations. The image of the Lizard, with all its other attractions, is incomplete without those little serpentine shops and their softly shining, easily carried, locally made souvenirs. Provided the prospectors can go on finding new veins as the old ones work out, and conservationists don't raise a ruin-of-the-natural-landscape hare some day, Lizard Town should be able to keep its most characteristic industry for the foreseeable future.

The 'miserable, bleak, dreary' village on the peninsula tip – the southernmost place in Britain, as its signs never tire of pointing out – deserves a better press than it has had. In homage to its favourite chronicler, here is the Rev. C. A. Johns, recounting an adventure on the nearby serpentine rocks of Kynance Cove with typical gusto and wealth of detail. He's stuck fast on a crumbling ledge nearly 100 feet above the sea, encumbered with book, bag and walking stick:

I found myself in a situation in which few I believe have ever been placed, except in the most terrific dreams . . . I had inserted the end of my stick in a crevice, and, being obliged to use both hands in clinging to the rock, I could not draw it out: and if my foot had slipped I should have glided over a few feet of smooth stone, and then fallen seventy or eighty feet, whether into the sea, or on to the shore, I could not turn my head to examine . . . I was supported almost entirely by the muscular strength of my fingers. The only possible support for my feet was six feet below the summit of the rock, and not more than half an inch wide. I managed with great difficulty to set my foot on this, snatched at, and caught hold of, the top of the rock with the ends of my fingers, and was suspended as it were between heaven and earth directly over the precipice, when – the ledge under my feet gave way . . .

How did he survive to write the story? You'll have to go to the library in Redruth to find that out, or stand someone a drink in Lizard Town.

17. Padstow

Closing time in the Golden Lion at Padstow on May Eve. The beer is beginning to tell on the accordion players and mouth-organists limbering up for action, and on the side-drummers and big bass drum-bangers waiting in the doorway. Reinforcements in the way of bottles and cans are being bought over the counter and stowed away in pockets, but red faces are already running with drink and tension. Outside in the cool night air the crowds stand packed shoulder to shoulder under the lines of bunting along narrow Lanadwell Street, chatting and joking, a tightly pressed avenue of bodies where you can hardly get a bottle up to your lips or raise a hand to wave to a friend. Down the middle of the crowd crouches a double line of women in white dresses or trousers, blue ribbons round their waists and across their shoulders, hemmed in and almost hidden. The air is taut with anticipation, a buzz of expectancy growing as more and more people squeeze down each end of the street.

At last the moment arrives. The door of the Golden Lion is pushed open and out come the musicians, easing their instruments sideways through the doorway. A great cheer goes up. Bodies in the crowd are jammed back against the shop-fronts, toes are freely trodden on. With an ear-jarring thump the drums bash out a slow rhythm and the accordions and mouth-organs swing into a jerky tune that comes bouncing back off the house-walls. The crouching line of women springs up, forcing the crowd further back, and begins a spasmodic dance. The dancers' hands punch the air from side to side, up and down. Their whole bodies follow the movements, waving and flirting with all their energy, a shadow mime of the real business that will come tomorrow morning when old winter in the shape of the 'Obby 'Oss will be brought out into the open for his funeral rites.

> Unite and unite, and let us all unite,
> For summer is a-come unto day;
> And whither we are going we will all unite
> In the merry morning of May.

Everyone roars it out: Padstonians as they have done for hundreds of years, seemingly drinking in the words with their mothers' milk; earnest folk-fanatics from all corners of the country, gleaming with solemn pride that they know the whole song by heart; tourists in shorts and sandals squinting at song-sheets by the light of windows. Between verses the music stops abruptly, someone in the thick of things shouts, "Oss! 'Oss!' at full bellow and the dancing women yell back, 'Wee 'Oss!' After ten minutes of thumping and roaring the long, clotted pipe of bodies begins to go by peristalsis – stop and start, squeeze and shove – down Lanadwell Street, spilling out and up into the Market Square to get as close as possible to the maypole in the middle. Ribbons and bunting string out in all directions above the bobbing, singing sea of heads, and most windows are packed with onlookers gazing down or swapping backchat with the crowd. Blue drifts of tobacco smoke spurt up and waver away above the singers. Fresh supplies of beer appear from somewhere, and yet more people jostle down from other streets. By midnight all free movement becomes impossible and everyone is bounced up and down in a scrum of similarly bouncing bodies, forced to surrender to exhilaration. The music thumps on, brassy and urgent, for twenty or thirty verses at a time, slowing down occasionally for a mournful section where the dancers kneel down, before leaping up and twirling on. It's a scene out of some Latin-American religious carnival rather than a grey and windy English spring night. One wouldn't be surprised to see the enormous effigy of a saint swaying above the crowd.

As May morning comes in, the crowd begins to thin out at the edges, parents carrying sleeping children away to save some of their energies for the frolics that will begin in a few hours' time. The 'night singers', however, have only been loosening up for the next stage. Now they gather the band together, throw away their chip papers and empty bottles and set off round the streets of the town to serenade the windows of long-established Padstow folk with a set of personalized verses:

> Arise up, Mr [So-and-so], and joy you betide,
> For summer is a-come unto day;
> And bright is your bride that lies by your side,
> In the merry morning of May.

Some verses are more personal than others, sung with especial gusto if there's a pretty girl in bed or at the window up there:

> Arise up, Miss [So-and-so], all in your cloak of silk,
> For summer is a-come unto day;
> And all your body under as white as any milk,
> In the merry morning of May.

Till three or four in the morning the night singing goes on; and by then there are only a couple of hours till the pubs are open again.

The salt would be truly without its savour if Padstow ever lost its 'Obby 'Osses. There are two of them that come prancing out on May morning, the Red Ribbon 'Oss and the Blue Ribbon 'Oss. The Red Ribbon 'Oss is the senior partner, certainly a survival of pagan spring, fertility and resurrection rites which have been lost beyond the recall of local historians. Most people seem to agree that the Blue Ribbon 'Oss party was a nineteenth-century secession from the true church of the Red Ribbon, brought about by the drunken and riotous state that the ceremony had got into. There was bad blood between the temperance Blues and traditionalist Reds, leading to hard words and blows. Nowadays the two parties seem to get on well enough, though their paths on May Day don't usually cross more often than is necessary. There's a nice irony in the choice of headquarters for each 'Oss. The Red Ribbon, with all that earthy past, is now based in the sober brick Padstow Institute; while the Blue Ribbon supporters (far more rollicking these days than their Red counterparts) hang out in the boozy Harbour Inn on the waterfront.

Padstow is an ancient port with a very long tradition of ship-building, trading and seafaring, and the 'Oss and his dancers may well go back beyond the sixth century when St Petroc, that much-travelled Welshman, arrived to build a church and bring the light to the benighted locals. When Padstow harbour silted up in the Middle Ages (the mermaids' revenge for the shooting of one of their number by the villainous 'Long Tom Yeo of the town of Padstowe') Doom Bar, wrecker of countless vessels, formed across the entrance and shut off the port from big ships. But Padstow continued to be an important place, shipping out voyagers across the Atlantic, passing Irish immigrants onwards to the big cities of England, dealing in lead ore, corn, timber and fish, and building ships. Padstow's vessels were used as far afield as the Newfoundland fisheries. The shipwrights' tools and little wooden half-models of ships' hulls can be seen in the crowded, jumbly small museum above the library in the Market Place. Here are seamen's knots and lobster pots, a pair of choughs above a sailor's bone-handled knife, a 'Grotesquerie' painted on part of a whale's ear, old photographs and amateur paintings to summon up Padstow of the past.

Powerful whiffs of hot blood and dark magic float with the excitement and crowd elation in the May Eve dancing and singing. The least fanciful participant feels it: a combination of a beat so loud you hear it in your stomach rather than your ears, leaping tune, leaping women, dark sky overhead, lamplight on flushed faces, beer and sweat. A Papua New Guinea tribesman would recognize the mood. All are beside themselves in one way or another.

On May morning it's pouring with rain. The car parks at the top of the town have been full since eight o'clock. Down in Padstow the old magic still dominates, but it's a different, lighter feeling. As you walk down the narrow, curving streets you can hear the bands already thumping away all over the town. People greet each other not with 'Good Morning', or 'Hello', but by shouting slogan and response:

"Oss! 'Oss!'

'Wee 'Oss!'

There are bluebells and cowslips in buttonholes, brown wallflowers, primroses and bunches of greenery round hats, in shop windows, behind brooches, on drum bracings. Young girls lay their coins down on the old-fashioned haberdasher's thick wooden counter for lengths of blue or red ribbon. The children's 'Osses are out straight after breakfast, getting tremendous applause as they twirl into pubs and down side-streets – more tasters for the big event and much photographed by the visitors who dash out from the dripping shop-awnings to get a good shot.

At ten o'clock the crowds are thick round the door of the Institute, television cameras and long microphones poking from between their heads. The rain still drives solidly down, but it doesn't matter. Here's the Red Ribbon 'Oss emerging from his stable as last night's tune bashes and crashes out again. He's no friendly old dobbin. This is a fiendish sight, a caped black disc of a body seven or eight feet across, with a savage mask at the front, fierce white moustache and fringe of hair under a pointed witch's hat trimmed with a tossing plume of horsehair. You wouldn't hold a lump of sugar under the nose of this 'oss – he'd snap your fingers in his long, clacking wooden jaws. Babies burst out crying when they see the 'Oss; they've been expecting something out of a paddock. In the old days, pretty girls were whisked under the cape of the 'Oss to have their cheeks rubbed with lamp-black. In the even older days those marks of favour may have been earned less innocently in the darkness of the black cape. As the 'Oss circles round, jerking up his behind with its tightly bound little wisp of tail, you can well believe the stories that say that a French invasion was once

Above: Lindisfarne Castle, still formidable in its striking position on top of Beblowe Crag.

Left: Norman magnificence in the ruined nave of the priory church on Holy Island.

Below: Top 'em, tail 'em and turn 'em over – Holy Island herring boats in useful retirement as fishermen's sheds.

Above: Easington Colliery's coal-blackened beach, with the dinosaur shape of the waste conveyor disgorging more of the same.

Right: Pit village perspective – the converging lines of Easington Colliery's brick terraces.

Below: Coal picking on Easington shore.

Above: Robin Hood's Bay lies cradled in the arm of the cliffs as they curve away towards distant South Cheek.

Below: Nothing straight and everything narrow in the side alleys of Robin Hood's Bay.

Above: The pleasures of South Sands, under the wooded headland that rises to Scarborough Castle.

Left: The coble *Adventurer* sets out from the harbour for a trip around South Bay, Scarborough.

Below: Below the lifeboat shed at North Landing lie the few remaining cobles of the Flamborough fishing fleet: an unimprovable design.

Left: The lighthouse looks down over the Sole Bay Inn into East Green – one charming corner among many in charming Southwold.

Right: The ship-like Palace Hotel drifts into rudderless dilapidation, its stylish elegance out of place on Southend's raucous seafront.

Below: The Kursaal's flashy promise of a sweaty good time once summed up 'good old Sahfend'. Now it symbolizes the uncertainty of Britain-beside-the-Sea; in search of a new role, as yet unfixed.

Above: Black swans on the mill leat in the heart of ancient Swanage.

Below: Ramsgate's West Cliff, with the Ramsgate Home for Smack Boys in the centre of the picture, and the Sailors' Church on the left.

Above: The church gate opens into the flowery graveyard of St Peter and St Paul, West Wittering.

Right: 'Harbour'd fafe below', Daniel Hack lies easy in West Wittering's green and pleasant churchyard.

Below: Henry Royce lived at Elmstead, West Wittering, while hatching plans for the Supermarine seaplane that won the Schneider Trophy in 1929.

Above: The disused lifeboat station in Polpeor Cove. Lizard Town fishermen store their nets in the shed these days.

Left: Lizard Town. David Hill goes to work on a block of locally quarried serpentine – the first stage in the process of shaping it into a highly polished barometer case of softly glowing red shot through with veins of white.

Below: The assistant keeper at the Lizard lighthouse, Philip Griffiths, with his wife and son in the Trinity House compound on Lizard Point.

Above: 'Unite and unite, and let us all unite.' The young Blue Ribbon 'Oss dancers of Padstow step it out, oblivious of the pelting rain.

Right: On Padstow's waterfront stands Abbey House, once the Guildhall of medieval Padstow merchants, at least five hundred years old and steeped in history and legend.

Below: A children's 'Oss gets rainy May morning off to a lively start at Padstow, whipped up by his High-Stepping Teaser.

Left: The gatehouse at Oxwich Castle, scene of the murder of Anne Mansell.

Below: Above the Mansell coat of arms on the gatehouse of Oxwich Castle is the slit through which uncomfortable items could be dropped on the heads of undesirables below.

Below: Dovecote outside the ruined walls of Oxwich Castle, where Anne Mansell was brained by Watkyn John ap Watkyn's well-aimed stone.

Above: The ungodly inhabitants of Oxwich offered smuggled gin to John Wesley when he came to stay at The Nook, but he settled for a nice cup of tea instead.

Right: Tall and handsome buildings overlook Tenby's little harbour.

Below: Victorian Tenby dominates the clifftops above Castle Beach: a view from the Caldey Island ferry boat.

Below: Freedom from traffic fumes and noise is guaranteed in Clovelly: this is the village's main thoroughfare.

Above: The obligatory shot – Clovelly's cobbled street as it first greets the eye, and the camera.

Right: 'The village like a waterfall.' Clovelly seen rising up its wooded cleft from the harbour.

Right: Last frolic
before bedtime on
Aberystwyth's beach,
behind which a
classic line of seaside
resort buildings
curves impressively
away towards
Constitution Hill.

Above: Looking
inland from the quay
towards the bridge
over the Afon
Rheidol and the
wide spread of
Aberystwyth.

Left: The Fortress of
Light, Dinas Oleu,
rears craggily over
the steep streets of
old Barmouth in this
lovely view from the
Isle of the Monk,
Ynys y Brawd.

Top: A promise of fun and laughter on the
side of a Blackpool tram. Not much fun for a
Blackpool carriage horse, though – just a
long, head-down wait.

Above: Grand hotels and groaning trams on
Blackpool's wide North Shore promenade.

Right: Toddler and Grandpa admire their
reflections in the Italian garden pool in
Stanley Park's quiet, unflustered calm;
everything you don't expect Blackpool to be.

Above: Yewbarrow Terrace, Grange-over-Sands, where the clock stands eternally at tea-time.

Above: Above the long, outreaching tongues of Whitehaven's harbour stand Candlestick Chimney and the dilapidated old cottage where Jonathan Swift spent part of his childhood.

Left: Young fishermen share the old wooden jetty at Rothesay with the Caledonian MacBrayne ferries that still bring small numbers of Glaswegians 'doon the watter'.

Right: Looking over the harbour to the houses of Anstruther, a town rich with fishing but gearing up for a future without it.

Left: BF 85 *Ocean Challenge* rounds the jetty at Macduff, coming in from a rough sea to the sheltered calm of the harbour's Outer Basin.

Right: The sea lock at Crinan, through which pass all boats on their way between the Crinan Canal and the waters round the Western Isles.

Left: Fishing boats in the inner half of the basin at Crinan, waiting for their crews to return from a weekend ashore.

scared off by the sight of the 'Oss capering on the cliffs at Stepper Point, surrounded by a crowd of Padstow women in their flapping red cloaks.

In front of the 'Oss gambols the 'High-Stepping Teaser', the high priest of this ceremony, aping the see-sawing of the 'oss with his own arm and body movements. He could be mocking a victim, but it looks more like sympathetic encouragement. 'Oss, teaser and band frisk and thump for ten minutes in front of the Institute before moving away a foot at a time between the packed pavements, oblivious of the pelting rain, to hallow the rest of the town. Everyone sings without restraint, and the teenagers you might expect to be most scornful of such a ritual are among the loudest singers and keenest dancers. Two-year-olds on their parents' shoulders murmur, 'Melly maw-ling a-May.' It's hard to think of any other example in our undemonstrative country of a community so closely knit together by a celebration.

When the Red Ribbon 'Oss is well on his way, the Blue Ribbon 'Oss is let loose from the Harbour Inn in the same sort of atmosphere, pickled in a good deal more alcohol. The Red Ribbon party wind their way up Fentonluna Lane to Prideaux Place, the long, crooked old sixteenth-century house at the top of the town where the Prideaux family (now Prideaux-Brune) live as they have done since the Place was built. The 'Oss and teaser perform their capers on the lawn, before bouncing down into the town again. Meanwhile the Blue Ribbon 'Oss is making his way along the harbour front past the bulging wall and bowed window-frames of Raleigh's Court House, as old as Prideaux Place, where Sir Walter Raleigh collected his dues as Warden of Cornwall before things went sour for him. Even the fishermen, normally intent on their own business to the exclusion of all else, are up on the wall above their boats to see the 'Oss go raving by. The Blue Ribbon party lead their ally/victim past the rain-soaked fairground and gyrate up a narrow alleyway into the higher, newer part of the town where the 'Oss will bring some old magic to the new housing estates where some of the longest-established Padstow families now live. Later in the day the Red and Blue Ribbons will be mingling, if all goes well, round the maypole in the Market Square, to sing another nail in the coffin of winter and of the old antagonism.

All is not sweetness and light, however. Away from the frolics, May Day means a lot of bitterness for some of the born-and-bred Padstonians. The lady in the bookshop gets very cross when outsiders 'presume'. If you just want to buy a book and go away, all well and good; but if you stop for a chat about the ceremonies, beware. She has a bucket of cold water ready to pour on any foreigner's enthusiasm for Padstow at 'Obby 'Oss time.

'What do you mean, exactly, everyone's having a good day? That's typical, if you don't mind me saying so. I suppose you've been trailing around after the Blue Ribbon 'Oss. Those people call themselves supporters, but how many true Padstonians have they got in their party? They're just presuming on our traditions, that's what they're doing. They come here from outside and take over the 'Oss, do all the arranging. There's hardly one genuine Padstonian among them.'

"Oss! 'Oss!' calls a cheery lady with bluebells round her hat, putting her head round the shop door.

'Wee 'Oss,' mumbles the bookshop lady, conscious of an outsider at her elbow. Being seen at her devotions by anyone not part of the native circle is an embarrassment. She doesn't like the boozing in the pubs, the bearded enthusiasts from Midlands folk-clubs who stand on the pavement swapping stories of previous May Days in Padstow. It doesn't make any difference to her that the 'Obby 'Osses of her girlhood were a decayed breed, the ceremony itself staggering limply on from year to year. She's well aware that it's the outsiders, with their enthusiasm for traditions not their own, who have prevented the Padstow May Day celebrations from dying out. They have 'presumed' her 'Obby 'Oss into new life, and at the same time made it into an alien beast. It's too bitter a pill to swallow.

'I was born in this town when it was a friendly little place with just a few visitors that everyone knew. On May Day we had the place more or less to ourselves. Outsiders wouldn't have dreamed of interfering. Now they come in and don't wait to be invited – they just join in, think they own the place. It's not the town I knew.'

The bookshop lady is not the only Padstonian to resent the dilution of the town's original flavour. I overheard this exchange in a grocer's shop the same day –

SCOTSMAN: I *did* enjoy that music. It's lovely.
OLD LADY: We want all you bloody foreigners to go away and leave us alone.
(SCOTSMAN leaves abruptly.)
SHOPKEEPER: There was no need for that, Milly. That was a customer of mine. When you go to Scotland or London they don't tell you to go home, do they?
(OLD LADY leaves abruptly.)
SHOPKEEPER: Oh, Lord! Now I've lost *two* customers.

138

Kept alive and kicking by whatever means, it's the 'Obby 'Oss that pulls Padstow together more sharply than anything else. The old town won't choke to death on its rich diet of outside money while such energetic emotions and such depths of loyalty are plumbed each year by that devilish black-caped totem. He means to Padstow what the lifeboat means to Flamborough village, or the serpentine to Lizard Town: something round which community pride can gather. Seaside tourist places that possess one of those rallying symbols have a lifeline to their own identity, no matter what influences the outside world brings to bear.

On the North Quay stands Abbey House, dilapidated, shuttered and weed-grown in 1987, waiting for someone with time and money to come and save it. Its dark walls of slatey stone are run through by great granite lintels and doorposts, and pierced by small slit-windows. When Raleigh's Court House was built in the sixteenth century, Abbey House had already been at least 100 years on its slab of slate by the Camel estuary. It was the Guild Hall and chapel of the medieval Padstow merchants. Legend connects it by underground passage to the monastery that stood where Prideaux Place now stands. Half-way up the front wall of this ancient house is an open balcony; here Annie Simpson used to lean out to lecture the crowds of holidaymakers. By the time she died in 1981, aged eighty-two, Mrs Simpson had become a local celebrity, haranguing anyone who stepped on her garden, shouting at passers-by, ringing a bell if she felt the crowd gathered below was not big enough. She didn't deal just in words, either – cabbages and buckets of water might come flying out of the Abbey House balcony. On other occasions she would bring down a can of beer or an orange, tenderly wrapped in tinsel, for the fishermen and boat callers, who had elected themselves her guardians and briskly saw off catcalling teenagers and 'see-the-madwoman-of-Padstow' coach parties. Annie Simpson was one of those eccentrics which places like Padstow used to assimilate and look after on their own terms. She wasn't a born Padstonian, though she had lived in the town for the best part of half a century. But she used to stand bolt upright and silently weeping every May Day, when both Red Ribbon and Blue Ribbon 'Osses and their bands, singers and dancers would stop under her balcony to let her know that she was still part of Padstow.

18. Clovelly

'You fight with yourself! You struggle with the devil in you! You grit your teeth! You will be strong! You will not give way! No matter how beautiful it becomes you will not say . . . Resist, resist, keep a tight hold on yourself! You will not . . .'

. . . utter the word 'quaint' while you are visiting Clovelly. All in vain, however: the dreaded encomium was coming out of H. V. Morton's ears by the time he had finished collecting local colour for *In Search of England*. The Clovelly he found in the 1920s was just as quaint as it is today, and just as crammed with seekers after the picturesque.

Take a narrow valley plunging 400 feet down to the sea between rounded red sandstone cliffs. Clothe those cliffs with superb woods of oak, beech, sycamore and sweet chestnut, and throw ten miles of cliff, estuary and moorland views in a great curve to the north-east. Now tumble a handful of pretty cottages down the cleft so that they come to rest on top of each other at all angles. Squeeze a winding, cobbled roadway through them, too steep and narrow to get a car down. Place a few cuddly donkeys half-way up the street. Smother the place in flowers, cover it over with an invisible, water-tight lid against the twentieth century – and see if *you* can beat the Morton challenge. Clovelly is ridiculously pretty, immediately breathtaking in a way that's the envy of every seaside village on this North Devon coast. For a tiny community of about eighty houses it looms large on road-signs; they beckon you in from ten miles away and more. Clovelly gets upwards of 300,000 visitors a year, more than any other place of comparable size and remoteness anywhere in the district. It groans, sighs and threatens to split at the seams when the summer holiday season comes round. That it survives intact and astonishingly uncommercialized is owing to the unobtrusive iron hand (well sheathed in velvet) that two successive family dynasties have stretched out protectively over the village from Clovelly Court for more than 700 years.

A glance at the map shows you what you are in for if you arrive at Clovelly in summer by the B3237 road: up to a mile of queueing to get into the car parks above the village. No wheeled traffic is allowed down the single cobbled street: everyone has to get out and do it the hard way. A much pleasanter alternative is to leave the A39 Bideford road at Hobby

Lodge, well to the east of Clovelly, pay a small charge and dawdle along the three glorious woodland miles of the Hobby Drive. The Hamlyn family held sway at Clovelly Court from 1738 until a few years ago, and it was one of these benevolent despots, Sir James Hamlyn Williams, who had the Hobby Drive laid out for his pleasure in the years immediately after Waterloo. Today it's a pot-holed track, a bumpy ride of right-angle bends along a narrow ledge in the hillsides, with the ground on your right falling steeply away into long ravines. Birdsong is the loudest sound here among the trees and bracken banks. Every now and then you turn another corner and are faced with a startling view of the sea as an inverted cone, its point rammed into the bottom of a V-shaped valley. At one spot, a bench at the roadside gives a wonderful prospect down over the treetops on to Clovelly's harbour lying at the foot of the cliffs. The village houses are hidden by trees and the flanks of the hill slopes, and the Red Lion Hotel at the landward end of the stone pier seems the remotest building in the world, trapped between cliffs and sea on a black, stony beach.

This isolated situation, backed by the enormous rise of the cliffs and fronted by a sea notorious for its storms, ensured that hard times and empty bellies were the rule in Clovelly before Sir George Cary came to power at Clovelly Court in late Tudor times. The Cary family had owned the village since about 1370, and continued to do so until they handed over to the Hamlyns, nearly 400 years later; but it was Sir George who stamped his influence most firmly on Clovelly. He built up the village and provided it with a proper pier and the warehouses and salting cellars that would turn it into a prosperous herring-fishing community. Clovelly was the only safe harbour in the rocky cliffs between North Cornwall and the Taw estuary, and most of the fishing and sea trade along these miles of dangerous coastline was centred here. There were terrible disasters for Clovelly's fishing fleet from time to time, such as the two great storms in 1821 and 1838 which between them drowned fifty-three men. When the visitors began to arrive here early in the nineteenth century they discovered one of those fishing communities forged into a tightly enclosed circle, tempered by common experience of danger, isolation and self-reliance. Sir Zachary Hamlyn had bought the estate in 1738 from the widower of the last of the Carys, but the pattern of domination by a single family continued to be woven as strongly as ever. Like Lynton and Lynmouth, Clovelly was meat and drink to artists and writers. Dickens loved the 'Steepways' of his

Christmas Stories, summing it up in the words of Captain Jorgan as 'a mighty sing'lar and pretty place as ever I saw in all the days of my life!' Charles Kingsley spent part of his boyhood in the village (his father was Rector here (1832–6), a man capable, according to legend, of out-fishing and out-sailing the local fishermen and still remaining popular with them – some feat) and brought many of his memories of Clovelly, as well as one of the Carys, into *Westward Ho!* Turner painted the village, as did Whistler. Clovelly had to face the fact that, once in the eye of the outside world, it was never going to be out of it again.

After the peaceful pleasures of the Hobby Drive, that outside world comes slap into focus in the big, crowded car parks at the head of the village hill, patrolled by a roving band of fee-collectors. The uninitiated heart tends to sink at this point – and sinks further at the sight of the spanking new Visitor Centre standing squarely athwart the village path-way. It is in fact possible to get into Clovelly another way (by walking down unmarked back roads), but most visitors flock obediently through the turnstile of the Visitor Centre. You pay a small – but annoying – charge here, a little levy to St Peter. Then the Centre does its best to seduce you into lingering and shelling out some more on souvenirs, food, drink and so on. The idea behind Clovelly's Visitor Centre is an excellent one, to explain the history and ambience of the village through audio-visual displays and information desks, while providing the lavatories, picnic areas and refreshments that everyone expects these days. The Centre building, though, is massive, forbiddingly blank-faced and made of some material already staining and blotching with the weather. It's a sadly unwelcoming gateway to Clovelly. But the Centre is all there is of unsmiling commercialism in the village. Once past the stall of O'Donnell's Famous Triple Diploma Winner Clotted Cream Devon Ices, you descend the cobbles into a place where the brightest colours are not day-glo plastic but aubrietia and geraniums. No shop signs intrude into the street. No rock music blares out. There are no cars to block the roadway, foul the air or batter the ear-drum. Clovelly, uniquely, is a tourist honeypot free from buzzing. You can actually hear the birds, the breeze and the far-off sea above the clack of stiletto heels on cobbles, click of camera shutters and murmurs of 'Oh, how qu—' (Yes, all right, Morton. Down, boy!) 'Unchanged' is the other word that springs to mind on first sight of the twisty little street going steeply down between beautifully restored and maintained houses. Take away a couple of television aerials, and you might be walking down into the nineteenth century. It's only when you come to Clovelly that you realize fully the enormity of the changes – noise levels, violent colours, jarring styles of architecture, road-widening, general tension – that have wrecked almost every other popular tourist place it's possible to think of.

The tube of visitors squeezes slowly down the hill, reeling off the Kodachrome. A following Martian would be intrigued by the ritual step-dance in progress, the Clovelly Camera Shuffle – five paces . . . stop! Raise the hands to the face . . . click! Clovelly is all laid out for photographers. For every level camera there are twenty held sideways up to catch that classic shot that will include varying roof-heights, chimney-pots, flower baskets and walls on both sides of the street, cobbles in the foreground and sea as a backdrop. The cameras work to jamming point when the little donkeys come out from the New Inn to carry departing residents' luggage up to the car parks. The donkeys don't constitute Clovelly's sole means of transport any more. There's a Land Rover service these days up the back road from the harbour. But Clovelly without its donkeys would be unthinkable. In their present semi-retirement they get more cuddles than ever. There's even a Donkey Shop just below the post office, given over to donkey models, drawings and brass knick-knacks. They symbolize the Clovelly that everyone comes to see: small, cute, lovable and passive under pressure. The theme goes on as you walk down the street to the kink in the roadway from which you can look down over the couple of trawlers and scatter of crabbing boats sheltering inside the pier. Tiny side-lanes run off from the street, all cobbled and uneven – not a complex of lanes like those at Robin Hood's Bay, Yorkshire's version of Clovelly, but short alleys that stop at house-walls and gardens or in the face of the hillside. The sideways span of Robin Hood's Bay is wide compared with that of Clovelly. The geography of the place funnels you slowly and irresistibly on down to the Red Lion Hotel and the sea. Then you turn round, gasp a Morton, take a snap of the 'village like a waterfall' tilted in its green crack above, and return to the car parks either by Land Rover on the back road, by a slow and sweaty climb up the cobbles or, more adventurously, by way of North Hill. This narrow lane runs up behind the village, its cobbles and steps much steeper but far less crowded than the main roadway, to bring you out among the trees high above Clovelly. And that's it. There's nothing else to do, unless you want a drink or a meal. One of Clovelly's chief attractions is that you don't need to spend much money; another is that the whole visit is neatly fitted into a morning or an afternoon – down, up and away again with a camera full of gorgeous shots.

To live here, of course, is to see another side of things. Hundreds of people apply every year to the Clovelly Court Estate, hoping for vacant tenancies in the dream village they've fallen in love with in the course of a morning's visit, yearning for that absence of traffic, those lovely views, the remoteness of the workaday world, the fresh air, the peace and quiet. Many of these starry-eyed applicants fail to take on board the reverse side of the coin. Clovelly as a retirement haven needs some thinking about. There are days in winter when that scenic cobbled street becomes a sloping sheet of ice. Mists from sea and moor often blot out the view and cling dankly to the woods and valleys. Shopping bags can feel like lead by the time they have been lugged down the street. Arthritic limbs don't take kindly to the steepness of the hill, or to hauling provisions over cobbles on a sled. And if you fall ill and happen to live in the lower part of the village, you'll have to be carried bodily up to the ambulance and then face a nasty, jolting journey over the cobbles before reaching the smoother roads above.

Younger people, too, soon find out that there's a swing for every roundabout. Children have to leave Clovelly to go to school, the older ones travelling a good ten miles to Bideford. Any form of entertainment outside the pub is either home-made or has to be sought miles away. For teenagers in particular, the village is a dead duck, as Madge brought home to me. She's a tiny, chirpy Londoner, well into her eighties, with eyes as bright and amused as a cat's, who came to settle in Clovelly just before the war.

'Our daughter left home when she was fifteen. She hated the place. Her father was on at her because she would talk to the boys down on the harbour. So she said, "Right, I'm off to somewhere where I *can* talk to boys, then." And she upped and went. She's married now, of course, with children and grandchildren of her own. They don't really like it down here, either. They prefer London, having a lively time. You have to be fifty before you really enjoy living in Clovelly.'

Madge and her husband have lived in the village for fifty years, 'if you can call that a long time'. There are still several families in Clovelly who can trace their roots here back over hundreds of years. For these people, mostly farmers and fishermen, the surge of tourists down their street is something they accept, and even look forward to every spring. 'Without the visitors this place would be completely dead' is the general view. It's the most recently arrived residents who get hottest under the collar about the late-night noise and the litter, posting imploring notices in front of their houses: 'So much has already been ruined – cuttings torn off – plants trampled – hedges and banks climbed by dogs, children and adults! We beg you to think how it would feel if thousands of people entered your garden.' To live in Clovelly is to live in a shop window against which hundreds of thousands of noses are jammed every summer. Only the iron determination of the Clovelly Estate prevents the world from bursting through and crowding out the whole shop.

When Christine Hamlyn took over the estate in 1884, some of the villagers wondered whether things would hold together under this young, inexperienced woman. They soon found that their new mistress had a rigid will and an unswerving determination to maintain Clovelly pure and undefiled. She reigned as uncrowned queen of the village for fifty-two years, her hawk eye everywhere, relentlessly keeping the inhabitants up to the mark. She was famous for drawing up battle-lines against the manifestations of the modern age which were changing the appearance of every other seaside village in that branch-line railway era: beach stalls, advertisements, electricity cables, motor roads, sheds, shacks and cheap housing. Woe betide any resident in her village who introduced anything out of place on to the scene. H. V. Morton got some good mileage out of describing the agitation up and down the street when the septuagenarian Christine Hamlyn came visiting: 'At frequent regular intervals the natives hear the tapping of her long cane on the cobbles, and they hurriedly hide Willie's second-best trousers, or any other blot on the landscape which might at that critical moment be defying the old-established "quaintness".'

Autocratic she certainly was, but Christine Hamlyn had made good use of her eyes and nose when visiting Clovelly in the early years of her reign. She gave as short shrift to overflowing cess-pits and crumbling walls as she did to vulgar extrusions. Modernization and improvement went hand in hand with her preservation of Clovelly immaculate. Many of the estate's houses carry the initials 'C.H.' and a date from somewhere in the half-century-span of her rule, recording their rebuilding or renovation. By the time she died, in 1936, few Clovelly houses were without their own drainage and water supply, and the residents lived in greater comfort and security than the tenants of many less-fortunate estate villages.

The face and character of popular seaside villages have changed almost beyond recognition since the 1930s, but life in Clovelly continues to be ordered exclusively by the Clovelly Estate Company from its office near Clovelly Court. Sections of this beautiful old house in the woods above the village date back to the fourteenth century, survivors of a fire in 1943 that all but wrecked the building. Wandering through the grounds of Clovelly Court in the utmost peace on a summer afternoon and hearing the trees whispering in a light sea-breeze, one could cheerfully put out leaves and stay rooted for ever in that delightful parkland. The present director of the estate, John Rous, can't afford to sit back in rustic bliss, however. Like his great-great-aunt, Christine Hamlyn, he never stops juggling the two opposing aims of improvement and conservation. Viewing Clovelly in all its timeless perfection, it's easy to get the impression that snug equals smug; but the estate management has a pretty clear idea of the precarious nature of its business. A lack of commercial enterprise and up-to-date facilities for visitors, and they'll take their custom to more accommodating places. Too sudden or strident a change, and Clovelly will lose its appeal. Too many incomers, and the born-and-bred Clovelly people will be swamped. Too few, and the village will in-breed to death. All the strings of decision still converge on Clovelly Court, as they have done for centuries; to pull one is to set a dozen others in motion.

This absolute power of say-so gives the Clovelly Estate Company complete control over the social mixture of the village. Not one of the houses is a second home – to get the tenancy of one of those coveted cottages, you have to be prepared to settle here and be part of the community in bleak February as well as in balmy July. Natives of Clovelly still make up about one-third of the village population, and the composition of the remainder is closely monitored. When, a few years ago, the estate owners felt that the balance was tipping too far towards an elderly community, preference was given to younger applicants for tenancies, and things evened out again. These days, with the increasing tendency of young people to move away from the village to find work, Clovelly Court looks favourably on applications from those who have a trade or skill to offer: fishermen, craftsmen, cottage industrialists and so on. This modest social engineering goes on discreetly from year to year, maintaining a healthy balance between the generations, ensuring that Clovelly doesn't enter any one-way tunnels. Everything is carefully controlled. As in Christine Hamlyn's day, shopkeepers have to get estate approval for any signs they want to put up, and even the contents of their shops are thoroughly 'discussed' with the management.

As for the future, the Visitor Centre, clumsy and unsightly though it is, shows the way: a pointer to change, as were the advertising brochures issued by the Estate Company for the first time in 1987. Competition from cheap flights to fun in the sun is making itself felt, even in adorable Clovelly. Holidaymakers aren't prepared any more simply to be grateful for what they are offered. They make demands, these days. Woodlands, village, farms and harbour all need that tourist revenue if they are to survive and prosper. Clovelly's residents know it. They're content to live under a protectorship that is so effective at filtering the eager world down to them in such manageable doses.

19. Appledore

The elderly drinker at the bar of the Royal George was well into his fifth or sixth pint of the evening, and opening up just a little. The talk had made its straggling way round to salmon-netting by night in the pool above Bideford Bar and, while the old man naturally had no idea in the world whether unlicensed netting still went on there, he was happy to tell a story against Appledore's perennial Aunt Sallies, the water bailiffs.

'Not so long ago a chap I know happened to be out there about midnight. All of a sudden he saw the bailiff's boat, and shot down over the bar and around the corner – just to be out of the way, you know. The bailiff – stupid bugger – went straight on, and smack! He was on top of the rocks. The tide goes over they rocks at three, three and a half knots. The bloody bailiff's boat was rocking up and down, this way, that way. My mate shouted out: "You might drown there, you know – I'm sorry if you do."'

With the tale-teller's face cracked into seams by laughter, the soft Devon rumble of his voice contrasting with the hard-heartedness of the joke, it could have been one of Henry Williamson's fishermen holding forth. Before he found fame, if not great fortune, with *Tarka The Otter* in 1927, Williamson had been living for several years at Georgeham, on the other side of the estuary of the Two Rivers, Taw and Torridge. He enjoyed visiting Appledore, drinking in the Royal George and yarning with the local fishermen. Many of them, along with their tall tales and deeds both everyday and underhand, found their way into short stories in such collections as *Tales of a Devon Village*, *Tales of Moorland and Estuary* and *The Old Stag* – books less well known and appreciated than they deserve to be, overshadowed as they are by the brilliance of *Tarka*.

Williamson was fascinated by the community he found in Appledore, isolated on the end of its peninsula, self-absorbed and suspicious of 'foreigners', its men and women speaking the same idiosyncratic dialect as their grandparents had done and, like them, getting a hard-won living out of the estuary while carrying on a kind of maritime guerrilla war against those symbols of an interfering outside world, 'they bliddy baillies'. As the village changed during his lifetime into an altogether smarter and more accessible place, Williamson grew to dislike it; and the feeling was largely mutual. Appledore people are quick to resent nosiness on the part of an outsider, as I found to my embarrassment when the old man in the Royal George spotted me making notes at a side table and told me, very loudly, just what I could do with the bloody old book he could tell I was writing.

His friend said it wasn't fair that Williamson should have made all that money out of the place. These days the seeker after memories of Henry Williamson is likely to learn more about the failings and foibles of that lonely, driven man than about the skill and sensitivity with which he set down the innocence, hardiness and cruelty of that all-but-vanished Appledore still thriving during his first years in Devon.

Appledore's long waterfront, curving for well over a mile in a semi-circle round the nose of land formed by the scouring waters of the Torridge, is much the same one that Williamson knew in the decade after the First World War. From Appledore Ferguson's shipyard downriver to Hinks's boatbuilding shed there's hardly a twentieth-century building to be seen. Confined to its toehold of land by the neighbouring village of Northam to the south and the sandy expanse of Northam Burrows to the west, Appledore couldn't put on a sideways building spurt if it wanted to. The Royal George stands directly over the estuary on Irsha Street where, under a thin skin of tarmac, the old cobbles of the roadway still slope inward to a central drain. Tiny cobbled courtyards, deep in shadow yet bright with flower baskets, run off between thick cottage-walls as they do along the other narrow, unevenly curving streets just behind the waterfront road, most of them not wide enough to admit a car. There are many small pubs but few shops in these long streets of plain-faced terraces whose height and closeness keep the sun out for most of the day. They put on no kind of a show to please visitors. The excellent North Devon Maritime Museum on Odun Road up the hill is the nearest thing to a tourist attraction that you'll find away from Appledore's waterfront.

Here along the village's one open face are some fine, large Georgian and early Victorian houses looking out over the estuary to Instow, and Appledore's handful of inns that do set out to attract the custom of holidaymakers. There are one or two trinket shops among the newsagent's and grocery stores, but visitors who make the detour off the new road-bridge over the Torridge are disappointed if they expect to find anything like a glittering resort out here beside the estuary. There is a tiny crescent of sand tucked away under the low cliffs beyond the old Custom House at the northern end of Irsha Street, but the pleasures of Appledore are chiefly the pleasures of leisurely strolls along the river, fishing off the slipways and gazing at the passing boats. Fishing is still an important business in Appledore, as are boat trips across the estuary or further out to Lundy

Island and around the North Devon coastline. Small trawlers and crabbing boats, ferries, old lifeboats converted to makeshift yachts, the modern lifeboat at its moorings, dinghies, rusty phosphate-carriers on their way up to Bideford's quay – the water is never clear of traffic of one kind or another. Bideford Bar, a ridge across the estuary mouth known to Henry Williamson's fishermen as the Shrarshook (according to Williamson – no one I spoke to had ever used or even heard the word), is an extremely dangerous hazard with its sharp tides and eddies, and the Two Rivers pilot-boats that guide strangers through this difficult obstacle course are handily based in Appledore.

The view over the estuary changes hour by hour, according to the state of the tide. At high water the whole channel is filled from bank to bank, a broad highway of water lying almost motionless between the dunes of Braunton Burrows and Northam Burrows. As the sea ebbs back into Bideford Bay, the mingled waters of Taw and Torridge chase it out with a far-off roaring over the bar, the flow speeding up and shrinking inwards until the Torridge under Appledore has dwindled away to a winding stream of contrary tides between vast mud- and sandbanks gleaming with drying pools of water. These contrasts and shifts of speed, depth and direction where three opposing water forces meet, a constant challenge to the skills of sailors and fishermen, glue onlookers to the waterfront railings in fascination for hours at a time. An added fillip to their enjoyment of the scene comes once or twice a year, when one of Appledore's two shipyards waves goodbye to another brand-new offspring.

In centuries past Appledore grew prosperous on profits from the Newfoundland cod fisheries and the import of tobacco from Virginia, as well as from its large fishing fleet. Those fine old waterfront houses represent the bricks-and-mortar investments of sea captains and merchants from the seventeenth to the nineteenth centuries. Along with these lucrative businesses, the sea brought another in the shape of shipbuilding. Appledore, with its long river-frontage, sheltered position on the estuary and proximity to the open sea, was perfectly placed to make a go of the dozens of small shipwrights' premises that, at one time or another down the years, set up shop at the head of their short slipways. These days only two still build sizeable vessels, but between them they employ well over five hundred men, nearly all of them locals. The basic nature of their business is all that the two shipyards have in common, for in every aspect of their operations Appledore Ferguson and J. Hinks & Son are as different as it's possible to be. Without them, Appledore as a living, working community would be as good as dead.

A long mile upriver from the junction of Torridge and Taw, Appledore Ferguson's enormous corrugated shed stands squarely on what was marsh and farmland until the yard was built in 1969/70. About 520 men work here, piecing together large, practical ships out of thin sheet and bar steel. Walking round the shed is like being inside a giant alarm clock. Things thump, whirr, clang and shriek all round you against a background din of piercing, insistent electric bells and hooters. Intense pinpoints of unbearably bright blue light flare out as the welders put together the separate sections of ship, brought to them from different departments by overhead cranes. It's no surprise to be told that the two most common industrial injuries here are deafness and arc-eye, this latter an especially nasty condition in which the eye's surface layer of cornea is shredded and burned away by prolonged staring into the mesmeric blue heart of the welder's electric arc. Everything is large-scale, much of it automated to the point where computer-controlled oxyacetylene burners can cut any shape ordained by their tapes out of the steel plate. Mild steel is remarkable stuff. A thick girder of it has enough give and inherent suppleness to be bent into almost any form.

When all the basic components are ready to be fitted together, the ship takes shape surprisingly quickly at the bottom of the dry dock at the river end of the yard. As cavernous as a good-sized concert hall, the dry dock can take two vessels side by side. The sections are swung down one by one, followed by engines, pipework, miles of electrical cable, internal fittings and electronic control-gear for the ship. Isambard Kingdom Brunel might be amazed at the technology that has gone into her planning and construction, but he would instantly recognize the underlying design, a floating box of plates and girders, pretty well unchanged since he pioneered it over a century ago. Suddenly the whole ship, perhaps a 4,500-ton dredger, lies there ready for launching. For nearly a year she has been an idea in a computer, a jumble of separate seventy-ton blocks of steel plate. She doesn't grow – she just appears in one long burst of assembly, has her bows splashed with bubbly by some company chief's wife, and is gone to make way for the next one. The shipyard workers don't admit to much affection for their creation, but many of them try to get to some vantage-point along the river bank to watch her go. 'You feel more for a boat, put a lot more of yourself into her, if you're working in wood,' one of them told me. 'But don't get the idea that we don't care what we do here. We like to see her go off looking nice. And we like to keep up with news of her, too. We've got one chap working here who's got a photo of every ship ever built in this shipyard, and he can tell you all their histories. A lot of us have put a lot of blood and sweat into this yard – our own blood and sweat. We want to see it live, properly, not go down the slide like a lot of others have done.'

Down at the other end of Appledore, Hinks's boatyard is a different world. The construction shed is a corrugated affair, too – but there all similarity with Appledore Ferguson ends. Hinks's shed rattles and moans with every passing breeze. Rust streaks its outside walls. The interior is a lofty cat's-cradle of wooden posts, beams and struts, with birds twittering up in the roof and pale bars of sunlight striking down from dusty windows and chinks in the shed-walls. About twenty local men work here, no one having to raise his voice to make himself heard. There's a complete absence of industrial racket in the cool gloom of the shed – the loudest sounds are the deliberate clink of hammer on chisel, soft 'chunk' of adze or dull thud of caulking mallet. Hinks's build wooden boats by hand, as they have done since 1844. Alan Hinks, the present principal, represents the fourth generation of his family to follow the business; and his daughter, Alison, hopes one day to step into his shoes in her turn. I needn't have been apologetic about taking up her whole morning when she showed me over the boatyard – talking about ship-building is like drinking champagne to Alison. She glowed with enthusiasm, pouring out technical details, facts and figures, building up a picture of an operation which calls for craftsmanship, precision, rule of thumb and an instinct for the way natural materials behave and misbehave.

Unlike the giant's Lego process of ship construction at Appledore Ferguson, a Hinks-built boat grows gradually outwards and upwards from the day the oak keel is laid along the floor of the shed. Tradition is embedded into each boat from the outset in the form of the hookscarf joints that interlock the keel sections – their first known use was in a burial boat discovered in the tomb of an Egyptian queen. When the keel is in place, the sternpost and transom are laid. Then the five sections of each frame or side-rib of the boat are cut out and shaped with adze and plane before being bolted together and set up. It takes about six weeks to frame up, using unseasoned oak (Alan Hinks's personal preference), after which the bare skeleton of the boat is finished. From now on it's a matter of filling in the gaps with planking of iroko, a hard wood from the rainforests of South America and Africa which has replaced the larch, elm or oak of olden days. Iroko has a beautiful dark colour and a dense grain. To Alison it smells of lemons, pleasanter than the whiff of smelly feet she detects on unseasoned oak.

Getting the planks on to the frame in the right shape and position is no easy job. They are bent to the required curvature in the steamer; then the men dash into the shed and squirm through the scaffolding, toting a smoking-hot plank, racing to get it into place and bolted to the frame before it cools. If they don't get it right first time, the plank has to be steamed and bent all over again. A full run of planking, stem to stern, is known as a strake and is made of two or three planks laid butt to butt. The thickest strakes go where the boat is most likely to be bumped – at the top, at the bottom and at the hull's widest point of outward bulge. The planks can't be fitted too tightly end to end or they'll split at the joints when swollen by seawater. A tiny gap is left between each plank and its neighbour, to be caulked with oakum (Indian hemp). The oakum arrives in bales like matted sheep's wool, greasy and sour-smelling, and has to be rolled between the palms and knees of workers to make strands thin enough to be tamped in loops into the seams of the planking with a caulking mallet and iron. Then it's stopped in with a mixture of putty and white lead. Caulking isn't a job for those with delicate nasal passages.

Now the four or five steel bulkheads are inserted into the planked-up hull, the engine and tanks for fuel and water are dropped in by crane, and the iroko-wood decking goes on like a lid. Deck seams are not 'stopped' after caulking, but are 'payed' with hot tar – different term, but much the same effect. At the same time, sub-contractors are busy fitting the plumbing and electrics. For the bigger boats that Hinks's build, such as the seventy-foot trawlers that Scottish skippers order from the yard, these final additions are the last work done in the shed. The completed hull is launched and taken round to the dry dock, half a mile upriver, for the wheelhouse and deck structures to be fitted and any outstanding work – painting, additional welding, cleaning – to be cleared up.

Launching day is the day when the boat comes alive. There's a new, exciting atmosphere in the shed which everyone senses as soon as they arrive. The boat is 'dressed overall' with flags, blessed by the vicar, named with a champagne bottle (well taped to prevent flying glass) smashed across her bows. It's goodbye to twelve months at least of everyone's utmost involvement; a moment when, according to Alison, 'Everyone cries, even the roughest and toughest.'

There is a long time to wait, and a lot of money to pay (upwards of half a million pounds), for what's essentially an outdated type of craft. Those trawler skippers think it's worth every month, and every penny, to take delivery of a boat that will 'give' in a rough sea and be cheaper and easier to repair than a steel box. At the bottom of their choice, however, lies some romanticism and a large slice of tradition. What suited their fathers suits them. Wooden boats are better, that's all. Alan Hinks agrees with them. He was brought up with wooden boats in the background of everyday life, going round the timber-yards with his father and absorbing technical talk from his earliest years. He joined the family firm during the Second World War when he was fifteen, cutting his ship-building teeth on the small clinker-built boats which in his opinion represent one of the highest forms of the craft. Their success or failure depends entirely on the skill of eye and judgement of the builder. His first job was a sixteen-foot rowing boat, put together at the age of sixteen under the watchful eye of his father. By the time Alan Hinks was twenty-one, he was in charge of the firm and of seven or eight workers. They took on all kinds of work – this was in the days when fibreglass had not been invented and steel was mostly used for bigger boats. When fibreglass came on the scene they tried it out, but there was none of the solid satisfaction of working in wood.

In 1967, as Alan Hinks was shifting his premises from the old, cramped location on Irsha Street to the present site, an order arrived from the Hudson's Bay Company to build a replica of the *Nonsuch*, the first ship to enter Hudson Bay exactly three centuries earlier, in celebration of the company's tercentenary. The *Nonsuch* that Hinks's turned out, complete in detail down to the last wooden pin, was a beautiful boat, considered by Mr Hinks to be probably the finest bit of work he's done. He gets a certain amount of wry amusement out of her present situation, captive in a museum in Winnipeg at the very centre of the Canadian prairies and about 1,500 miles from the sea in either direction. More exotic orders followed on the heels of the *Nonsuch* success: a replica of the *Golden Hind*, built between 1971 and 1973, and another, two years later, of the Gokstaad

Viking ship discovered during the last century and exhibited in an Oslo museum. Alan Hinks went across to Norway to study the original, and was intrigued to note that the art of clinker building had changed hardly at all in the past thousand years.

This kind of work is the jam on the bread and butter of trawlers, yachts and Customs launches that keep Hinks's boatyard a going concern. Not long ago Mr Hinks and Alison had plans to convert the shaky old boatyard shed into a working museum, but car parking difficulties strangled the scheme at birth. However, they can't see the traditional wood-built boat dropping into past history unless and until the strength and pliability of fibreglass can be drastically improved. For the foreseeable future, therefore, it will be business as usual at Hinks's boatyard if the determination and dedication of father and daughter can keep it so.

A working museum at Hinks's would certainly attract far more tourists to Appledore than come here at present. There was something of a vogue for the village among the Bright Young Things of the 1930s, but it has never become anything like a popular resort. Until recently it was too remote to attract many commuting settlers or second-homers, but improved dual-carriageways slicing into the West Country have brought the rest of well-heeled Southern England within range. Places by or near the sea, especially ones with strong individual flavours and nice old houses, are suddenly in demand. Already Irsha Street in Appledore has seen a mini-invasion by Bideford and Barnstaple commuters, and few of the other streets of the village remain even half in Appledore hands. These incomers, while not exactly instant villagers, are (many of them) Devonians and all of them working, spending and socializing locally. Along with them, however, has come a sprinkling of those magnets for resentment in small seaside villages, the second-home owners. You don't have to sit in the Royal George for very long to hear either: 'What's killing this place is the bloody second-homers,' or: 'This village is half dead in the winter.' There are few Devon accents behind pub bars and shop counters in Appledore, another cause of irritation and estrangement.

Judged by the axiom that a village that has stopped grumbling has started dying, Appledore is still alive and kicking. While so many of its people still fish for a livelihood, or are employed on their own doorsteps at Appledore Ferguson and Hinks's, the village stands a chance of preserving its integrity. There's no Henry Williamson industry here, no Tarka

Teashops or handy guides to Williamson Country. Too many local people brushed with his hedgehog personality and are still rubbing the pin-pricks. They can deal out a handy jab or two themselves to ward off outsiders who presume too far. These niggles are just bubbles in the yeast, evidence of vitality at the heart of Appledore. If the day ever comes when a prying stranger can find out all he wants to know without either getting an evasive answer or being bitten off short, then Appledore will have given up the last of the spirit captured by Williamson. Until then, that Jeremiah among prophets will continue to have little honour in his own adopted country.

20. Lynton and Lynmouth

All approaches to Lynton across the broad green crown of Exmoor are spectacular: a succession of plunging, wooded cleaves or stream valleys on each side of the road, followed by a hill that has your car nearly standing on its nose. In the days when the tiny tank-engines of the narrow-gauge Lynton & Barnstaple Railway still rattled their crimson-and-white coaches into the station high above the town, the journey must have been something special. For many of today's elderly holidaymakers who came here as children, Lynton lost a tithe of its magic on 29 December 1935, when the little railway, so slow that you could lean out of the carriage windows and pick flowers from the cutting sides as you inched round the bends, gave up the battle with the accountants.

In the 700 years between Domesday Book's reckoning and the town of the nineteenth century, the population of Lynton had increased by about 80, without yet reaching 500. Those steep hills folding one into another had combined with the forbidding emptiness of a nearly trackless Exmoor to deter outsiders from venturing down to the self-contained community on its saddle of ground 500 feet above the sea. Then came the first seekers after wild and lonely places, among them William Wordsworth and his sister, Dorothy, with their friend, Samuel Taylor Coleridge. The Wordsworths and Coleridge wandered far over the Exmoor coastline and hills from their cottage at Nether Stowey, thinking high and talking big, revelling in wilder surroundings than they had enjoyed since leaving the Lakes. What poured from their pens was elixir to English travellers barred from continental adventures by the Napoleonic Wars. Suddenly eyes were focused in a new way on scenery which had hitherto been dismissed as grotesque, freakish or terrifying. By the time Victoria came to the throne, Lynton was on its way up in the world, no longer a sheep-farming community but an expanding resort. The approach roads were improved – a little – and the customers came in ever-increasing numbers. They found the tiny fishing village of Lynmouth on the shore below Lynton. They scrambled up the boulders and glens of the East and West Lyn rivers, and went on Romantic Rides into the desolate Valley of Rocks, just along the cliffs. They painted those great sandstone cliffs rising like red knees 500 and 600 feet from the sea. They wallowed in Savage Grandeur and Awful Splendour. And when R. D. Blackmore brought out *Lorna Doone* in 1869 they just couldn't keep away.

The Lynton that you stroll through today holds the very essence of that nineteenth-century boom. The narrow, steep lanes of the old farming village are still there, winding away opposite St Mary's Church, down Queen Street and along Market Flats; but the gridded lines of roads running north and south between Lee Road and Lydiate Lane are pure Victorian in their solidity, solemnity and style. The magnificent Valley of Rocks Hotel was built to cater for the newcomers in 1807 and embellished with all kinds of elaborations as their demands for comfort and dignity grew. A portal featuring Corinthian pillars sprouting out of floral urns leads you into a cavernous central area with wrought-iron balconies and columns leading up to a stained-glass skylight overhead. The balconies have been filled in these days with simpering portraits on fake walls, and the crinolined ladies and curly-brimmed gentlemen of the old photographs supplanted by today's coach-tours of Americans and Australians, but the spirit remains the same. So do some of the shops of Lynton, like Reg. T. Reeves, Stationer and Printer. These dark premises on Lee Road, dispensing dog food, photos and printing paper, have come straight from the nineteenth century. Lynton is a place where you change down a gear for a nice long tea in the glassed-in conservatory of the Greenhouse Bakery and Restaurant. Sauntering is the way to get around. The town has kept its family-run butchers and grocers alongside the gift shops. Lynton children can still go to their own school. In winter the place doesn't die; it just switches over from the servicing of holidaymakers to the WI, pub clubs, lectures and church activities that fill every evening for the year-round residents.

As the Victorian holiday trade turned Lynton's face towards new ways and new prosperity, the old traditional life of the Exmoor farmers flowed strongly on in the hills and valleys all around. These days, no corner of the moor remains unvisited or unchanged, but strands of the same old ways – hunting the red deer, winning a livelihood from the slopes of combes and cleaves, disregarding as far as possible the dictates of Westminster – still run through the lives and customs of local people. The trappings and the machinery have changed beyond recall, however, replacing horse with tractor and peat fire with Aga. When turnip hoe and griddle irons are finally thrown out, the chances are that they'll end up crammed into the already wildly overcrowded Lyn and Exmoor Museum, housed in the eighteenth-century St Vincent Cottage in Market Street. Established in 1962, the museum has managed to gather into its small, low-ceilinged rooms enough relics of Exmoor's past to give a really evocative idea of the way things used to be in what was a completely isolated part of the country. Not that there's anything approaching a coherent, chronological exhibition to be studied at St Vincent Cottage. Everything lies, stands and hangs everywhere. Chimney hooks swing in the fireplace, otter traps in the out-house. On the chimneypiece is a jar of gooseberries bottled in 1919 by Mrs Harris of Cross Street, still looking delicious. Cider presses, table lamps, knife-cleaners, peat ploughs and hedging tools elbow one another. After an hour you begin to take it all in. These over here are family treasures, lent to the museum after heart searching; those in that corner are derelict old implements rescued from the dungheap. Everything is meticulously labelled, some with funny little comments:

'Old Tin Opener – Stone Age Model.'

'Mouse Trap of Unique Design – But it works!'

'Exmoor Farmer's Weather-Glass – When Jar Empty It's a Drought. BBC Please Note.'

The museum has a ghost, too – a crying baby who haunts the room upstairs now filled with stuffed birds. Over the fireplace in the central room on the ground floor hangs a painting of a well-known Exmoor character. He sits brick-faced and scarlet-coated astride his beautiful grey hunter on the crown of the moor, surrounded by hounds, staring out towards Dunkery Beacon, Master of the stag hunt and lord of all he surveys. Stories about him and most of the rest of Exmoor pour out of Mr Henry Sutton, the first secretary and onlie begetter of the Lyn and Exmoor Museum. Mr Sutton could cheerfully talk the hind leg off a red deer – talk full of Exmoor villages, valleys, hills and people. Listening to him is like digging your hands into the rich red earth of North Devon.

'Tom Parracombe is a straightforward, down-to-earth, honest-to-goodness Exmoor farmer. Ever shaken hands with him? Hah – you'd know it if you had. He's got a grip like iron. Tom and I have run together since we were boys. He was quite a lad in his younger days, you know; but I'd never give him yes if I felt no. When he became a JP he said to me, "What would your advice be to me now I've got this position?" I said to him, "Tom," I said, "the very first time you look across and see some poor devil in the dock, you just say to yourself, 'There but for the grace of God'."'

Mr Sutton has no time for the local councillors and fund-holding authorities who won't recognize his museum for what he sees it to be: the beating heart of old Exmoor.

'"Oh, there won't be the interest," they told me when I first brought up the idea. But I'm pretty well known up by Brendon. I went round to all the farmers up there. "Can I have a look in your barn, Jack?" – "Why, whatever for? What're you after, Henry?"

'I'd go in there, put my hand up on a partition or behind a loose stone in the wall. Never knew what I'd come out with – a pair of sheep-shears, a storm lantern, a pair of boots. "Oh, them old things!" – "Thank you, Jack," I'd say, "these'll just do nicely."

'Some of them thought I was mad, but most of the real locals were interested. It's been the National Park and such organizations who couldn't give a brass button for us.'

One of the buildings whose contents Mr Sutton would love to have got his hands on was Hollerday House, the Victorian mansion built on Hollerday Hill near Lynton by the publisher, Sir George Newnes. Hollerday House burned in a great fire and was subsequently pulled down, but Sir George's influence is still plain in the town that benefited from his generosity. He put his money into the Lynton & Barnstaple Railway; and he built the great pile of the Town Hall on Lee Road, a block of turreted bays and half-timbered wings pierced by a wide arch. The interior of the Town Hall is all parquet flooring and heavy, dark carved wood. In the upstairs chamber Lynton holds its dances, discos, film shows, banquets and public meetings. A local builder and inventor, Bob Jones, also found an enthusiastic backer in Sir George when he put forward designs, late in the 1880s, for an inclined railway to take the sting out of the 500-foot drop down the cliffs between Lynton and Lynmouth. Bob Jones's scheme for an opposing pair of cars worked by the weight of water was such a success that it's still in operation, unchanged since its opening in April 1890. The cars, like small mobile conservatories with their bases angled at 45° and their tops horizontal, rumble up and down a gradient of one in one and three-quarters, the car at the top filling its 500-gallon tank with water as its twin disgorges at the bottom of the slope. Gravity does the rest, with a lot of shaking and rattling as sauce to the journey. The cables buzz over their rollers, the cars jerk and shudder; but you reach Lynmouth at the bottom in safety, like everyone else before you since the cliff railway first began work.

The travel problems posed by bad roads over steep hills at the outermost edge of a wide moor kept Lynmouth, like Lynton, from discovery by the world at large until the beginning of the nineteenth century. The herring arrived at the same time as the romantic explorers, and Lynmouth began to grow fat on profits from both. Until the cliff railway was built, it was still a tedious business to get down to the village by the sea, but the wonderful views up into the dramatic clefts of the East and West Lyn rivers more than made up for the difficulties of the descent down the muddy hillside tracks. Robert Southey fell in love with the houses perched directly above the two rivers; Gainsborough painted the village; the Wordsworths and Coleridge came down and adored everything they saw. Percy Shelley stayed here in 1812, and had fun sending polemics in defence of the working man out to sea in bottles or up over the moor on balloons. Lynmouth working men thought their would-be champion was a crackpot, but they soon caught on to the advantages of living in what came to be known as 'the English Switzerland'. Hotels opened, fishermen's cottages were packed with visitors in summer. Lynmouth entered upon its golden age of prosperity.

From the cliff railway you walk along the Esplanade towards the harbour where the Rhenish Tower stands chunkily on the end of the pier. This square block of stone topped with mini-battlements and walkways was put up in the 1850s by General Rawdon, who had settled here and wanted a suitably picturesque storage-tower for seawater to supply his baths. Standing by the Rhenish Tower, you can see why those early incomers were so attracted to Lynmouth, a double line of buildings curving gracefully at the feet of the tree-covered sandstone cliffs, its rivers trickling past the houses to meet and flow into the sea over the beach of boulders. The contrast between the peaceful homeliness of the village and the ruggedness of its surroundings is irresistible. But in Lynmouth nothing is quite as it first appears.

This north-facing coastline of Devon and Somerset, so mild and friendly in summer, grows teeth when the winter gales set in up the Bristol Channel. It has taken a heavy toll of shipping through the years, and the lifeboats, which were stationed at Lynmouth between 1869 and 1944, between them made hundreds of rescues. One in particular has lodged itself in the lifeboat service's collective memory as the supreme example of determination against all odds: the overland launch of the lifeboat *Louisa* in January 1899. The story, a nail-biter if ever there was one, is laid out in a permanent exhibition in the Exmoor National Park Information Centre on the Esplanade. Here you can see photographs of the crew of the *Louisa*, some of whom took part in that extraordinary adventure, sparked off by an emergency message from Porlock on 12 January 1899: 'Urgent. Lifeboat. Large vessel distress offshore Porlock. Urgent.' Heavy seas roaring up the Lynmouth slipway in a full gale made it impossible to launch the *Louisa*; but her coxswain, Jack Crocombe, was made of stern stuff. 'We launch from Porlock!' was his response, a gritty statement which the exhibition has taken as its overall slogan. The lifeboat crew and their volunteer helpers embarked on a thirteen-mile slog up the one-in-four Countisbury Hill, over the top of the moor through lanes so narrow that the boat had to be dismounted from its wheeled carriage and heaved along on skids by hand and horse, down Porlock Hill (even steeper than Countisbury Hill) and through hastily demolished cottage-garden walls to the sea at Porlock, all at night-time in the vilest winter weather. On Friday, 13 January, nearly eleven hours after setting out from Lynmouth, the *Louisa* was rowing her way out to the 1,900-ton *Forrest Hall* which was pounding to pieces out in the gale. *Forrest Hall* survived, in fact, to limp across to South Wales; the crew of the *Louisa* accompanied her there, and got back to Lynmouth the following day. They collected £5 and a presentation watch each for these prodigious efforts.

From the Information Centre, the Esplanade curves round along the harbour front to open up a view of the double line of Lynmouth's houses, shops and hotels running up to the river bridge. On the right, the narrow pathway up Mars Hill mounts to become a zigzag track up to Lynton. Climbing up Mars Hill, you pass the low, thatched, black-and-white Rising Sun Hotel, in part dating back to the fourteenth century, to round a corner and look down over Lynmouth. The red-brick roadway of Lynmouth Street makes a shallow arc with Riverside Road, both roads lined with shops and cafés. The wooded hills behind press in above the village on three sides, the Tor Hotel overlooking everything from its superb position high among the trees in the face of the hill opposite your viewpoint. It all looks as if nothing can possibly have changed in centuries; there's no obvious sign of the disaster that fell on Lynmouth on 15 August 1952. The physical scars have been carefully disguised and nearly forgotten, but the emotional wounds inflicted that night on some of the villagers still surface in conversation, raw and painful.

The story of what happened then has been told with once-and-for-all exactness in a book you can buy in any one of a dozen shops in Lynmouth, *The Lynmouth Flood Disaster* by Eric Delderfield. Written a year after the tragedy, from eye-witness accounts and with meticulous research, it brings the whole terrible event up before your inner eye in sharp-edged detail. Briefly, what took place was this: after several days of heavy rain had filled Exmoor as sopping full as a sponge, nine more inches fell in one night. The feeder streams to the East and West Lyn rivers could take no more water, and the two rivers simply poured everything down through Lynmouth. A ten-foot wall of water came rearing down the West Lyn River, bringing with it ten-ton boulders, whole trees, broken bridges and an avalanche of silt which blocked the natural outfall where the rivers met in the centre of the village. The West Lyn River surged aside and pushed its way like an enormous, impatient fist through the body of Lynmouth. Whole houses were smashed apart, front walls ripped clean off, hotels demolished, cars, belongings and people swept away. All this took place in blinding rain and pitch darkness, the electricity supply having failed, to the accompaniment of what most survivors agree was the worst part of the whole event: a horrifying, paralysing roar of wild water and rumbling of boulders. The houses along the main street stood close together, rising straight from the old river-bed: a picturesque huddle in the worst possible situation.

With a copy of Eric Delderfield's book in your hand, you can look down from the bend in Mars Hill and compare what you see below with the photographs taken the day after the disaster. Lynmouth Street was blocked at its far end by a mound of mud, boulders and rubble that reached thirty feet up to the windows of the buildings still standing. All along the street were houses with their front walls gone, bathtubs suspended over snapped floorboards, roofs sagging to ground level, window-frames and doors scattered far and wide, piles of wood, iron and stone all mangled and lumped together. Some survivors in mackintoshes and wellingtons, others still in dressing-gowns and slippers, wandered around in a daze, unable to take in what had happened to their village. These photographs might just as easily be those taken after the Coventry or Plymouth bombing raids. That was the comparison in the minds of most villagers and rescuers, only seven years after the Second World War had ended.

The enormous and long-drawn-out task of repair to the devastated village was carried out so well that today the new Lynmouth stands solid and whole. Where the river flowed before the flood, Riverside Road now runs, with the new river course widened and strengthened against any danger of a repetition of the disaster. A car park stands at the old junction of West and East Lyn rivers, plugging that weak point for ever. A few stumps of walls are all that remain of the houses burst apart by the flood. Others, less badly damaged, were repaired to their former state. The Rhenish Tower, which was flattened by the surge of water at the river mouth, was restored identically down to the last detail. But the price of that night was not counted only in bricks and mortar. Thirty-four people lost their lives in those smashing waters, fifteen of them from Lynmouth. Another eight of the victims were from neighbouring villages and hamlets. The deaths tore a hole in the community which no amount of restoration work could repair. Now, nearly forty years after the flood disaster, a new generation of villagers lives in Lynmouth, a high proportion of them incomers. But those deaths still lie heavily on the older people who were caught up in the tragedy.

'You do get over things like that,' one of them told me. 'Time's the healer. But we do still remember. We had a memorial service here the other day, in the stream bed. Some of the same members of the Salvation Army who were first on the scene with their soup kitchens and the inevitable cups of tea – they came and provided the music. Most of us were moved to tears. We don't forget the ones who died, and never shall.'

Lynmouth has moved a long way in spirit from being the remote little long-stay resort it was before the disaster. These days, Lynmouth Street is one long line of gift shops. People tend to come across for the day from Exeter and Taunton, fitting in an hour in Lynmouth between visits to Lynton and the Valley of Rocks. There are fewer families prepared to spend a couple of weeks in a place with a pebbly beach and almost no undercover instant attractions; more shopkeepers who come, make money and move on. 'The Flood 1952' is a common slogan on posters, cards and bookstalls, a source of tourist income to Lynmouth, rationalized into a piece of history which might hold the visitors' attention a little longer. It's a way of coping with what happened, allotting it a place in village mythology where it can be safely examined. The old lifeboat house under Mars Hill has been turned into the Lynmouth Flood Memorial Hall and contains a display of accounts, newspaper articles and 'before-and-after' photographs. In a way, Lynmouth is as proud of its Flood as it is of its Overland Launch. But that's an onlooker's perception. You don't have to talk for long to anyone who was there at the time, before the shutters go up and the conversation is turned, politely or abruptly, to something else. What tore Lynmouth to pieces on 15 August 1952 goes on tearing many of its people. They keep the Lynmouth Flood Memorial Hall immaculate, in memory not only of the thirty-four victims but also of the village they knew, a different place from the one they live in today. And in spite of the seemingly invincible new flood defences, when rainstorms burst over Exmoor, some of them are still gripped by a terrible anxiety.

WALES

21. Southerndown
22. Oxwich
23. Tenby
24. Aberystwyth
25. Barmouth

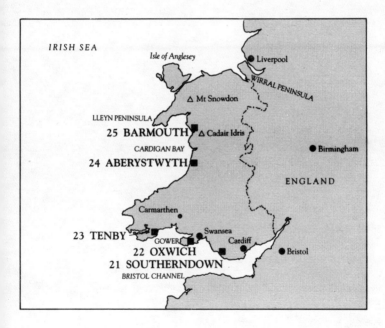

21. Southerndown

Driving along the Glamorgan coast, on the B4524 road between Ogmore-by-Sea and St Brides Major, you could easily pass through Southerndown and miss the village completely. The road swings right, runs south for a couple of hundred yards past a few old houses and an elegant ex-hotel, swings left by a pub on the corner – and that's it. Southerndown is so un-touristy, its atmosphere so matter-of-fact, that it blends with no sharp edges into the landscape. The whole place can slip quietly into your net and out again in the time it takes to change gear twice on the bends.

Even walking through the village, and taking your time about it, you can be through from one end to the other in two minutes. At the top end is a solid Victorian building with fleur-de-lis hoods round the windows; half-way along, a much larger one with towers and sharp witch's-hat turret roofs. These were Southerndown's hotels – the Marine and the Dunraven respectively – until business declined and costs climbed too far to keep them open. There's a tiny modern church, a reasonably priced restaurant and the Three Golden Cups pub on the corner. No shop, no post office, no trinket emporium – just the solid old stone-built houses going down the street and on down Beach Road for a few yards, their white walls and grey roofs chiming restfully with the green of the surrounding fields. It's hard to imagine a more modest village. Although several houses show Bed-and-Breakfast notices, there's a complete absence of any of the signs of modern seaside tourism. Ogmore and St Brides have both succumbed more or less to new building developments and the influence of their holidaymakers, but Southerndown is an oasis of ordinariness between them. Looking from the village street over the surrounding grazing fields and stone walls, there's no hint that one of the most beautiful and interesting bays in South Wales lies less than half a mile away.

Beach Road leaves the houses behind and dips over the crown of the ridge below Southerndown, to fall steeply to the neat little car park in Dunraven Bay. At the peak of the holiday season in fine weather you'll probably find every space full and have to park your car up in the field on the far side of the valley. But even at these times, though the deep half-moon of sand between the cliffs can be crowded beyond enjoyment, almost everyone here has come from somewhere in South Wales. Anyone in search of loud fun can get it in Porthcawl, just up the coast. At Dunraven Bay there's only a tiny beach shop selling ice-cream, sweets and a few beach toys. End-of-the-day ice-cream wrappers and picnic leftovers are whisked away as the visitors go home, leaving the whole place spotless. It's still very much a Welsh day-visitor's beach, prized by its users for its quietness and lack of anything like a commercial approach. They come to Southerndown and Dunraven Bay year after year, sure of finding things just as they were when they left them last time. It's the sort of permanence that you might expect to find on the remoter coasts of Scotland, but here in one of the most popular tourist areas of Britain – and one easily accessible since the motorways telescoped time and distance – it's remarkable, to say the least.

Southerndown's miracle is worked from the unlikely surroundings of the old Seamouth Café, which stands in the bottom of the valley just inland from the beach car park. A long, low building, plain and squat, it's the headquarters of the Glamorgan Heritage Coast Project which stands guard over fourteen miles of this coast, from Newton Point just east of Porthcawl down to the giant power station at West Aberthaw. They can't do a great deal – though they try – about the industrial effluent from Port Talbot and the sewage from scores of coastal towns and villages that at certain times make Dunraven Bay, like all other beaches hereabouts, not the nicest place to bathe from. But whatever clearing, restoring, negotiating, arranging, educating, pleading, threatening and planning can achieve above low water mark in their patch, they do. Since the project was set up in 1972 they have managed to exclude from these fourteen miles almost all the excesses that loopholes in planning regulations and lack of foresight have visited on less energetically championed stretches of coastline. You won't find rashes of intrusive new housing, badly sited caravan parks or sharp new amusement strips to gladden ten and sadden a hundred. You will find restored buildings, beaches as clean as they can be, information where you'd most like it, absence of aggressive sights and sounds, miles of unspoilt countryside to wander in and other miles without access even by footpath, where wildlife stays undisturbed. If this all sounds idyllic, that's what it is. But the idyll is maintained only by hard work all year round. Establishing the Glamorgan Heritage Coast has been a mile-by-mile, landowner-by-landowner affair. At Southerndown, the Heritage Coast Project and the Dunraven Estate, which owns the bay, the cliffs and a good deal of the village, have managed between them to nurture a marriage of tolerance that says a lot for both sides in the arrangement.

As you stand looking south from the beach in Dunraven Bay, the view is cut off by the long, pointed promontory of Trwyn y Witch, the Witch's Nose, rising to a green top a couple of hundred feet above the water. With far views over sea and land it's an obvious stronghold, and one that has been in almost constant use since Iron Age defenders built a fort there. Caractacus may have used the site in his defiance of the Romans, and Norman castles on Trwyn y Witch were burned and knocked down by both Saxons and Welsh. One of these was in the manor of Dunraven given to Arnold, the cup-bearer of Ogmore Castle, by his Norman master as a thank-you present for beating the Welsh raiders away from Ogmore while the lord was elsewhere. Arnold formalized his job-description into the surname Butler, and the family held successive Dunraven castles until Tudor times. The Three Golden Cups pub in Southerndown still displays the tools of Arnold's trade as part of its sign.

On the lower, inland slopes of the Witch's Nose, a long box of castellated stone-walls rises among the salt-stunted bushes of the valley. The walls look bleak and half ruined from the beach, and the impression grows as you walk up towards them and see the choke of brambles, elder bushes and ivy that grow around and up them. But get through the door in the wall and you'll see the Heritage Coast Project in action. This great fortification was built to keep out not Welsh or English, but sea-winds and spray. These were the walled gardens of Dunraven Castle, a mass of weeds and crumbled stonework when the project's workers took them over in the 1970s, now being carefully restored and laid out again. The Tudor walls with their nineteenth-century upper layers have been rebuilt, the gardens replanted to show the development of gardening through the ages. There's a medieval herb-garden, a fruit orchard, a plant-hunters' garden full of species brought back from overseas by explorers and plant-gatherers, a glassed-in vinery, a Victorian garden where the practical need for food and medicine gives way to a horticulturalist's ornamental creation. In the south-eastern angle of the walls is an ice-tower, built to look medieval but probably several centuries younger, which stands above the underground chambers where ice was stored in winter, to be used during the summer in the kitchens of Dunraven Castle. But you look in vain for the huge fortified manor house that stood above its walled gardens at the top of Trwyn y Witch.

From Butlers to Vaughans to Wyndhams through more than four

centuries; enlarged, added to, castellated, tinkered with as finances and fashions dictated, changing from an earl's residence to a military hospital and a holiday centre, finally standing empty and decaying, Dunraven Castle dominated the beach and valley as its owners dominated the village of Southerndown. But the bills mounted, and the family's need for it declined. The Wyndhams who had acquired it in the seventeenth century had their main estates in Ireland, and Dunraven became an increasingly expensive embarrassment. In 1963, after local objections had blocked Lord Dunraven's plan to sell the pile to developers who had golf clubs and caravan sites in mind, he called in the bulldozers. Within a month the house was a pile of rubble and timber. Its ground-plan, outlined in stone and brick, still sprawls across the turf above the gardens, a splendid viewpoint from which to look over Dunraven Bay to the grey-and-white line of Southerndown curving over its ridge of green fields.

The relief model of a woman's crowned head adorns one side of the doorway at the Heritage Coast Centre in the old Seamouth Café. Some say it's St Bridget who gave her name to St Brides Major; some think it might be Diana, the huntress. That would be appropriate, as the building started life as the kennels of the Dunraven Hunt. However, it's possible that the little head represents Caroline, the first Countess of Dunraven and a formidable chatelaine of the nineteenth century who reigned here for a good half-century. Those were the days when all goods had to be carried up fifty-two steps to the castle on the backs of servants who were forbidden the use of Dunraven's drive; when all estate retainers had to bow or curtsey when a family carriage passed them; when a flag flew royally from the castle to advertise the presence of the owner. The family owned coal-mines in South Wales and were not exactly strapped for cash, but they knew how to let the pounds look after themselves. Lord Dunraven owned a good slice of the Great Western Railway and, when the hunt kennels were converted into a laundry, one of his perks was to have the dirty washing brought over from his Irish estates by train to be laundered at Dunraven – an economy on a scale grand enough to leave his neighbours gasping. Stories of the parties held at the castle in those golden years still go the rounds among locals with long memories in the Three Golden Cups. Not just parties, either: there's a weight of misery attached to the best of all the Dunraven Castle stories.

The family of Arnold the butler intermarried with the Vaughans some time early in the sixteenth century. The Vaughans' tenure of the castle, lasting more than a century, ended when Walter Vaughan sold it to the Wyndhams. If Walter was sick to his soul of Dunraven, he had good cause. The story is grippingly told in the Heritage Coast Centre's leaflet *The Wreckers of Dunraven*. In brief: Walter Vaughan, as magistrate, orders the arrest of local gang-leader Mat. During the struggle Mat's hand is cut off. Mat takes to wearing a hook and nurses vengeance in his heart. Later on Walter, embittered by snubs, turns from a decent man into a sour old curmudgeon. He spends all his money, kills his wife by breaking her heart and drives his eldest son overseas. Soon he's up on Dunraven cliffs wrecking ships and looting cargo along with Mat of the Iron Hand, having forgotten their previous brush. But Mat hasn't. Terrible things happen to Walter. Along with all his servants, he watches from the cliff as two sons drown, then returns to the castle to find that his youngest son, left unattended during the tragedy, has also drowned, in a tub of whey. Then the final act: a stormy night – a ship lured by lights – wrecked in the bay – a sole survivor retching on the beach, found by Mat of the Iron Hand and promptly murdered to shut his mouth – lantern-light on a familiar face – Mat's fiendish grin of revenge – a corpse's hand severed by Mat's knife – shown to Walter – look! that ring! it's his long-lost son!

Today's Dunravens live in Ireland, but they and their estate managers keep a close eye on what's happening over here. The agreement between the Dunraven Estate and the Heritage Coast Project keeps the whole of Dunraven Park open to the public: a change for the better from the days when estate employees would come down to the shore to warn off anyone trying to walk on Dunraven property, and when permits hand-written by Lord Dunraven had to be carried by the few fishermen allowed on to Trwyn y Witch. It was John Howden, the first Heritage Coast warden and a persuasive character, who managed to prise open the oyster of the Dunraven Estate. His early work on the dilapidated grounds and gardens was carried out with the help of working parties from local prisons. These days, it's Manpower Services Commission labour that keeps the project going. Funds come from at least six different sources; most of the 'permanent' employees are on short-term contracts. It doesn't add up to a rock of security for the Heritage Coast Project.

Southerndown village, too, belongs in large part to the Dunraven Estate. Less than ten minutes from the centre of Bridgend and half an hour from Cardiff, it has attracted commuters to its single street of strongly built old houses. A certain amount of cautious selling off by the estate has brought in outsiders, far more protective of their undeveloped village than the local farming families. Even the 'foreigners' who own and rent out houses in the village have helped to preserve it, for these beaches are famous among surfing fanatics, many of whom are local lads. They club together to take winter lets of houses that would otherwise have a fair chance of standing empty from autumn until spring. It's a tight, proud little community with no visible chinks in its armour. But here, as elsewhere, the price of security is eternal vigilance. One of the Southerndown farmers has signalled his willingness to part with some of his land, and there's a steady stream of applications to the council for planning permission for a bungalow estate. A couple of fields have already been bought; they are outside the Heritage Coast boundary, so it's only the well-marshalled objections from the villagers that stand between Southerndown and a nice little fringe of new buildings and the nice little shops that go with them – and the nasty little shops that come later. As soon as the village gets wind of a planning application, the door-to-door petitions are organized. By now it's a well-oiled operation. The Southerndown inhabitants have learnt from the experience of other seaside villages all over Britain: the thin end of the development wedge, once inserted, has never yet failed to dig out the heart of such places. So far, the objections have kept development from Southerndown, but the villagers can't afford to let any application go unchecked. It seems ludicrous that they should have to defend themselves in this way, or that people should even be allowed to apply for development permission in the case of a place like Southerndown. For the locals it's not a question of smugness or snobbery, but of preventing their village from becoming one more bland, indistinguishable slice in the cut white loaf of the seaside. Their self-defence activities also have the valuable side-effect of drawing together natives and incomers in a common cause.

The danger with carefully preserved villages – even those preserved by their own people – is of disappearing in a warm bath of inactivity. It's not worth anyone's while to keep a shop open, for example. When most villagers have a car and can fill up on essentials in the nearby towns, what can you stock except luxuries or the little, cheap things that people are always running out of? These don't make a profit. Southerndown's post office and shops, traditional forums for the exchange of news and gossip, have all fallen victim to the superstore and the motor car in recent years. Frolics Restaurant with its excellent, cheap pasta plates and other more expensive dishes is for visitors or celebrations. The tiny modern church half-way up the street provides a get-together for a few people for a couple of hours a week, and there's a cricket club operating on a beautiful little ground just above the church. But there's only one place in Southerndown where local money and local chit-chat get turned over every day of the week. The Three Golden Cups is where the spark of village life is centred. The lounge bar is like a museum of Southerndown history, with its photographs and relics of wrecked ships; and in the public bar what social historians call the 'oral tradition' comes pouring out with the pints. Here you can learn about the horse-drawn brakes that brought expensive visitors from the railway to the classy Dunraven Hotel, the lemonade tent that was pitched by the beach, the Sunshine Home for Blind Babies that occupied the old Marine Hotel for many years; and how local people view the future of the village. One or two of the older farmers think the Heritage Coast Project and the conservation of Southerndown is a lot of old rubbish. They are the ones who hold the key to the village's prospects, together with the Dunraven Estate. Demand for those fields on the fringes of Southerndown grows year by year, and so do the offers. But those who don't have any time for the conservationists are outvoted and out-manoeuvred – for the present – by the new-wave inhabitants who have settled here. Most of the long-established villagers agree with the incomers: they would rather keep the special flavour of their thin slice of coastline, even at the sacrifice of a large helping of that tasty, smothering development jam.

22. Oxwich

There's a tacit agreement between visitors and locals to keep the Gower Peninsula just the way it is. No one wants to lose that unique atmosphere of a place at the edge of things. When you have passed through Swansea and entered the Gower across its neck of connecting land, the wide heath you drive across is the gateway into an area still largely unspoilt by twentieth-century development. Everything is small-scale, but everything is here: cliffs, sandy beaches, woodlands, hills, winding lanes, heath, farmland, marshes, tiny villages, old churches, people happy to switch off their tractors or put down their gardening shears for a nice long chat. Visitors draw a deep breath of relief once they are past Swansea airport, and let themselves relax. Here there are no theme parks or amusement arcades. It's all like Cornwall must have been before the railways arrived.

Oxwich, cradled by its bay on the underside of the peninsula, has been lushly but accurately called 'a beautiful movement in the symphony of Gower'. In August, when the children are out of school and the sun shines, it's not the easiest of villages to reach. You can sit in a traffic jam on the narrow A4118 road for a couple of hours and still not get there. Once the car park by the dunes is full, the police turn late arrivals away. You have to be down the lane and on the beach by nine o'clock in the morning if you want to spend the day at Oxwich. At such times Gower's problems are on the surface. How does such a popular yet intimate area keep its head above the tourist tide, except by moving the incomers on? But come here out of season or on a cloudy day, and you can have the village, dunes, beach and bay more or less to yourself. There are tight, brackeny lanes to explore, footpaths that take you up through the woods on to the coastal path along the cliffs, three miles of uninterrupted sand, a nature-reserve on Oxwich Burrows reckoned to be one of the best-run and most varied in Britain. You'd have to go back to pre-motor-car days in most other seaside places to equal the exhilaration of a May morning at Oxwich.

The village straggles down a narrow lane, all the new development penned up at the top end. Here are the camping and bungalow parks which siphon off the weekly and fortnightly holidaymakers. There are a few Bed-and-Breakfast places in Oxwich, and more expensive accommodation at the Oxwich Bay Hotel on the beach, but most visitors put up at these holiday parks. 'NO touring caravans . . . NO motor bikes . . . NO unsupervised young people . . . NO dogs . . . NO cats' say the notices at the camping park; but it's a pleasant site on two large, open fields with long views over the bay and the spine of Cefn Bryn, the ridge that divides Gower almost in two. Nearly 600 people can be fitted in here, and about the same number in the ranks of bungalows under the woods on the other side of the lane. The villagers weren't happy when this land was sold for development a few years ago, but time has demonstrated the advantage of having almost all the holidaymakers up here rather than down there.

Oxwich was later than most comparable places in Gower in being designated a Conservation Area, and a certain amount of free-for-all building went on before such development was stopped. As you walk down the lane, there are some remarkable exhibitions of individual taste (no names, no pack-drill) featuring crazy-paved house-walls, piazza-style terraces and glaring black-and-white frontages on which bright red burglar-alarms catch and transfix the eye. But these soon give way to the few old houses that make up the older Oxwich village. You pass tiny Margaret's Cottage and the whitewashed house called The Nook which is everyone's dream of a country cottage, with its tiny windows under heavy brows of thatch, hanging flower baskets and low doorways. A slate plaque in the wall records the visits to the house of John Wesley, who came five times to lodge here with the bailiff of Oxwich and preach salvation to the locals. He found them an irreligious lot and spurned an offer of smuggled gin on his first visit in favour of a dish of tea. Next down the lane is the old post office, closed in 1978 and now a craft shop, and at the crossroads another whitewashed house with a pantiled roof which runs a shop from one end – it used to be the village's Bull Inn. On the far side of the crossroads is the old school, which shut down in 1963. All these closures – post office, pub and school – drained the life-blood from Oxwich during its slump years before the nature reserve and water sports began to re-awaken people's interest. The village all but died in the 1960s and '70s as the long-established families moved away, unable to educate their children, buy a pint or do their shopping locally. But at the same time the commuters were moving in with their money and their tender concern for conservation. The decay stopped, and life of a different sort returned. There's a new post office now, and a couple of shops. The most recent sign of Oxwich's revival has been the opening of the Oxwich Bay Hotel at the bottom of the lane as you reach the bay. It's become a meeting place for water-sporters and societies enjoying a night out, with bars, accommodation and a restaurant.

What the Reverend John Collins would think of the use to which his fine rectory is being put is open to conjecture. As the present Oxwich Bay Hotel, it has sprouted excrescences on top and behind, notably a roof like a Second World War gun emplacement, with slit windows and a featureless breadth of grey slates. But the outlines of the dignified building put up in 1788 can still be made out, 'delightfully situated on the shore near the sea, so as to command an awful prospect of its extensive surface, calculated to excite in the reverend pastor of a flock, and the rising olive branches round his table, daily sensations of wonder and filial obedience towards the Creator of the Great Deep'. Mr Collins was perturbed by the fondness of his flock for smuggled gin, as his journal for 1794 records: 'Thursday 13 March – Smugglers chased into the bay at Oxwich by the "Speedwell" cutter and taken. Sixteen men landed and saved some casks &c. &c. – several of parishioners got very drunk with gin.' Two days later, on 15 March: 'Poor Thomas Matthew died owing to drinking a quantity of gin on Thursday.'

Some 200 people turned up to the funeral in St Illtyd's Church that Sunday. The church with its tall thirteenth-century tower stands hidden by the trees beyond the hotel, built around the cell of a hermit who took refuge here during the Dark Ages. The old bell in the tower inscribed 'Ora Pro Nobis Sancte Maria' was probably hung there when the tower itself was built. Oxwich was a lawless place when Mr Collins was vicar, a smugglers' stronghold where most of the local farmers, fishermen and limestone quarry workers had a finger in the free trade pie. These sharp-toothed cliffs and the dangerous tide-races off them claimed a good number of ships during winter storms, and the villagers made the most of the cargoes that were washed up on their beach. It was this tradition of looting wrecked ships that led to a tragedy at the gate of Oxwich Castle.

A steep, leafy footpath runs up from the village street through the woods to Oxwich Green where the impressive castle ruins stand in sixty-foot curtains of broken wall, their blank, decaying faces full of small windows. 'Castle' is the right word for this sixteenth-century fortified manor-house, about to be opened to the public at the time of writing after twenty years of painstaking restoration. There are one or two homely touches, including the farmhouse crouching into the walls and the round, many-ledged dovecot just outside, but the message is one of defiance to allcomers. A pretty cheerless place, cold and harsh, but an improvement for Sir Rice Mansel when he moved here in the 1540s from nearby Penrice Castle.

Disputes between neighbours could easily get out of hand in those days of private armies of retainers and universal carriage of arms. When a French vessel drove aground at Oxwich on Boxing Day 1557 and word got round of her valuable cargo of raisins, figs and wool, the stage was set for a scramble for the goodies between Sir Rice and a gentleman from Swansea, Sir George Herbert, both of whom laid claim to the booty. Sir George ended up facing a court, accused of complicity in murder and robbery.

The records of those Tudor court proceedings have survived, and they give a very full and graphic account, from the testimony of eye-witnesses, of the tragedy as it unfolded. At dawn on 28 December, Sir George and a party of supporters had gone the rounds of the Mansel estate houses where the looted cargo had been stored. The gang 'ryfled' the properties, 'and toke awaye also two french p'soners, a barrel of resons, a sack of woll, 3 peces of Figges, at the risenge of the sunne'. Then, knowing that Sir Rice was away from home and had left his teenage son Edward in charge, Sir George and his merry men made for Oxwich Castle. Edward Mansel was a brave young man, confronting the aggressors in the gateway beneath his father's coat of arms with the challenge: 'Howe nowe, are ye com hyther to robbe and invade me?' Sir George Herbert tried to discompose the young defender by taunting him for his youth, bragging 'that he wolde bynde Edwarde Manxell like a boy, and wolde send him to his father like a coke'; but Edward seems to have kept his cool until 'Wm Herbert bastard', one of the jeering crowd outside the gate, drew a sword and wounded him in the arm. The boy, his pride pricked by the mockery he'd had to take, began laying about him with his own sword. His aunt, Anne Mansel, who had come out into the gateway to support her nephew, caught him by the arm and tried to dissuade him; but it was too late. A Herbert follower, Watkyn John ap Watkyn, 'toke vpe a stone, and threwe it, and therewithall strake the saide Anne downe to the grownd. Then they within the gate cryed owte mvrdder, mvrdder. Vpon whych throwe and crye, the said Sr. George Herbert called his men away.'

Mvrdder it was: Anne's brain had been pierced by Watkyn's stone, and she died shortly afterwards. At the end of his trial, Sir George was imprisoned and forced to make reparation to the Mansels – but what happened to the hapless Watkyn, a pawn in this landowners' game of piratical chess, we don't know. The gatehouse where Anne Mansel met her death still stands, the family coat of arms in relief over the gateway below a cleverly concealed slit from which discouraging objects could be dropped on the heads of attackers. Unfortunately the Herbert party never got far enough under the arch on that winter morning to be caught by this device. One nice touch from history, showing how myths shape themselves in every age: from the time of the Profumo scandal onwards, Sir Rice Mansel has been known locally as Sir Mansel Rice-Davies.

Walking down the lane to Oxwich from the castle, there are glimpses between the trees of a flat, marshy belt of low-lying country stretching inland from a range of grassy dunes behind the beach. This is Oxwich National Nature Reserve, a showpiece among such places – which is not to say there's anything static or self-satisfied about it. On the contrary: warden and reserve workers bubble with energy and enthusiasm, and work like beavers all year round to keep things moving, growing and improving. The warden, Michael Hughes, lean and incisive, wouldn't agree to give me the two minutes of his time I asked for. However, he'd be pleased to give me two hours – he couldn't put things in perspective in any less time. Crunching up the cockle-shell path over the dunes, Michael led the way to a high point from which the whole reserve was spread out in view. 'There she is,' he said, waving an arm over twenty-five years of intensive work, planning and imagination.

When the National Nature Reserve was created here in 1963, the sand dunes were badly eroded by sliding and trampling visitors and breached by blow-outs, gaps in the vegetation that uncover loose sand for the wind to blow away. They had also been cut up by RAF practice bombs and the tracks of American tanks rehearsing for D-Day. Behind them lay an area of marshland which had once been drained and reclaimed for grazing but was now reverting to a freshwater marsh. The Nature Conservancy Council leased the reserve area – dunes, fresh- and salt-water marshes, some woodland and most of the beach – from the Penrice Estate in 1963, but it wasn't until another twenty years had elapsed that they could buy it outright and make firm plans well into the future. During those twenty years the dunes were stabilized by planting marram grass and screens of pine branches to trap the sand and hold it steady. Looking across the reserve from the sandy little knoll, I absorbed a lesson from Michael Hughes about dunes, and another one about marshes.

The Oxwich dunes were probably formed by great sandstorms in the Middle Ages, and again from about the time of Sir Rice Mansel onwards.

Dunes are remarkably varied things in places like Oxwich Bay, not at all the bone-dry, featureless pyramids of sand you might imagine. They are full of bits of seashell, rich in the lime that a wide variety of plants enjoy. Great pink and yellow patches of bloody cranesbill and evening primrose grow across them. They provide many different micro-habitats – the dry tops exposed to the sun and wind; the damp 'slacks' or hollow backs of the dunes where the wind has blown out the loose sand down to the solid wet stuff further in; parts facing the sea which are constantly sprayed with salt water; areas which get little sunlight; areas where fresh water collects. The dune slacks in particular, where rainwater and lime trickle down the sides together with other minerals, get covered in bushes and flowers, including several kinds of orchid. They need careful managing, though. If you just let things go, the bigger bushes take over at the expense of the small, sun-loving plants. The cockle-shell paths that run across them have to be renewed frequently as wind, rain and visitors' feet wear them away. The visitors themselves have to be reminded not to slide down those tempting mini-mountains, hollowing out channels for the wind to get to work on.

The reserve workers can't just let the marsh go, either; wild and natural though it looks, it's the result of selective cutting back, drainage, ditching, clearing and channelling. If the Oxwich reserve's marsh was left alone, reeds would spread, unchecked, across it, choking up all the pools and watercourses. Alder and willow would follow the reeds until within fifty years the whole area would be a boggy woodland known as 'carr', unattractive to most of the wildlife it supports at present. To prevent this, Michael and his colleagues spent an enormous amount of time and energy hacking back the reeds and water-greedy trees, and redirecting the marsh drainage through the dunes into the sea; an expensive business that they could only justify undertaking once the reserve had been bought and its future guaranteed. More than 150 species of birds have been recorded in the reserve, about half of them on the marsh, including bittern, water rail, purple herons, firecrest, marsh harrier, hobby and great crested grebe. There are over 600 kinds of flowering plants, nearly thirty of butterflies, fifteen of dragonflies.

The price of all this richness and diversity of habitat and life is eternal vigilance and forethought, allied to hard, back-aching physical work. All sorts of people come to the reserve, up to 10,000 a day at the height of the season. They range from botany students to parties of schoolchildren and families out for the day. There's a well equipped centre in the car park, with displays, leaflets, a lecture room, maps, relief models and a marine aquarium. But everyone wants to be out on the dunes, or in the woods or the bird-watching hides on the marsh, either on the guided walks organized from the centre or just by themselves. Over-use, and the trampling, erosion and disturbance to wildlife that it brings, is the biggest threat to the reserve, and visitors have to be encouraged to understand that threat and to co-operate with Michael Hughes and his staff.

Michael gets a good deal of quiet amusement out of acknowledging the realities of his job. 'Let's face it,' he told me, 'the main reason why a family comes here is because it's the lowest common denominator of interest. Dad wants to go to the pub, Mum wants to be on the beach, the kids would rather be playing the video machines – so they compromise and all come here. It's these people that I want to get through to. My job isn't to educate them, but to stimulate them and inspire them. If they come to the reserve thinking, "Oh, well, might as well give it a try," and go away saying, "Gosh, yes, that was interesting," then we've succeeded.

'The Nature Conservancy Council has been rather too concerned with the scientific community in the past, people who know what it's all about anyway. There's been a tendency to preach to the converted, and see the general public as intruders. But one of the best days of the year was when we had a party of schoolkids here when it was literally pissing with rain all day. Half of them came without any waterproof clothes, in fashion jackets and trainers. We took them all out, blindfolded them so they could listen and touch, had them smelling things, feeling things, going over a patch of dune with a magnifying glass. They all got soaked. They loved it.

'We've got a lot of leaflets in the centre, and you can learn a lot from them. We're trying to rewrite and improve them all the time. But I'll tell you the most important thing in them. It's those first three words that you see when you open the visitors' map – Welcome To Oxwich.'

23. Tenby

Tenby is such an exciting place to discover for the first time. You arrive from the everyday world, by road or railway, to come suddenly face to face with a medieval walled town standing high on a cliff above the sea. Somehow these grey stone walls – towers, battlements, arrow-slits and arched gateways – still cradle two sides of the old town seven centuries after they were founded. From South Parade you might be looking at a knights-in-armour film set. Twenty or thirty feet high, Tenby's town walls bar you out. You can enter the heart of the town through the south-west gate, known as Five Arches from the five archways whose connecting columns clutch the pavement like the roots of a mangrove; but the dramatic way is to walk down White Lion Street to emerge on the top of the cliff.

There can't be many prettier harbour views than this one. You look down from where the seaward walls ran before they decayed and were demolished during the eighteenth century as Tenby began to come to terms with its new role as a seaside resort. The disappearance of these clifftop town walls laid the whole sea view open. Below you is the sandy little harbour, cupped between stone pier and cliffs, sited northwards out of the weather and lined round with tall, three- or four-storey Georgian and Victorian buildings in blues, greys and milky browns, all facing inwards in a tight semi-circle. On the sheltered sand of the harbour lie dozens of sailing boats beside a cluster of solid stone warehouses. Beyond the pier rises the green knoll of Castle Hill where the ruins of Tenby Castle perch right above the sea. From the harbour a sweep of dull golden sand stretches north, broken by rock outcrops, to the jagged head of Monkstone Point; then the view arches away to the east into the enormous curve of coastline around the top of Carmarthen Bay, completely enclosing the horizon from this viewpoint. If you're a photographer or an artist, look no further – satisfaction is guaranteed without moving another step.

Tall, dark, crooked old Crackwell Street leads down from here to the harbour, passing the Sun Inn whose side alley into the High Street is so narrow that there's less than five feet of space between its oversailing medieval walls each side. Crackwell Street descends into Bridge Street before bringing you down into Castle Square at the head of the harbour, a meeting place of all the strands of Tenby's history. It's also the spot on which all holidaymakers converge, to make their way down to the beach, climb up to the castle and town museum, book a boat-ride round the islands or just lean over the harbour wall in time-honoured fashion and watch the world go by. Apart from the beach, the main attraction is the ruin of the castle keep, all that remains of the stronghold built by the Normans against their invaded but unpacified Welsh subjects. The castle survived a visit by Llywelyn ap Gruffydd in 1260 during which most of Tenby was destroyed. This was the final straw of insurrection that led to the building of the town walls and the consequent obsolescence and neglect of the castle. Tenby, with its immunity from attack and its sheltered harbour, became a great trading post in Tudor times, exporting the produce of the farmlands behind the town – wool, hides, corn, coal and cloth – and bringing in those items that temperate Wales couldn't supply: spices, wine, fruit, salt, oil. What lovely smells there must have been in that prosperous little town. As well as trade with the Continent, Tenby also had profitable links with the West Country ports of Bristol and Barnstaple. On Quay Hill, just inland from the harbour, stands a surviving house from those great days, a merchant's old dwelling, tall and thin, of knobbly stone blocks crammed into an alleyway of steps and close walls. But Tudor profit and good living turned into Stuart and Hanoverian slump and decline. By the time that eighteenth-century sufferers were beginning to turn to the seaside for relief from their gout and stomach upsets, Tenby was in a bad way, its streets decaying, houses falling down and town walls crumbling.

In 1781 Dr John Jones of Haverfordwest began to advertise the benefits of bathing in Tenby seawater. Since the Middle Ages the local fishermen had given prayers before their expeditions, and thanks at the end of them, in the little chapel of St Julian on the end of the harbour's stone pier. Now the chapel was turned into a bathing establishment, and the splendid houses which stand all round the harbour were built. Sections of decayed town wall on the clifftops were demolished – along with their ancient gateways – and new wide promenades and roads were laid out. North of the old walls rose the fashionable suburb of Norton. Tenby became quite the place to be, though the local people still stuck to their old ways, to the distress of observers of refined sensibilities like Louis Simond. In 1810 he noted with distaste: 'The use these Hottentots make of the beetling brow of the cliffs, the very place for poetical raptures and philosophical contemplation, is too vile to be named.' The chapel baths soon proved to be too small to deal with the influx of visitors. New baths, together with assembly rooms, were built under Castle Hill at the landward end of the pier. The baths burned down, but were quickly rebuilt. Tenby couldn't do without them. The building, known as Laston House, still stands by the pier, plain and classical in design, with a curved and grooved front bay – the world's earliest essay in Art Deco. A quotation from Euripides is inscribed in Greek above the door: 'The sea doth cleanse all man's pollution.' These were splendid baths: warm rooms, cold rooms, ladies' and gentlemen's baths, a cupping room, bedrooms for invalids and a 'spacious vestibule' where the servants could wait while their employers splashed, groaned, flirted and chattered.

A path runs up from the harbour to the museum on Castle Hill where you can trace Tenby's boom as a resort in a fascinating collection of pictures and painting books. Here are grand oil-paintings showing the town from every angle, high and low; amateur water-colours by visiting ladies in love with the cliffs and caves; the lithographs and pen-and-ink sketches of Charles Norris that capture the mood of the early resort days; lovely intimate paintings done by E. J. Head a century later of old salts playing dominoes and Edwardian families stiffly posing on the beach in long dresses and black hats; drawings and paintings of family and friends by Augustus and Gwen John, Tenby's own heroes. There are also books of carefully pressed seaweeds, laboriously assembled by amateur naturalists on mid-Victorian holidays when the study of the seashore had become a craze among the leisured classes. Tenby was a mecca, too, for serious students of seaside ecology such as Thomas Huxley, who honeymooned here with his sickly wife Henrietta (she got better and bore him eight children), and Philip Gosse, whose book *Tenby: A Seaside Holiday* became a favourite when it was published in 1856. Poor Gosse caught one of history's branch-line trains to oblivion with the book he brought out the following year, though. An admirer of Charles Darwin's methods, he couldn't bring himself to accept the theory of natural selection over that of divine intervention, and in *Omphalos* tied himself in knots trying to bring the Genesis story to bear on natural history. But his work inspired thousands of Victorians to look more closely at the seashore. Some were not as scrupulous as Gosse, and there was a good deal of indiscriminate specimen collecting and tearing apart of hitherto unspoilt places. Gosse felt himself responsible for opening up Eden to vandals, and it caused him a lot of heartache towards the end of his life – a sad harvest for such a careful and skilful naturalist.

Tenby, fortunate in the beauty of its views of town, harbour and coastline, is also blessed with four fine beaches. The north and south beaches run for miles in both directions, great bars of sand where there's always a space on the busiest summer weekend if you walk out for ten minutes or so. Between these are two smaller, sandy stretches – the one inside the arm of the harbour, and Castle Beach at the foot of the incline down from Castle Square. At low tide you can walk out from here to the rocky, green-headed St Catherine's Island just offshore, topped with the square block of a fort built in the 1870s to warn off Napoleon II. The fort, equipped with eleven guns and sixty men, was a white elephant, and still is today. For a time it was a zoo, and there have been great plans to turn it into a swanky hotel; but somehow the money never quite materializes. You'd certainly have a memorable stay in the Fort Hotel if it ever came to pass, cut off by the tide twice a day and passing the time with the wonderful view out over the bay and back to Tenby on its cliff. The cliff-faces are full of tiny ornamental gardens, reached by flights of steps from the upper promenades of the Esplanade and the Paragon. In the second half of the nineteenth century the town bulged out south and west from its walls in a line of hotels that dominate the heights, giving more emphasis to an already striking inland view. Beside St Catherine's Island is the landing stage on wheels from which you can take a boat ride out to Caldey Island, a couple of miles south of Tenby, where a handful of elderly Cistercian monks are struggling to keep their community going. The monastery runs a farm, a dairy and a post office on the island, and the monks make and sell chocolate and perfume. One visitor in three to Tenby makes the short sea-journey to the island, and the crossing business keeps several local boat-owners in work, as well as giving the monks some financial leeway. But young men don't fancy the isolation and hardship of the monastic life in such a lonely place; and without new blood the future of the community looks bleak.

South Beach makes a long curve away from Castle Beach to the rocky nose of Gilter Point. Behind this great expanse of sand rise the dunes of The Burrows, smothered in sea buckthorn which was planted there in 1930 to combat erosion and has taken over in a big way to the detriment of variety in the plant, insect and bird life. This is a great place to wander with sounds of the beach overlain by wind and larks. You might be miles away from a busy holiday resort. Dune gentians, tiny dull purple spikes of flowers, were discovered here in the 1920s, the first time they had been recorded in Britain. There are many unusual plants growing near Tenby, and the fate of one in particular would have broken Philip Gosse's heart. Since things warmed up at the end of the last Ice Age, the Tenby daffodil had been growing all over the surrounding countryside, and nowhere else as a native plant in the whole of Europe. When the Victorian enthusiasts learned about Tenby daffodils, they couldn't get enough of them for their gardens and woodlands. Local people, knowing a good thing when it hit them, set to with trowel and spade digging up the bulbs and sending them off on the trains to London – a quarter of a million every year in the 1880s. Soon the daffodils were seen no more in the Tenby fields, wiped out by the bulb robbers and the development of ploughs that could bite down to where the remaining bulbs were. Ironically, the Tenby daffodil is now beginning to re-colonize wild places from the private gardens and woods which became its only refuge.

While the outer fringes of Tenby spread out in all directions by beach, cliff and Victorian building expansion, the heart of the town remains a tight huddle of medieval streets inside the town walls. The High Street is the widest, with the large and beautiful St Mary's Church standing above Tudor Square. It's a cavernous, cool and quiet building with a fifteenth-century wagon roof made of irregularly sized and aligned timber struts among which are nearly 100 carved bosses and a figure of God surrounded by angels with their eyes tight shut. On the south wall there's a black slate memorial tablet to Peggy Davies, erected by some of the ladies she obliged during her forty-two years' service as a bathing attendant. 'Her good humour, respectful attention, & Gratitude [ah, yes! that essential virtue] made her employers – Friends.' Peggy died on the job in 1809, aged eighty-two, when 'seized with Apoplexy' while she was in the water, still attending her ladies.

Upper and Lower Frog Street, running parallel with the High Street, are delightful. Tenby Pottery stands here, where you can watch the vases and plates being made and buy samples glazed in brown and white; and Tenby Market, large, shabby and cheerful, where the stall-holders have the time and inclination to rib their customers as they sell them cheese, fruit, Welsh woollen clothes and old books. There are covered arcades of shops in cobbled courtyards full of trees and hanging baskets. These are the friendly, old-fashioned streets promised by those protective medieval town walls. But here, too, are the over-bright colours of the trinket shops, signs of the times that Tenby people resent deeply. They stand two or three together, each one replacing a family-run business which the locals remember and hanker after. In winter they close and the owners decamp, many to sell up to another strange face. These gaudy shops are a conspicuous focus for the unease that the residents of most small seaside resorts feel about what outsiders are doing to their town.

Tenby tries hard to give its visitors what they want. The Radio One Roadshow takes over the South Beach car park every now and then to please the teenagers for whom pretty, polite Tenby is deadsville. There's scuba diving and water ski-ing from Castle Beach, a small amusement arcade on North Beach and another one in the town centre. But it's the 'quaintness' of the town, a label the tourist office would like to see fixed all over Tenby, that's the goose that lays the golden egg of tourist income here. Places like the Dirty Shop just outside the town walls – 'Disgusting Gifts for the Dirty Minded' – are what tourism promoters and local people don't want to see. They prefer what they call the 'bucket and spade brigade' in summer, and the conference trade that is Tenby's winter nest-egg. Winter brings its own problems, however. The boat-owners, having gathered all they can in the fat summer months, go on the dole or find other jobs. So do the staff at the tourist information centre. The young people hang around the pretty streets with nothing to do. Those lovely houses by the harbour, from Laston House round the curve, have almost all been turned into holiday flats. After the season their windows go blank and the harbour, so vigorous and lively in summer, becomes a dead place. This is par for the course for the majority of small seaside towns, and everyone accepts it as a fact of life. But it means that the harvest of summer activity has to be energetically reaped, stubble, thistles and all. Tenby's problem is the one that every other popular seaside place has to tackle: how to get the good grain in without letting the thistles take over the field.

Each winter the tourist centre sends a travelling exhibition promoting Tenby to the places where most of its non-Welsh visitors come from: Preston, Doncaster, Sheffield, Nottingham, Birmingham and the major Irish cities. The hotels of the town couldn't possibly cope with the number who arrive in summer, even if they were cheap enough to be in the market.

Saundersfoot, the next resort up the coast, has the same difficulty; so the hinterland between Tenby and Saundersfoot has become one almost continuous, sprawling caravan and camping park. These three miles of former farmland house tens of thousands of people every week in the season. The Pembrokeshire Coast National Park, in which Tenby lies, keeps a very close eye on the proliferation of caravan and camping sites, but needs must where the devil drives. At the time of writing there are nine of these places between Tenby and Saundersfoot, and another one, Kiln Park, above The Burrows. There are big schemes afoot for Kiln Park: a boating lake, a fun centre and so on. Nothing has been decided yet. The Tenby Civic Society and the town's other conservation groups wouldn't like to see much more popularization of the area. But better outside the town walls than inside. The trouble is that a kind of Parkinson's Law operates in these circumstances – caravan sites, unless confined by a corporate act of will, tend to expand to fill the space available.

Where Tenby is lucky is in its position out at the end of West Wales. It's the region's most popular resort by far, but it's still quite an effort to get there. The extension of the M4 motorway has made things easier in recent years. But casual visitors don't tend to happen upon Tenby. The people who come (*pace* the travelling exhibitions), come either because they've heard of it from friends or because they've been coming for years. It's the narrow streets and friendly shops, the town walls, the views, the safe bathing from long, clean beaches that most visitors value. While they're here they may buy farting powder in the Dirty Shop or plastic Welsh dollies in the trinket stores, but they would vote with their feet if Tenby ever became the Blackpool of West Wales. That's not likely to happen, given the vigilance of the National Park and the other conservation bodies interested in keeping the town out of the fast lane of tourism. Tenby is full of charm, as it was for those beach-combing Victorian visitors. But those caravans need watching.

24. Aberystwyth

In 1865 Aberystwyth hosted the National Eisteddfod for the first time. All those who took part in that great annual expression of Welsh pride and Welsh culture were well aware that the old barriers between Wales and England were fast breaking down. The enemy was already within the gates – the railways and the Victorian tourist's craving for wild, romantic scenery had seen to that. One of the speakers warned his countrymen to face up to the future, advising them: 'Learn to speak English, or stay where you are and eat brown bread.' By this yardstick, Aberystwyth is very much a brown bread town, and proud of it. Here you'll find record shops dealing exclusively in Welsh-language recordings, bookshops whose windows display not a single English title, and pubs where – outside the height of the tourist season – you won't understand a word of the conversation if you come from east of the border. It's a cultured town, in no way out of touch with the modern world – very much the reverse, in fact, containing as it does the University College of Wales and the National Library of Wales, the Welsh College of Librarianship, the headquarters of the Welsh Books Council and the Welsh Language Society. Aberystwyth is effectively the capital of 'Welsh Wales' and guards that heritage jealously.

George Borrow in the early 1860s found 'a place called Aber Ystwyth, where stands a lovely town of the same name, which sprang up under the protection of a baronial castle, still proud and commanding even in its ruins, built by Strongbow the conqueror of the great western isle'. As not infrequently, Borrow in his enthusiasm got it wrong – Gilbert Strongbow's original earth-and-timber stronghold stood at the mouth of the Afon Ystwyth but, after the usual multiple and violent changes of ownership, it was burned down (by a Welshman) in 1208. The stone castle whose ruins stand superbly on a grassy knoll facing the sea was a stronger affair altogether, begun in 1277 by Edmund, brother of the English King Edward I, no less the Hammer of the Welsh than of the Scots. Many Welsh leaders besieged it; Owain Glyndwr took it in 1404 and lost it four years later. Parliament besieged it during the Civil War, captured it in 1646 and blew it up in 1649 to put an end to the insurrection that had always surrounded it.

Around the castle the medieval town of Aberystwyth grew up, hemmed into its cramped site by marshes, cliffs, mountains and sea. From the sea came prosperity by way of the town's great herring fleet, and later on the lead-mines up in the hills to the east which sent their produce out through the port. But all the mountains of mid-Wales lay between Aberystwyth and the outside world; the trackways that crossed them were bad at the best, impassable in winter. Stand on the clifftops to the north or south of the town, and it becomes obvious why Aberystwyth remained so Welsh for so long. Every gap in the landscape is plugged by a river or range of hills. Before the coming of the railways, few outsiders without a very good reason would be tempted to try the hazards of a land journey to Aberystwyth. Daniel Defoe, one of those who did get through, was not particularly charmed with what he saw: 'This town is enriched by the coals and lead which is found in its neighbourhood, and is a populous, but a very dirty, black, smoky place, and we fancied the people looked as if they lived continually in the coal or lead mines. However, they are rich . . .'

They became a sight richer after the discovery, towards the end of the eighteenth century, of the resource that every seaside town longed to find on its doorstep: a chalybeate spring, rich in iron and suitably unpalatable. Now Aberystwyth could join the spa town set, with its wonderful scenery and sea bathing as an added attraction. The ill wind of the Napoleonic Wars blew Aberystwyth plenty of good, too, denying continental travel to the well-heeled classes and turning their attention to what was on offer this side of the Channel.

The legacy of this expansion into elegance is laid out in full view as you walk north from the castle and round the corner of seafront by the pier. The tall, handsome hotels and houses that curve round the bay right into the cliff under Constitution Hill are the fruits of an imported culture that threatened for 100 years to weaken the roots of Aberystwyth's Welshness. This is just how you want a seaside resort's shop-window frontage to look: brave, distinguished, facing the sea like a line of flags in pastel blue and green, beige, yellow and white, with bright interludes of brick-red and ochre. The sands are where they should be, right in front of the long crescent of Marine Terrace, bounded on one side by the pier and on the other by the little cliff railway climbing Constitution Hill. From its summit you can enjoy a wonderful panorama: south over the town and its coastline, and north to the backbone of the Lleyn Peninsula running west on the horizon, a chain of mountaintops looking like islands and ending in a real one, Bardsey Island, nearly forty miles away.

Behind Marine Terrace is the town that grew up to cater for those

191

eighteenth- and nineteenth-century visitors. Some of the narrow medieval streets were widened, large sections of the old town walls knocked down and new streets of shops, hotels and boarding houses put up. Aberystwyth remained the preserve of the genteel holidaymaker until the railway, that great leveller, arrived in the town in 1864. Soon the network of Welsh railways had been ramified to link the Cambrian's Aberystwyth line with the crowded industrial valleys of South Wales, and the handsome station in silvery stone became the gateway to a seaside holiday for the coal-miners and steel-workers and their families. Aberystwyth's streets are full of tiled and glazed buildings, over-decorated in late-Victorian and Edwardian style. The White Horse Hotel off Terrace Road has bunches of grapes and wine jars round its swirlingly engraved art nouveau window, above which 'REA'S BAR LOUNGE' stands proudly out in raised lettering. On the corner of Terrace Road and Cambrian Place, T. J. Davies's jewellery and silversmith's shop stops all clocks with its lumpy effusion of terracotta mouldings and old-fashioned wood-framed shop window. And in Terrace Road itself is the fabulous Coliseum, built in 1904 and splendidly restored as a museum in the form of the music hall-cum-theatre that it once was. In the wrought-iron, horseshoe-shaped balconies are exhibitions of maritime Aberystwyth (ships in bottles, sextants, telescopes, old photographs) and bygone Wales (box beds, mock-ups of cottage interiors, dressers jammed solid with jugs and plates) among many others. On the wall are old playbills from the Coliseum's great days, lively and varied enough to suit all tastes: MDLLE. BARTENELLI, Most Wonderful Lady Gymnast & Contortionist; *Yeomen of the Guard* performed by Aberystwyth Amateur Society; The BROS. ARNOLD, Funny Patter Comedians; THE ATLAS BIOSCOPE with all the Latest Animated Pictures, including The Life of a Cowboy, Saved By Bluejackets and The Orphans, or, A Sister's Devotion, in 12 scenes!

Lest all this frivolity should divert minds from higher things, great sombre chapels were built to admonish both residents and holidaymakers. Douglas Hague, in his excellently arranged *Aberystwyth Town Trail*, says it all when he notes of these gloomy temples that they 'display their great gable ends richly, if illiterately embellished, to compete with their neighbours'. The chapels were not the only reminder that, under the skin of foreign influences, the Welsh heart of Aberystwyth continued to beat during Victorian times. Between castle and pier stands the enormous

Castle House, built in 1795, which was in the process of being turned into a hotel in 1872 when the newly founded University College of Wales was housed here. With its rosette windows, pinnacles, peaks, turrets, columns and archways, it's as if St Pancras station had come to Aberystwyth and pupped. Nowadays UCW occupies a campus high up on Penglais, the hill at the back of the town, but it was the influence of this wonderfully overblown Gothic building by the sea that made Aberystwyth more than just another handsome seaside resort. Walk south from the castle and stand looking inland from the quay beyond South Terrace, and you can see both old and new Aberystwyth rising from the bridge over the Afon Rheidol: packed slate roofs and narrow streets opening out to the green spaces of Penglais where the University buildings stand above the National Library of Wales. When this huge barracks of learning was founded here in 1907, Aberystwyth truly gained the position it holds so proudly today as the capital of Welsh Wales.

It's the remarkable harmony between the lives of university and town that gives Aberystwyth such a strong sense of identity. There are more than 3,000 students on the campus up on Penglais, but their presence is seen by most of Aberystwyth's residents as very much enhancing the atmosphere of the community. There's little of the town-and-gown mutual antagonism that sours relationships in many university towns. The University College of Wales works hard at its image – a good deal of the social life of the town, especially in winter, takes place on the campus. Townsfolk are encouraged to use the recreational facilities. Now that most of Aberystwyth's own cinemas have closed, and the King's Hall on the seafront round which most social activities used to revolve is a redundant hulk, Aberystwyth people look to Penglais for their films, rock music, plays and sporting occasions. Out of season there are discos in the pavilion on the pier and any number of pubs in the town, but they can't really compete with what's on offer up the hill. It's not all one-way traffic, either – the town council has its share of student representatives, and they don't hesitate to make their voices heard. Theatre groups come down into town to put on plays and events in any hall they can get into. Conservation projects attract enthusiastic support from the students. All this mutual commerce of ideas and action gives Aberystwyth a wide-awake atmosphere which most other seaside resorts would envy.

Aberystwyth's sense of itself as the guardian of Welsh nationalism is reinforced by the presence in the town of so many groups and societies involved with purely Welsh affairs. The Welsh Language Society holds its annual get-together here, where views are sometimes aired which foreigners might not be too flattered to hear. In the 1950s, Welsh was generally reckoned to be a dying language, and it's the vigorous campaigning of the Society that has been largely responsible for making it a live issue. Now that Welsh is being taught in schools on an equal footing with English, and local government tops and tails its correspondence in Welsh (if it doesn't write the whole thing that way), it's unlikely that the language will be threatened again. In Aberystwyth they've made a thorough job of it – at the railway station you hire a 'tacsi', and Banks's beer is transliterated outside the pubs as 'Bancs'. But the Welsh Language Society has attracted fringe groups whose passion has been inclined all along to spill over from hot words into hot action. Road-signs were the rallying point a few years ago, and a lot of paint-daubing and uprooting went on before the establishing of the dual-language signs that you see all over Wales today. Unfortunately it's only a short step in the mind of the general public from such rash but basically harmless activity to the transformer sabotage, weekend-cottage burnings and bomb threats of more extreme groups. Inevitably, some of the mud flung up by these events sticks to the Society, to the alarm of most of its members; and some clings to Aberystwyth. As a focal point for Welsh national identity, the town gets both a good and a bad press, depending on who has been saying what most recently.

Aberystwyth inhabitants aren't immune from these strands of public opinion when they surface. When something upsetting or violent is done in the name of Wales, local people review their feelings about the students of the University College. But these on the whole are ripples on the surface of a remarkably even relationship. UCW is an essential ingredient of Aberystwyth's rich mixture of culture, varied architecture, activity and pride in itself, all bottled up in superb sea and mountain surroundings. 'Aberystwyth is one town where you could be content to lead your entire life in Welsh,' the local-studies librarian said to me, and that sums it up neatly.

25. Barmouth

Barmouth is more West Midlands than West Wales in summertime, if the accents in the streets and on the beach are any yardstick. 'Brumbeside-the-sea,' say the locals, but without rancour – a century of railway connection with the Birmingham millions has made them fatalistic about the annual invasion. The sign by the recreation ground at the edge of town invites you to play 'bowlio', or if you've brought your golf clubs some 'pytio', but the emphatic Welshness that fires so many of the towns of West Wales has come to an accommodation here with the foreigners, their expectations and their money.

It wasn't always so. 'All day long the old guttural Welsh is heard about the hill,' reported the journal of the Guild of St George in 1901. The Guild, a utopian exercise in social reform, had been set up in Barmouth thirty years before by the zealous John Ruskin. In the piled-up cottages of the old town under the hill he had established groups of spinners, weavers and wood-carvers to toil honestly for honest rewards and the dignity of labour. There was something about Barmouth that well-meaning Victorian outsiders wanted to get their improving hands on. One look at the cramped and dirty streets of the steep little town, and moral sleeves were rolled up. 'A. R.', in his 1870 guidebook *On And Off The Cambrian*, relays a conversation he'd enjoyed on an earlier visit with a local doctor who had remarked of the town: 'Like Joppa it is excessively dirty, and as at Joppa, the filth that comes down from the upper galleries of houses into the street below is devoured of animals – the animals in the east being dogs, here pigs.'

Thank goodness, though, there were a few people of the right sort in Barmouth. 'Well, five years have elapsed,' chirps A. R., 'and, in justice to Barmouth, we must say that very great exertions have been made by the more intelligent inhabitants to promote cleanliness amongst the poorer classes: the pigs have disappeared, and much of the dirt.'

The view from the Dolgellau road into Barmouth is one of the most striking in a country full of wonderful views. It unrolls itself gradually as you drive along the widening estuary of the Afon Mawddach between rock outcrops: first the great railway bridge, half a mile long, whose legs stride right across the sandy rivermouth; then the solid stone houses and quays above the fishing boats and yachts in the harbour; then, as you round the corner, the old cottages climbing up the near side of the central grey slate block of houses, and a line of tall white hotels at the far end gleaming off to

195

the north over an enormous yellow sweep of beach. Tall, rocky-faced cliffs drop like a curtain behind the town, the buildings jammed hard back against them. In front lies the wide circle of Barmouth Bay. It's an exciting sight and one that has had writers reaching for their pens, though not all have been enchanted ('a horrible town, like a granite slug'). Enthusiasm for this breathtaking prospect is surprisingly hard to unearth – even such a great descriptive writer as Cledwyn Hughes could only come up with a rather bald 'Barmouth: grey-stoned and little harboured . . . a sea wall on the one side and the rising height of the cliff at the back. In between, the town.' And *Nicholson's Cambrian Traveller's Guide* of 1840 was similarly matter-of-fact: 'The houses are disposed, either on the sands in a low situation, or are reared at different heights on the side of a vast rock.' It reads like an estate agent making the best of a not very inspiring property, and this from the pen of a writer who stuffed most of his guidebook with furious torrents, dark wooded glens, abrupt crags and rude precipices. There are certainly enough of these in view around Barmouth, set as it is at the seaward feet of hill-ranges leading east to Cadair Idris and north to the mountains above Ffestiniog. The railway viaduct hadn't been built when the *Nicholson's* writer was here, so he never had the opportunity to stand high above the middle of the river and wax lyrical over one of the finest views in Britain, up the dark wooded glens and abrupt crags of the valley of that furious torrent, the Afon Mawddach.

Out in front of the harbour lies Ynys y Brawd, the Isle of the Monk, a hump of sand dunes connected to the promenade by a causeway. From here you get the best view of the town itself and the rock-faces towering behind it. They have beautiful names: Craig y Gigfran ('Raven's Rock') at the northern end above the tall terrace of hotels; Fron Felen ('Golden Breast') behind the slate-grey centre of Barmouth; Dinas Oleu (the 'Fortress of Light'), with the steep lanes of fishermen's cottages clinging to its lower part; Carreg Gribin (the 'Rocky Crest') overlooking the harbour. Barmouth's own name has suffered some sea changes over the years, from the original Abermawddach through Abermo and Bermo to Barmouth. In *Wild Wales* George Borrow confused the Mawddach with the Maw, to the detriment of his characteristic piece of pedantry about 'the place which the Saxons corruptly call Barmouth, and the Cumry with great propriety Aber Maw or the disemboguement of the Maw'. There's a steep zigzag footpath, the Panorama Walk, leading up to the top of the Fortress of Light and a full-circle view down into the chimneys of the town and round over mountains, river, sands and sea. English nineteenth-century romantics loved Barmouth: Tennyson was inspired to write 'Crossing the Bar'; Ruskin invested his dreams and his money; Wordsworth called the scene 'sublime', a tag for which the local pamphlet-writers have been truly grateful.

Abermawddach was at a low ebb when the visitors began to arrive, towards the end of the eighteenth century. There was just the cluster of old cottages under Dinas Oleu, remnants of a prosperous port that grew during the Middle Ages. The local people fished, built ships and exported a woollen cloth called 'webs', hand-spun from local wool in the cottages and sold in large quantities to slave-owners in the New World. The first thing new arrivals noticed about the town was that the streets were full of pigs and rubbish. Soon the new part of Barmouth was being run up under the cliffs, hotels and lodging houses appearing; though sand still covered the roadways. Sand has always been a problem for Barmouth, blocking up the river mouth, barring the harbour entrance and blowing in great sandstorms over everything. 'The sand at Barmouth is proverbial,' warned A. R. in 1870, 'and it is a common remark that it penetrates everything you eat there, except eggs, and these you must dispatch quickly.' It's still a job to keep the railway line clear of sand drifts, and if there's any sort of a wind blowing you'll find yourself walking about with constantly slitted eyes. The sand piles up into ridges along the promenade, clogs your nose and crunches underfoot in the shops. With all twentieth-century man's inventiveness and all his technology, he still hasn't really found a way to control this elusive stuff. The brown, yellow and pink city children capering on Barmouth beach can't get enough of it, but for the railway-men, ice-cream sellers, sailors and fishermen of the town it's a damned nuisance.

As the estuary sands dry out at low tide, the Afon Mawddach shrinks to a narrow ribbon winding under the legs of the railway viaduct. In the beds of sand around those 114 groups of sturdy-looking timber piles lurks a small but potent threat to the continued existence of Barmouth's railway lifeline from the Midlands. *Teredo navalis*, or Common Shipworm, brought here in the hulls of wooden trading vessels when Barmouth port was flourishing, took such a fancy to the viaduct's wooden legs that when the damage was discovered early in 1980 it looked as if the whole structure would have to go. British Rail could never have found the money to replace it, and

Barmouth would have lost half its customers. Sheaths of 'seacrete' around the viaduct piers, reinforced with worm-proof fibreglass, have done for the bridge what copper plating did for ships back in the days of sail: defeated *Teredo* – for the time being anyway.

Until 1972 the Afon Mawddach reached the sea through two channels. The south one, which formed the main entrance to the harbour, curved sharply north to skirt the sandbar that made this passage tricky for sailors without local experience. It was the more northerly of the two channels that posed the main danger, however. At ebb tide the river water raced along the edge of the beach below the seafront car park, unseen and immensely powerful below the surface of the bay. Its force was such that you could stand on the ferry landing-stage – a solid stone structure – and feel the whole thing vibrating beneath your feet as the tide went out. There is superb, safe bathing at the northern end of the town, but it was this death-trap of a beach that people saw as they parked their cars. Ignoring the red warning flag, they would hurry across the beach and into that inviting, calm-looking sea, to have their legs sucked from under them and find themselves being dragged away. In the worst incident in this deadly tide-race, seven people drowned in the course of a single Sunday. Now the Ynys y Brawd causeway shuts off the northern channel, and the river goes out in one sluice over the bar.

The tide-ripped shallows along the beach are still a nasty place to be caught in a small boat, however. Evan Jones, the coxswain of the Barmouth lifeboat, was awarded the Bronze Medal of the RNLI for the rescue a few years back of two fishermen who had abandoned their boat when they got into difficulties in a westerly gale. Mr Jones had had to drive the lifeboat over the shallows near the bar, storm waves breaking all round her as she bumped and grounded across the barely covered sand. There's a photo in the Lifeboat Museum on the quay of Evan Jones and his mechanic, Dewi Davies, going to collect the medal from the Duke of Kent. Mr Jones retired as coxswain in 1979 after forty-two years' service, and now watches the present lifeboat crew with a tolerant if critical eye. The old order of a crew made up of local fishermen has given way to a new membership more representative of today's dwellers in Barmouth: a shop-keeper, a garage owner (he's the coxswain), a postman, a doctor. There are about thirty men competing for seven places in the boat, two-thirds of them incomers to the town. Evan Jones thinks they're all good lads doing a good job. Through the years that's been the pinnacle of praise from one member of this most modest of callings to another, and Mr Jones is a bit wary of those newcomers with no family tradition of lifeboat service behind them who want to cut a dash. 'Some of these lads come down at the weekend and wear their bloody jerseys with "RNLI" on their chests, and their little badges, and do a lot of talking in the pub about what they've done. In my day we couldn't afford any of that gear. I went to the boat when I started in my working jersey and boots. People just knew you as a lifeboatman, not as a hero; and that's how you thought of yourself.'

Mr Jones was not only coxswain of the lifeboat; he was also Barmouth's harbourmaster for many years. In his lifetime he has seen the Barmouth fishing industry follow the same pattern of decline as everywhere else – the herring fleet between the wars gradually losing its stocks in the northern part of Cardigan Bay, the lobsters being fished out after the Second World War, the 1970s' boom in scallop fishing to the south when beam trawlers came from all over and articulated lorries rushed the catch away to market until they'd sucked the beds empty. Now there are five boats, one fifty-foot trawler for scallops and the others for lobster. As in almost every small harbour round Britain's coasts, it's sea-fishing trips for visitors that subsidize the meagre commercial fishing available to small boats. As a boy, Evan Jones helped on the ferries that worked over the estuary mouth from Fairbourne. Sheep would be brought over to the slaughterhouse in Barmouth, lying in the boats with their legs tied together or swimming alongside while the ferrymen held them up to prevent their waterlogged fleeces taking them to the bottom. The hotels in those days were full of well-to-do holidaymakers who came by railway and stayed for a month or more with their children and nannies. Now they come by car, most for a day or a weekend. The people who do stay for long periods are those who have turned the picturesque cottages of Old Barmouth into holiday homes. Most of the little grocers, bakers and butchers that Barmouth once supported have gone out of business, unable to compete with the holiday homers' carloads of provisions bought cheaply in the city supermarkets and brought down to the freezers in their cottages. Many of those old-fashioned family-run food shops have become trinket emporia in response to the demands of the casual day-visitors.

The town's economy has been changed, though not necessarily harmed; but the same can't be said of its traditions, to Evan Jones's regret. 'One change since I was a boy is that you hear very little Welsh spoken. People of my generation prefer to speak Welsh to each other, but there's not so many of us around as there were. And there's no singing in the pubs like there used to be. In those days, put two or three lads together in a bar and you'd got a choir.'

Here around the quay are gathered the old buildings of Barmouth: the little round stone lock-up built in 1834 to cope with drunken sailors from the incoming boats; the early-nineteenth-century bath house (now a café, run by a Birmingham refugee); Pen-y-cei, with its outside stone staircase, which the Lifeboat Museum shares with the harbourmaster's office; Ty Gwyn y Bermo a little further along, five centuries old at least, where young Henry Tudor – or perhaps his uncle, Jasper – is supposed to have hidden out while planning the campaign that brought him the crown of England at the Battle of Bosworth.

Here below the old town's cottages, in this small enclave of their tradition, the born-and-bred inhabitants of Barmouth come to chat – in Welsh – and look at the boats. If they admit to a sense of being part of a culture under siege, it's balanced with a good dose of realism. Barmouth makes a big effort to accommodate the habits and tastes of its visitors from across the border as much as those from nearer at hand. There's a small funfair packed neatly into the centre of the seafront to liven the evenings, and plenty of souvenir shops – too many to please Evan Jones and his contemporaries. But there's also an excellent museum on the quay, expeditions based on the town for would-be conquerors of Plynlimmon, Snowdon and Cadair Idris, canoeing lessons and outings, the thriving Merioneth Yacht Club, an Arts Festival in September featuring items from as broad a spectrum as Welsh folk-music, Harold Pinter plays, ballet, Beethoven, the Midland Youth Jazz Orchestra and the Barmouth WI tea-party. Such aspects of modern-day Barmouth life may be well and truly infiltrated by incomers, but these tread rather more lightly nowadays than did the improving Ruskins and A.R.s of Victorian times.

'We can put up with all this change,' said the lady behind the display in the Lifeboat Museum. 'It may not be the old Barmouth we knew as children, but I'll tell you something – a lot of people have forgotten just how dull this place used to be in the winter, with never a new face. What would Barmouth be today without the visitors? A dead little town, falling to pieces, in a beautiful setting – that's what would have become of us.'

NORTH-WEST

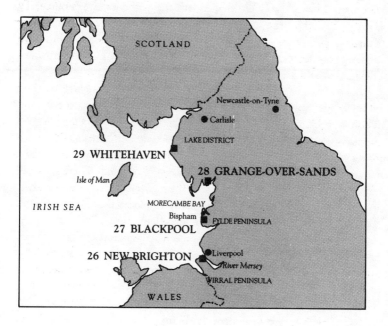

26. New Brighton

The best thing about New Brighton in the 1960s was how easy it was to get there from Liverpool. A short stroll down to the ferry from the dockland terraced houses, twenty minutes across the Mersey, and there you were. Liverpool was throbbing with the excitement of Merseybeat, and the rock fans could be relied on to pack the ferries when their idols were playing New Brighton.

NEMS Enterprises present

LITTLE RICHARD

at the

TOWER

Friday 12 Oct 1962: 7.30 to 1.00 a.m.

*

**with a sensational line-up of 10
Top British Rock Groups including**

THE BEATLES

**The Greatest Rock Night
Ever Presented on Merseyside*

Those were the days. Prestige was what Brian Epstein was after for his four mop-tops, with 'Love Me Do' about to be released: and New Brighton's Tower Ballroom had it. One of the most popular dance halls in the area, sited in Liverpool's own 'Blackpool on the Mersey', there was no better place for an up-and-coming group to top a supporting bill.

Many of the fans would be back the next day, Saturday, rowdying around the funfair in the Tower's pleasure-grounds or chasing along the sandy river beach among the day-tripping families. New Brighton was laid out to give you what you wanted: sand, promenade strolls, seaside food and entertainment, river cruises on board the *Royal Iris*. A day out in New Brighton was a Liverpool tradition, an escape to space and sea-breezes from the cramped terraces of dockland. New Brighton was old hat in many ways, not much changed since grandfather's time; but at least you could put the width of the Mersey between you and everyday life for a few hours.

Not that New Brighton was exactly the place for peace and quiet; it hadn't been like that since the Bank Holiday Act of 1871 gave everyone a taste and the means for a good day out. Six ferries were kept at full stretch on good weekends, and half a million people might come. A new drummer had joined the Beatles a couple of months before that Little Richard show in 1962, and he had some wild stories to tell of his days as a barman on the New Brighton ferries. At the time Ringo was pulling pints, the afternoon trips could get pretty rough. Hard Liverpool Teds would climb on board at three o'clock closing time, drink all afternoon in the floating bars and stagger off on to New Brighton pier as the pubs were opening again. The funfair and seafront were not the places to stare too long at anyone at such times. But the weight of the generations, the sensible families enjoying the beach, usually acted as a brake on the roughest customers – as did the likelihood of having your excesses reported to your father by someone from your street who had been keeping an eye on you.

The New Brighton promenade is a poignant place to stand today. The view across the Mersey hasn't changed a great deal since the 1960s, at first glance anyway. The dock cranes seldom move and there are few ships on the river, but the red-brick Victorian warehouses and long runs of stained sea-wall still front the thousands of ranked terrace houses. Up the river, the Liver Birds still stand on their pinnacles as landmarks for incoming sailors. From south to north, Toxteth to Crosby, there's eight long miles of waterfront laid out in front of you, and another four of seashore up to the sandy nose of Formby Point. You don't have to know much about the decline of Britain's greatest port to see something amiss in the enormous silence and motionlessness of Merseyside. And the disease is catching. To understand why the New Brighton dog-walkers and shopkeepers are so avid for conversation about the way things used to be here, you only have to stand by the pierhead on a hot summer weekday and look around you. One or two parked cars, a couple of old men leaning over the promenade railings, a group of lads larking in the Marine Lake on the shore – that's the sum total of animation in today's New Brighton.

Rounding the point of land at Perch Rock where the Mersey meets Liverpool Bay, and walking west along the seafront, the eeriness of the scene grows stronger. There are fine hotels rusting away, the empty tidiness of the Victoria Gardens next to the shabby Floral Pavilion theatre with its plastic lettering chipped and hanging. Then two great symbols of 1930s' prosperity and optimism, lime-green Wilkie's Covered Fairground amusement hall and the bright white Lido swimming baths – 3,000 capacity – both wonderful and contrasting examples of art deco at its most confident, and both clanging with inactivity. The Promenade that leads on into the distance might have been built for the triumphal entry of an army, red-surfaced, thirty or forty feet wide, as straight as an arrow. It looks as if most of Liverpool could stroll there and still have elbow room. But there's only the occasional cyclist or jogger looking at the wading birds at low tide. On a sunny weekend the day-visitors who come to use the slot machines and swimming pool do perk things up a bit. But they ought to be here in their thousands in the middle of Wakes Week when most of Lancashire has closed and come away on holiday. Wherever those holidaymakers are, it isn't here.

Some of the landmarks of that old golden New Brighton can still be made out from the Liverpool shore – Wilkie's Fairground and the Lido: Fort Perch Rock, 'Gibraltar of the Mersey', built in 1827 to guard the rivermouth and standing massively out in the sea along with its lighthouse: the Red Noses, sandstone outcrops that marked the shoreline before the promenade was built in the 1930s. It's at the angle of land where the Mersey joins the sea, the place where everyone came ashore, that the resort's vitality has disappeared along with its most characteristic symbols. Where the pier and landing stage jutted out into the river is a hole; where the Tower buildings and funfair stood there's now a blank, grassy bank sloping up to a new housing estate.

'Of course, the old tower came down in the 1920s,' George told me as we watched his mongrel dog digging in the bank. 'About a hundred feet higher than Blackpool's. I can just about remember it as a kid.' He kicked away the grass to reveal a sawn-off stump of iron. 'That's one of its legs. They went down sixty feet into the rock. The ballroom in that place had a sprung floor. It was beautiful. My uncle worked there as a brickie when they built it, and he took me down under the floor one day in a little five-foot space. Do you know, that whole floor was on hundreds of leaf springs, right across. We watched someone walking over above us, and you could see their tracks making each part tremble as they went over it. But that floor could hold 3,000. You could dance all night on it and never get tired.

'Down by the prom there were bobby-horses, a mermaid show – a Figure of Eight Railway over here. I used to come over on the ferry every Saturday and Sunday with the family. Two bob it cost us in them days. Lovely. All Liverpool used to come over on the boats. There used to be a one-legged diver waiting for them up the end of the pier – oh, as high as that crane. He'd get a crowd around and then make his dive, down like an arrow into the river. Then he'd hold out a big bag on a pole for their pennies. He made a bomb, that man.

'My sister had a fortune-telling booth in the funfair, and my wife's cousin had a shooting gallery over there. The whole family worked here at one time or another. You could look down at the end of the day, and it was nothing strange to see them queueing ten deep for a mile right down the prom to catch the late ferries back to Liverpool. Now it's just dead. Dead.'

More even than the familiar buildings, it's the noise, movement and life of the crowds of Liverpool working-class day trippers that New Brighton people miss. New Brighton started out in the 1830s as a speculation by a retired merchant, James Atherton, who bought up 170 acres of sand dunes and marsh to create 'a most agreeable and desirable place of resort to the Nobility and Gentry of all the neighbouring counties'. There was never much chance of New Brighton staying that way once the railways had arrived and Liverpool's workers were free to come across on their newly established days off. When Francis Kilvert of Clyro came here on 20 June 1872, having boarded a ferry 'in dancing spirits', he noted that 'there are beautiful sands stretching for miles along the coast and the woods wave green down to the salt water's edge'. Kilvert found the sands covered in 'middle-class Liverpool folks and children out for a holiday', and had some fun at the expense of the riders of hired horses, 'pitiable objects, bumping up and down upon their saddles like flour sacks . . . The ladies as a rule rode without riding habits and with crinolines. The effect was striking.'

Ah, the laughable Northerners, aping the pastimes of cultured folk. But within twenty years that foreshore was lined with a collection of cheap stalls and eating houses known as the Ham & Egg Parade.

'The Ham & Egg Parade!' George winked at me. 'Well, now. My uncle fought in the Boer War, and he said that when soldiers out in South Africa found out where he was from, the first thing they'd talk about was the Ham & Egg Parade. You see, there was brothels in the backs of those little shops. The girls would stand out on the prom and tug young men by the sleeve. Everyone knew it. My word, yes. So naturally they pulled it down.'

Part of New Brighton's cleaning-up act was the building between the wars of the Marine Promenade along the sea frontage of the resort. It served a double purpose as both promenade and anti-erosion defence. The dunes of this shore badly needed protection from the sea, trampled as they had been by a century's visitors. But in making the Marine Promenade, New Brighton cut its own throat – a long suicide, but a sure one. Sand allows the sea to surge in and out, depositing more sand. Concrete repels both sea and sand. The force of the tides was redirected along the new defences and into the mouth of the already narrow Mersey. Within a couple of decades the sea-wall was being eaten away by the suction. More defences were put out, ribbed barriers off shore that broke up the tide before it could reach the wall. More power was diverted into the Mersey channel when the tide was making: more power came sucking out on the ebb.

What happened to New Brighton's beaches, both sea and river, should have been foreseen. Away went the precious sand, to form useless bars out in the water: and away went the families to Formby and Southport. New docks were built directly across the Mersey at Seaforth, narrowing the river still further. Out went more sand, and out went more customers. Today the river beach where George and his childhood friends would jump over the promenade railings on to a carpet of thick, soft sand is a hard stretch of the underlying mud rock, now exposed. The fossilized mud looks beautiful – swirls of grey, purple, blue and pink – but it's no use to families with children. Round the corner, the Liverpool Bay beach has shrunk to a tiny crescent of litter-strewn sand in the shelter of Fort Perch Rock.

But there was another effect of the changed tide that was even more devastating for New Brighton. Below the level of the mud rock at the edge of the Mersey, the outgoing sand and silt had been piling up under the ferries' landing-stage beside the amusement pier. By 1971 the ferries could no longer get close enough to land their passengers, and that life-line to

207

the spenders of Liverpool was cut. Two years later the pier itself was closed down, its legs rotted and weakened beyond repair. Here the Beatles had played in their pre-Hamburg rough-and-ready days for thirty bob in the dance-hall pavilion set half-way along the pier above the river. Without the ferries the Merseysiders' favourite resort began to curl up and die. By now Liverpool was hard hit by recession, most of its workers feeling the pinch. The old dockland communities were dissolving, their inhabitants being resettled on huge, bleak estates far away from the waterfront. There were tunnels under the Mersey, but many Liverpool people couldn't afford to run a car. There seemed no point in taking the whole family on the long journey by public transport from the new estates down to the ferry still running three miles upriver, then up the other side to a beachless New Brighton, when you could reach the sands of Formby and Southport just as quickly and cheaply. The Tower ballroom had burned down in 1969, the pier was gone. Now the funfair closed, starved of custom. That whole lively, rowdy corner of the river was suddenly dead.

Not everyone in New Brighton was sorry to see it go. Up above the hurly-burly of the shore, the smart houses of the Victorian commuter town stand well spaced in large gardens. From the western end of Marine Promenade there's a strong resemblance to Rye in Sussex, in the way they rise to crown the hill with their red-tiled roofs and white walls. Here is the pleasant, comfortable middle-class Wirral resort that James Atherton had in mind when he issued his prospectus for New Brighton. And from here come the crossest of the letters to the *Wallasey News* about Victoria Road.

In its present listless, hangdog state the New Brighton waterfront is a sitting target for speculators, and Victoria Road is the outward and visible sign of its vulnerability. The road rises directly from the pierhead up the hill, a thriving street of shops, pubs, bingo halls and cinemas, until some smart ideas for its future went wrong. These places are not just closed down and derelict; their paintwork, plaster and even architectural details are bleaching out into an awful grey-white blankness, streaked with rust dribbles. The grocery shops and tobacconist's that still survive among these pale shells look unnaturally bright and clean by comparison. Victoria Road is literally fading away. A few years ago there were plans for it to become a shining example of old into new, a street of shopping arcades built at first-floor level like The Rows in Chester. But the speculator put his money into Liverpool's dockland Garden Festival and went bust – after he had bought the bottom end of Victoria Road. There have been other grand schemes, too, notably one to turn the whole length of Marine Promenade into a gigantic Disney World funfair. But the money just isn't there.

At present New Brighton is at the bottom of its trough. The town is exhibiting all the signs of depression: pessimistic, resigned, unable to imagine better times or to appreciate its own good points.

'Who wants to come to New Brighton these days?' shrugged the lady behind the newsagent's counter in Victoria Road. 'It's a mess. What's the point of coming all this way and finding a place like New Brighton is today at the end of your journey? People don't want *this* any more – they want plenty of fun and a bit of class. I see people walking up this road and looking around, and you can hear them thinking: "Oo, what a scruffy old place. I'm glad I don't live here." The trouble is, *we* do.'

Two hundred yards above her shop, where Atherton Street crosses Victoria Road by the railway station, there's a demarcation line between downtown and uptown New Brighton. Below the line it's decay and depression: above the line stands the magnificent, enormous Hotel Victoria with a plush bar as big as a ballroom where dwellers on the middle-class heights sit and look out over one of the best seaport panoramas in the country. With a view like that on its doorstep, the Wirral's golf courses and green spaces at its back and fine, extravagant architecture in its heart, there must be brighter days ahead for Liverpool's old resort. At present they are dredging sand from the banks out in the bay and dumping it back under the sea-wall to re-create the beach that vanished. If they can get it to stick, New Brighton could be in business again. If they get the ferries going again. If someone comes up with some money. If New Brighton's seafront folk can come up with a few smiles.

27. Blackpool

Mavis, puffing a fag as she waits at the tram station at Bispham, has been coming to Blackpool with her husband three times a year for the past thirty years. She wouldn't dream of going abroad and doesn't care for coach trips, so it has to be Blackpool. Not that Mavis and Arthur use the great glaring town centre much – just the occasional tram ride down to the cheap food and clothes shops to stock up for their return home to Manchester.

'Bispham's nice. You don't get all that hurly-burly and litter out here. We stick to the same lodging, with Mr Ackroyd – he's a beltin' feller. Seventy pounds a week all in, and tea and biscuits when you want them. Blackpool's changed since we've been coming. It's too flashy along the seafront now. We feel right at home in Bispham.'

Bispham's wide main street runs inland opposite the tram station, lined with neat brick shops and houses – groceries, furniture shops, cafés, poodle parlours, estate agents. It's about the nearest you can be to Blackpool and still live a normal life. Pensioners bike along the roads with shopping baskets perched on their handlebars. There's not a flashing light to be seen, not a drunken shout or over-excited shriek to be heard. People come to Bispham for the peace and quiet, while still rubbing shoulders with all that hurly-burly, three miles to the south. The 'sandgrown 'uns' (born-and-bred Blackpool people) don't have a bad word to say about Bispham's visitors, unlike some others they could name. Bispham was a thriving clifftop village 200 years ago when 'Blackpoole' was just a muddy mere by the shore, and in the locals' eyes the relationship hasn't really changed since then.

The south-going tram comes rattling into Bispham Station. There's grime on its green-and-cream paintwork, rust patches on its body and salt spray tracks down its windows. The woman driver exchanges her ritual chant with each passenger in turn:

'Yes, please?'

'Starr Gate, please.'

'Eighty pence, please . . . thank you!'

The old workhorse moans up a rising scale as it jerks off down the tracks. It rocks and swerves along, clacking over the rail joints, like a cross between a branch-line train, a country bus and a London tube. The passengers bounce gently up and down in unison on the old hard seats as they chat or look out of the smeary windows. The neat suburban streets of Bispham fall behind, replaced by more and more small hotels as the tram approaches the North Shore cliffs. It passes the enormous Miners' Convalescent Home, set back like a sizeable chunk of Versailles over a bank with 'MCH' picked out in raised letters of grass. On the seaward side a little further down is the curlicue-encrusted lift entrance down to The Cabin. Here in the early nineteenth century the gypsies had their encampment; but as Blackpool began to swell, they were pushed out to make way for the favourite pleasure spot of Uncle Tom's Cabin with its fairground, pavilion, refreshment stalls and *camera obscura*. When the sea claimed Uncle Tom's Cabin from these unstable clay cliffs, a new and even better version quickly replaced it.

Now the grand, overblown, splendid hotels of the North Shore pass the windows of the tram – the Cliffs Hotel, a plums-and-custard mixture of art deco and classical Greece; the modern Pembroke like a purple factory; the great conference-attracting pile of the Imperial, flags flying. Splashland goes by in yellow art deco blocks, its wall gripped by the curling tube down which the customers scream in the agonies of the Knucklebuster waterslide. The tram passengers shuffle along their seats to squeeze newcomers in as the tram slopes down to Promenade level by the cast-iron shopping arcade under Butlin's elaborate monstrosity of a hotel. Back in 1795, when Bailey's Hotel stood here, you could get full bed and board for 3s. 4d. a day and enjoy an evening among those holiday pioneers whose 'hilarity and wit are enlivened by the superiority of the viands and the wine'. A few bumpy yards more, and here we are on Central Beach where Roberts' Oyster Rooms stand opposite the tram-stop, still in business, the name embossed along the front wall, a true touch of 'Old Blackpool'. The tram halts with a wheeze of folding doors to let half its cargo off, then sets off again along the loud delights of the Golden Mile.

Here on this narrow strip of shore is everything you think of when you think of Blackpool. On your right stretch out the famous sands, intersected by the three piers, their deckings crammed high with pavilions, slot-machine halls, photographers and funfair rides. Sandcastles, donkey rides, paddling – it all still goes on down there on the yellow beach between the piers. Middle-aged couples stroll slowly along the wide Promenade above the sands, old folk sit out of the wind in the ornate shelters. The trams ply up and down, some (like this one) shabby and grubby, others revitalized veterans in shining new paint or up-to-date versions shaped like boats and outlined in twinkling lights. Beside the tram-tracks stand the carriage horses, heads resignedly down, their drivers chatting and joking as they wait for custom.

Over on the other side of the Prom runs the lucky rainbow of the Golden Mile. It sprouted here when the stall-holders and cheapjacks were uprooted from their beach strongholds by Blackpool Corporation in Victorian times. Here the glitter-and-glory tradition of Blackpool grew up and thrived in the town's heyday, and here it bravely continues. Those early visitors in the 1750s put up at Forshaw's Hotel on the corner of Talbot Square where the New Clifton Hotel now stands. In those days the Promenade was just a strip of grass above the beach, where it was the custom for health-recruiting strollers to ignore the inmates of rival hotels. Once the textile barons of Lancashire had discovered Blackpool, however, health gave way to wealth; and when the railway reached the town in 1846 the floodgates were open to allcomers. The New Hotel, the Beach Hotel, the Prince of Wales Baths and Theatre, the Alhambra with its 3,000-seat theatre, the Grand Pavilion, the Aquarium and Menagerie, the Palace – the pleasure domes and hotels jostled, outdid and replaced one another along the magnetic mile. If you tired of the Winter Gardens' skating rink, theatre, music hall, ballet, floral gardens, switchback railway and fairy grotto, you could take up the invitation issued by the flamboyant manager, William Holland, to 'come to the Winter Gardens and spit on Bill Holland's 100-Guinea Carpet!' In 1894 the seal was set on Blackpool's pre-eminence as the trippers' paradise when the 518-foot Blackpool Tower was put up, the centrepiece and symbol of the whole fantasy. This was the place for a Rochdale or Bolton or Blackburn mill-hand and his family to step out of their everyday existence for a few precious days and spend, eat and drink like lords and ladies – a sweetener for another year's drudgery. To accommodate them, the famed and feared Blackpool landlady came into being, her lair the parallel streets of cheap boarding houses behind the shining face of the Promenade. On into the 1920s and '30s the Blackpool boom continued, as buses, charabancs and private cars helped the trains to bring in the holidaymakers for their short and rowdy visits and the retired couples for the rest of their lives. Building accelerated inland, and the green fields beyond the North Shore were tamed by bricks and mortar until Blackpool could lay its cheery hand on the reluctant shoulder of Bispham village.

The Golden Mile is an unsettling, agitating sort of place, even from the comparative security of a Blackpool tram. The incredible noise comes booming in as you travel down the Promenade: not just the squealing and shouting of any resort seafront on a sunny day, but an ever-changing assault of entreaties, directions and encouragement hurled out of the slot-machine halls and fun parks. Amplified callers have replaced the old barkers as rock 'n' roll replaced skiffle – infinitely more effective, and infinitely more intrusive. There's no hiding place for the ear; and no retreat for the eye, either. From the galleried red bulk of the Tower building to the art deco Pricebusters store to the car park architecture of Coral Island amusement arcade to the modern starkness of the Golden Mile Centre, the eye jerks along, whisked from one demand to the next with no rest and no time to take in what each has to offer. Louis Tussaud's – the Jager Bier Keller – Jimmy Tattoo Artist – It's Here: Chris's New Bingo! – Cheap 'n' Cheerful Gift Shop – Foxhall Café: flights of balloons, stacks of pink rock, beach hats, souvenir mugs, fluorescent green toy animals. It's a relief when the small hotels begin again, flank to flank along the Promenade towards the South Shore.

The showman's heart of Blackpool still beats in the Golden Mile. All that colour, all those trinkets, all those crashing appeals to swap money for fun were Blackpool's life-blood from the start, and still are. Here you can plunge in and let the everyday world go hang. When you bring your money to Blackpool you know exactly what you're going to find – that's why you come. Blackpool's predictability is its strongest asset. But predictability has its drawbacks for a holiday town these days, especially for one that has little else to offer its visitors but that glittering show.

Blackpool may not have changed since those golden years of the seaside resort, but the demands of holidaymakers have. The tourists still come flocking in – well over one in ten Britons visits Blackpool every year. The up-to-date laser-operated Illuminations, five miles of them, still pack the boarding houses solid every autumn. Between them the visitors spend hundreds of millions of pounds. But most of them are chips off the old traditional bedrock on which the town's prosperity has always rested: the elderly folk like Mavis and Arthur who come because that's what they've always done; families from the North, the Midlands and Scotland who arrive by train or coach, having saved hard and painfully, prepared to spend hard and quickly. Few foreign visitors put Blackpool on their lists, few younger and better-off holidaymakers choose Blackpool if they can afford to go abroad to get what the town can't offer: guaranteed sunshine, cheap wine and exotic surroundings. Outside Blackpool itself, in the flat Fylde peninsula that surrounds the town, there's little in the way of lovely countryside or historic houses and castles, little variety in the landscape. In the old days it was just a stretch of country that had to be got through before the train arrived in Blackpool. No one cared very much what it looked like; all eyes and hearts were fixed forward on the seaside. But these days it won't really do.

'Ugly, foolish and flimsy,' growled Paul Theroux in *The Kingdom by the Sea*, '. . . perfectly reflected in the swollen guts and unhealthy fat of its beer-guzzling visitors – eight million in the summer, when Lancashire closed to come here and belch.' When this sort of thing gets written about Blackpool, the town can no longer afford just to jingle its money bags in reply. In 1972 the Corporation commissioned a survey of its visitors and what they really thought of Blackpool. The results confirmed what everyone could sense, that the old Box of Delights was looking rather empty. There was a tremendous feeling of loyalty: more than half the visitors questioned had come to Blackpool ten times or more. The criticisms, on the other hand, pinpointed just where it was failing as a modern resort: too loud, too flashy, too crowded, too expensive; polluted, tatty, isolated; old-fashioned and backward-looking; less warm-hearted than in the old days. The report on the survey had various remedies to suggest. Blackpool should attract more short-break weekenders, should acquire more caravan parks and self-catering accommodation, should promote itself as the place to stop over for foreign tourists on a car trip through Britain. But, concluded the report, 'Blackpool's strong identity and appeal as a lively resort calls for enhancement of what it already possesses: it needs to continue to be good at what it is.'

Away from the seafront are a few attractions that the town doesn't over-publicize. The antithesis of the Golden Mile is Stanley Park, tucked away a couple of miles inland. Here grandfathers kneel by ponds with their grand-daughters, students from the Blackpool schools and colleges come sketching, old ladies sit in twos and threes on the benches for a chat and a bask. There are little clipped and labelled exhibition hedgerows, water gardens, woodlands, a well-used bowling green and a formally laid-out circular Italian garden at the heart of the park. Its fish-pool, fountain and statues are overlooked by an enormous old café of the Nuremburg Rally school of architecture. Stanley Park is lovely. But it doesn't have squeal appeal.

Beyond the South Pier sprawls Blackpool's chief bid for future survival, the 'swinging, spinning, sliding, swirling, sensational PLEASURE BEACH!!!' The tram groans to a halt outside 'Europe's Greatest Amusement Park' and the folding doors wheeze back. 'Have a nice time, love,' smiles the driver. She lets in the lever and the dusty old green-and-cream rattletrap whines off, leaving you to be sucked through the entrance into the Pleasure Beach's heartless whirlpool. Here, as along all of Blackpool's seafront, things are just as they have always been, only more so. The South Shore was always the raffish end of the town, the kind of place where a group of wild lads would go to get drunk, thrilled, cheated and laid. That's exactly its function these days, though under a glossier coating. It's a riotous teenagers' paradise *par excellence*; but toddlers come here, too, for a rainy afternoon's roundabouting, and so do mob-handed factory outings for a chicken dinner and a rude show. Through the fog of sensation so aggressively spread round the Pleasure Beach a few details stand out – the nerve-scraping irritation of the manic mechanical laughter from outside the Fun House; the all-pervading hot sweet scent of candy-floss; the rapt faces of children queueing for the most terrifying rides, watching their doom approach; the patience and good nature of the souvenir-stall ladies. Round and over and under the walkways of Funshineland loop the tracks of the rides. Many are seriously frightening and carry notices warning off those with bad backs or hearts or other 'physical limitations' such as lack of youth – these rides are reserved for the master race. Little cut-out manikins stand by the entrances – 'If you are not as tall as me you cannot ride.'

The apotheosis of Pleasure Beach macho is the Revolution, a red-painted vertical loop of track in which for one sickening second the riders hurtle upside-down in their open cars, screaming their heads off. A line of notices up the entrance stairs turns the tension screw:

'From this point onwards YOU are on YOUR OWN!'

'This is one experience you will NEVER forget!'

'We wish you GOOD LUCK!'

There must be a wonderful inverted view over Blackpool from the apex of the curve, but no one ever sees it – G-force and terror clench all eyes shut. You do it forwards, then backwards. At the exit stands a 'Test your Scareability Now' machine, measuring your rate of heartbeat and grading the results from the coveted 'Hello Supercool!' down to the humiliation of 'Is That Just Ants In Your Pants?'

Revolving slowly 160 feet in the air inside the perspex chamber of the Space Tower, you get a staggering view over all Blackpool – piers, sands and Golden Mile, the red-brick streets crowding away inland behind the seafront, the Tower's crimson finger and the grand hotels climbing the North Shore cliffs towards distant Bispham. Below you, the Pleasure Beach flashes, whirls and shouts, a bright bank in which the town has invested most of its future survival. The old barker is still enthusiastic. For the moment, with a good deal of sweat and stridency, he's just about holding the attention of his loyal public. But the uncommitted customers are developing a taste for the sweets of very different stalls in the tourist fairground.

28. Grange-over-Sands

A narrow footpath leaves the Windermere Road just north of Grange-over-Sands and climbs steeply up between the ash, beech and yew trees of Eggerslack Wood to run out on to the windy top of Hampsfell. If you can resist the temptation to look around until you have reached the little hospice on the summit and have climbed its outside steps on to the roof, the view will transfix you. Thirty miles to the north rise the blue outlines of Lakeland's most famous fells: Scafell, Bow Fell, Skiddaw, Helvellyn. Swinging round eastward, you look over High Street and Shap Fell down to the great humps of Whernside and Ingleborough at the edge of North Yorkshire, then south to the grey blobs of Lancaster and Morecambe. The long Fylde coast runs away through Fleetwood to the pencil line of Blackpool Tower, with a glimpse far beyond on the clearest days into Wales to the white cap of Snowdon nearly 100 miles away; and, off in the west across the Irish Sea, another mountain tip – Snaefell in the Isle of Man. It's a panorama that lays the north-west of England out for inspection at your feet, a view to make you late for whatever else you'd planned to do this day. But one piece of the jigsaw is missing. Hidden from sight below the green brow of Eggerslack Wood, Grange-over-Sands sits tucked modestly into the side of Morecambe Bay, quite happy not to be noticed.

An enormous sweep of flat sands knits together the view from south to east, seamed across with the silver curves of watercourses and sprinkled with congregations of wading birds and geese. If you have a couple of hours to spend up here on Hampsfell, you can watch the sea come sliding in to reclaim all this territory as the bay rivers swell and spill over, swallowing the sand-spits one by one until the whole flat tongue of sand between Silverdale and Grange has reverted from land to water. The birds fly from one roost to another, delaying the inevitable moment when they will have to give up the game and make off for the marshy fields inland. The rusty old tractors of the fluke fishermen rock away shorewards through the widening pools, and walkers in the bay quicken their stride. The middle of Morecambe Bay is not a good place to be caught by a rising tide.

Clinging to the eastern side of the Cartmel Peninsula and cut off from mainland Lancashire by the long tail of the River Kent, Grange stayed in its little corner down the centuries, undeveloped but far from lonely. Those wide sands on its doorstep – 117 square miles of them exposed at low tide – yielded flatfish, cockles, mussels and shrimps for the fishermen of the hamlet; they also provided the shortest way (if not the safest) of getting from southern Cumberland to Lancaster. By carriage and cart, on horse-back and on foot, the travellers arrived at Kents Bank, Grange's neigh-bouring hamlet, to call at Cart Lane for the guide and set out across those seven or eight treacherous miles of shifting watercourses, sinking holes and quicksands. The sand guides, established shortly after the Norman Con-quest and still in action today, marked out the safe routes across the bay with sprigs of laurel known as 'brobs' – and woe betide travellers foolhardy enough to go it alone. Their bodies ended up in the graveyards of local churches, their belongings deep under the sands, to be disgorged on the shore months afterwards. Hundreds of reckless walkers and riders decided to dispense with the services of the guide, and ended their lives in the quicksands and tide races. During the last century one young couple, due to be married the following day, were drowned, along with their seven companions, when their cart tipped over in the notorious Black Scar hole. The cart was salvaged, and local people continued to ride across the bay in it – until, several years after the accident, twelve young men took it out for a trip over the sands to Lancaster Fair. As they reached Black Scar, over went the cart again and all twelve were sucked down to their deaths.

It's not so easy these days to get into trouble on Morecambe Sands. Cedric Robinson, the energetic Sands Guide who lives, as his forerunners did, near the shore at Guide's Farm where Grange meets Kents Bank, keeps a telescope in the house trained out into the bay to give him good warning of anyone in difficulties. The crossings of the sands which he leads several times a year bring thousands of visitors to Grange. Others come with binoculars and bird-books to revel in the bird life of the bay, an enormous larder of shellfish and invertebrate creatures for what is claimed to be the largest concentration of wading birds in Britain. At almost any time you can spot dunlin, curlew, turnstone, lapwing and the red-billed oystercatchers which have been known to cram up to 150 cockles into their crops at one sitting. Whimbrels arrive in winter, and bar-tailed godwits stay for most of the year except during the summer months. Other visitors are greenshank, ruff, sandpiper and stint. Spoonbills have been seen out on the sands. All told, there are probably upwards of 150,000 waders in winter, as well as gulls, cormorants, geese and ducks, getting to grips with the great food store of Morecambe Bay and attracting bird-watchers to Grange and the other villages around the coastline.

A winter's day in Grange is likely to be far less harsh an experience than in most other places in this part of England. Sheltered by Hampsfell from north and west winds, fronted by the vast humidifier of Morecambe Bay, encircled at a convenient distance by mountains which catch all but a few inches of each winter's snow, the village relaxes in its mild climate like a warm bath. All sorts of exotic plants grow in and around Grange, among them such wonderful items as strawberry trees, pocket-handkerchief trees, weeping ash and weeping elm, Indian bean trees, Jerusalem sage and New Zealand hemp. One field on the outskirts of the village was surveyed by local naturalists, who found fifty species of meadow plants, including six kinds of orchid. In summer, Grange's ornamental gardens soothe you with their scents and colours, until sitting down on a bench becomes a declaration of intent to snooze the afternoon away. You'll be in good company, however, for Grange is full of snoozers. That mild climate, the old-fashioned little shops and tearooms, the promenade above the bay and the wooded slopes clustering all round the village attract holidaymakers sick of seaside noise and crowds. You can get all that till it chokes you over in Morecambe or down in Blackpool; in Grange the clock turns back a century and the blood pressure falls in sympathy. There's a settled rhythm to the day here: a swim in the open-air pool that stands out over the sands, a stroll past the rockeries of the Promenade, a visit to feed the ducks in the ornamental gardens, tea in one of the cafés under the ornate cast-iron awning of Yewbarrow Terrace. 'Not fast nor boisterous nor overcrowded like some places one might name . . . its attractions are situation, walks, excursions, dry soil and mild climate' – that was Grange in 1867, but the description might have been written yesterday. As a small place well off the usual Lake District tourist track, Grange's appeal as a gentle, clean, unflustering haven for seekers after peace and quiet is vital to its prosperity. The Grange Hotel puts on 'Victorian Afternoon Tea'. The tourist brochure murmurs seductively of 'an Edwardian flavour'. But northern Victorians did not stop short at gentility. It was their hard-headedness and eye for brass that ushered in Grange's biggest time of upheaval on the back of the Furness Railway.

Visitors had been coming to the village on the sands for fresh air and saltwater bathing (when the tide was in) since the early years of the nineteenth century, but until the 1850s they found a place not much affected by the seaside boom bursting out all over Britain. The Crown Hotel had opened in 1789, and there were lodgings to be had in other parts of the village; but Grange was still a place for those in the know, left isolated in its peninsular fortress when the new turnpikes had been built further north. The shoreline ran well inland of its present position, high tide lapping where Yewbarrow Terrace now stands. The iron rings set into the pavement under the awning of the terrace are said by locals to be the old mooring rings for the fishermen's boats. There was only one source of fresh water, a well in the marshy area on the shore known as Grange Bog. Most goods had to be brought into Grange down steep lanes on the cart of Peggy Keith, the 'formidable old pipe-smoking carrier'.

In 1857 came the Furness Railway. Planned as an outlet for the iron ore of West Cumberland, the railway's other potential as a shifter of tourists was too good to be ignored. Grange's tin-hut station was soon replaced by the beautiful, solid little building that stands today on the northern edge of the village, its Victorian atmosphere enhanced by the elaborate ends of the platform benches with their grape-munching squirrels among cast-iron leaves, and by the steam trains that come puffing through from the Steamtown museum at Carnforth. The arrival of the railway brought Grange within reach of holidaymakers in Lakeland and the Morecambe coastline, and cotton barons from the Lancashire textile towns began to plan their retirement residences here. Solid, respectable villas went up inland and along the shore, and more hotels were built. The railway company lent £14,000 in 1866 for the building of the Grange Hotel directly opposite the station, and also financed the building of the Promenade along the shore below the village. The Hazelwood Hydro (now the Cumbria Grand Hotel), a great pile of gables and chimneys, appeared in 1880 among the trees to the north of the station as another of the pegs from which Grange hung its promise of comfort, quiet and good health. Grange Bog and its freshwater well vanished under the carefully laid-out Ornamental Gardens. Gentility arrived; and so did the dreaded day-trippers, venturing over the bay on steamers from Morecambe to dis-embark at two newly built piers and yawn away the afternoon complaining about the lack of excitement in Grange. At least there was a local joke to smile about, generated by the premises in Main Street of Mr Mudd the fishmonger –

'I say, I say, I say! Why is Main Street like a river?'

'I don't know – why *is* Main Street like a river?'

'Because it has a Bank on both sides, and Mudd at the bottom!'

The building of the railway brought another benefit to Grange, too. The hilly surroundings meant that the line had to be laid as close to the shore as possible, raised on a continuous embankment to keep it well above the water. The new embankment gave Grange a permanent seafront and promenade, and put an end to the frequent high-tide floods that had washed into hotels, houses and the village school. The low-lying marshland at Meathop to the east of Grange, now protected from the tides by the railway's barrier, could be brought into full cultivation.

The building and expansion went on more slowly well into this century, but Grange never developed into anything like a popular resort. It was just too quiet and too far away from the tourist hot-spots – and those Sands, this far up the estuary of the River Kent, are in truth made up of just as much mud as sand. The piers were closed and dismantled, and the village settled down to give itself over to its small number of walking, riding, nature-watching, ozone-breathing regular visitors, and to the increasing numbers of retired people who were looking for exactly the sort of atmosphere that Grange is steeped in.

In 1982 Grange Parish Council produced a report, 'Grange-over-Sands Town Appraisal', which highlighted the problems of trying to be a Victorian resort in the face of contemporary pressures to change. The heart of the matter is that half the village's population is over sixty years of age, and wouldn't swap the Grange they know and love for any other version. It isn't really a question of any threat posed by tourism – those who want the gentle pursuits that the place offers so abundantly will keep coming and want to change nothing; those who don't will stay away. The difficulties for the present and future lie in preventing Grange from slipping from a living community of mixed generations into a moribund village, peopled by old folk but unable to look after them.

Not that Grange's over-sixties are helpless, or anything like it. There are nearly seventy clubs and societies flourishing in the town, for everything from gardening and rambling to art, local history and old gentlemen's a-chat-and-a-drink gatherings. Everyone likes the dark, cluttered old Victorian shops along Main Street, where the folks behind the counter have time to enquire after your husband's tomatoes and how your daughter is doing in her new job. The spanking new library on Grange Fell Road, the little tearooms and the out-of-fashion robe shops all do well in and out of season. The most frequently voiced complaint is about Grange's lack of a hospital – rather a glaring lack, with the average age of the population rising all the time – but the enthusiastically supported 'share a car' scheme means that you don't necessarily have to rely on the trains and buses to get to Kendal and the local big towns. There's money in the community, a spirit of self-help and a great desire to keep things going. But put up the idea of bringing in light industry, or opening an amusement arcade for the young people of the village, and you tap a deep vein of distaste. At the top of Main Street stands the grey stone hulk of the old Grange Cinema and Ballroom, built in the boom time of the 1920s to seat six hundred patrons. When it closed in 1963, starved of custom, there were many plans for the building. Early in the 1980s the Brookwood Leisure Centre operated there, a privately owned and run retreat for Grange's youngsters with a café and some facilities for swimming and playing indoor sports. But in 1986 it closed, leaving the teenagers of the village with the choice of putting up with an hour's journey by bus to Kendal Leisure Centre or filling in the evening hours hanging round the Crown Hotel. They do their best to entertain themselves with the local rock bands that play in the Crown every so often, and with home-grown fun like the All Grange Budding Male Models Boxer Shorts Competition. But there's not really much to keep the youngsters in Grange during the evening, and not much for them there in the daytime, either. At secondary age, they go off to schools in Cartmel, Lancaster, Kendal or Ulverston, and few can look to their home village for the hope of a job when they leave school. The parish council's report doesn't turn a blind eye; it contains plenty of quotes from local people, both young and old, deploring this lack of facilities and urging the powers-that-be to make use of the derelict old Yewbarrow Lodge. In May 1941 this handsome grey stone house was burnt out after being hit by an incendiary bomb unloaded from a German plane whose crew had mistaken Grange for Barrow-in-Furness. After the war the owner gave it to the council, to use as they saw fit for the benefit of the village; but forty years on it still sits, slowly falling apart, in its beautiful gardens above Yewbarrow Terrace.

There are two symbols that really sum up the civilized past that Grange holds so dear and the uncertain future it looks towards so warily. Among the juniper trees and limestone pavements on the summit of Hampsfell stands the little hospice whose roof makes such a wonderful viewing platform over the north-west of England. It was built by the Vicar of

Grange, the Rev. Thomas Remington, in 1834 when Grange was still what today's visitor brochure styles it: 'Lakeland's Best Kept Secret'. Mr Remington intended the hospice to be a simple shelter for benighted wayfarers crossing the bleak fell, but he blessed it with his gentle, learned humour as well. Over the eastern doorway he inscribed in Greek 'The Rosy Fingered Dawn', and inside he put up some notices to amuse and instruct those with a long, chilly night to while away. One displays a poem composed by him but lettered by someone less formally schooled:

> This Hospice As An Open Door,
> A Like To Welcome Rich And Poor;
> A Roomy Seat For Young And Old,
> Where They May Screen Them From The Cold.
>
> Three Windows That Command A View,
> To North, To West And Southward Too;
> A Flight Of Steps Requireth Care,
> The Roof Will Show A Prospect Rare:
>
> Mountain And Vale You Thence Survey,
> The Winding Streams And Noble Bay:
> The Sun At Noon The Shadows Hides,
> Along The East And Western Sides:
>
> A Lengthened Chain Hold Guard Around,
> To Keep The Cattle From The Ground;
> Kind Reader Freely Take Your Pleasure,
> But Do No Mischief To My Treasure.

On the opposite wall hangs a cheeky reply in the same metre, dated 'Cartmel 1846', scoring a number of points off the reverend poet with verses such as:

> The 'Flight of Steps Requireth Care'
> Then Why Not Have A Hand Rail There;
> That Feeble Old And Timid Fair
> May Mount And View The Prospect Rare.

Ah, the days when ramblers could construe Greek, sleep on spartan stone benches under unglazed windows and write poetry! Mr Remington enjoyed the raillery enough to have the whole counter-poem hung opposite his own effort; but even in those days there were enough vandals around to

223

justify another splendidly resigned request to such persons 'to respect private property, and not by acts of wanton mischief and destruction show that they possess more muscle than brain. I have no hope' sighs the warning notice 'that this request will be attended to, for as Solomon says "Though thou shouldest bray a fool in a mortar among wheat with a pestle yet will not his foolishness depart from him."'

From the roof (its steps now hand-railed) the whole saucer of More-cambe Bay lies open below you. In the 1970s a plan for the bay was considered, whose mere mention in the tea-shops of Grange brings audible shudders all round. An enormous barrier was projected, running from Hest Bank, to the north of Morecambe, right across the mouth of the bay for twelve miles to Baycliff, about three miles south of Ulverston. Behind the barrier the entire bay would have become a giant double-reservoir filled by the two rivers Leven and Kent, split in half by the Cartmel Peninsula, with a storage capacity whose reckoning in gallons trails twenty noughts behind it. The benefits to the area would have been a major road along the top of the dam, giving greatly improved access to South Cumbria (a new guise for the old Sands crossing, in effect), and some crumbs of tourism from water sports on the reservoir which Grange might have picked up. A planner's dream, in fact; but, like most such dreams, it would have been a nightmare for those who would have had to live with it. The feasibility report made it quite clear that among the effects – the foreseeable effects – of building this monster would have been the end of most of the Morecambe Bay fishermen's livelihoods, the silting up and demise of Heysham harbour as a fishing and ferry port, the loss of almost all the invertebrates under the sands and a desertion of Morecambe Bay by its unique population of wading birds, and the creation of vast areas of what the report terms 'mere or polder' off Carnforth and the tip of the Cartmel Peninsula, unworkable but with possible use for 'nature conservation, amenity and recreational purposes' – nice vague phrases for unfortunate by-blows. There was also a likelihood, not mentioned in the report, that Grange would have kissed goodbye to the mild climate that brings it good weather and rare plants, and would have had to face whatever climate twenty noughts of new water might have created. And, of course, the whole character of the little community on the edge of its ever-changing world of half-water, half-land would have been fixed in a completely new mould.

Once some of these considerations had been hoisted on board, along with a projected cost at 1972 prices of £61 million (sure to double at least, during construction), the planners' maps began to change shape. The line of the barrier moved further and further north up the drawings, split into two round the Cartmel Peninsula and formed a circle off the tip, paused briefly higher up the estuaries of Kent and Leven, and finally vanished away into a file. The people of Heysham, Morecambe, Carnforth, Silverdale, Arnside, Grange, Flookburgh and Ulverston could breathe again. But nobody in Grange feels quite sure that the file won't be opened again some day.

Surrounded by its mosses, marshes, sands, farmlands and fells, Lakeland's Best Kept Secret still hasn't been whispered abroad too loudly. Grange people hope with all their hearts that it will stay that way. As long as you can take tea in peace under the awning of Yewbarrow Terrace, and pop into Postlethwaite's (hardware, gifts, toys, joinery and funerals – everything from the cradle to the grave) for a pound of nails and a chat, everything will be all right. But some of those youngsters flashing their boxer shorts in the bar of the Crown Hotel have another title for the village that raised them but can't keep them: 'Grange-over-Sands – Lakeland's Best Kept Fossil'.

29. Whitehaven

The best view of Whitehaven is from the very end of West Pier, standing by the old lighthouse and looking inland across the harbour at the town spreading up its cliffs and back into its valley. At first glance, Whitehaven's waterfront might have been brought wholesale to the West Cumbrian coast from some Dutch town. The elegance of those tall old warehouses and the streets of three-storeyed Georgian shops and terraces behind them make a satisfying composition, backed by a green ridge and fronted by the stone arms of the harbour. It takes a second and longer look to spot the signs of decay: the boarded-up windows and peeling walls, weeds growing along the dock railway lines and an absence of bustle and clatter. The town stands behind its harbour like a shopkeeper behind his counter; but the counter is pretty well bare these days.

> . . . an ample bason pours
> Her waves swift-rolling on the western shores,
> While num'rous masts beneath delight the eye,
> The growth, WHITEHAVEN, of thy industry.

Thus enthused local poet James Weeks in the 1750s, when Whitehaven waterfront was a hive of activity – as befitted the shopfront of the second busiest port in England – with shipyards turning out fishing and trading vessels; sailmakers and chandlers, ropemakers and millers; dockers unloading the incoming ships and packing the warehouses with sugar, tobacco and rum from the New World. And, on each outgoing tide, boat after boat loaded with Whitehaven's own black diamond – coal. Thirty years before, Daniel Defoe had noted that the town 'is now the most eminent port in England for shipping off coals, except Newcastle . . . 'tis frequent in time of war, or upon the ordinary occasion of cross winds, to have two hundred sail of ships at a time go from this place for Dublin, loaden with coals'.

The journey of those coals across the Irish Sea may have been a long one, but their trip from pit-head to dockside was short enough. Whitehaven stands between cliffs which are lined with coal, dropping in well-separated seams 1,000 feet and more, and running out for perhaps twelve miles under the sea. There's a fine cut-away relief-model of these in the Civic Hall museum. Men had been scratching at that coal since Norman times, when Whitehaven belonged to the nearby St Bees Priory, but when the Lowther family bought up the priory lands early in the seventeenth century great things began to happen to the little port. Sir Christopher Lowther built the Old Quay with its round lighthouse; but it was his son, Sir John, who took Whitehaven and dragged it to the centre of the commercial stage. Under his orders a whole new town was built in the shallow valley between the cliffs, its streets laid out in a criss-cross grid pattern. The harbour was enlarged and extended with new piers, quays and stone jetties, and the trade came pouring in and out. During the eighteenth century, fine large terraces were put up along the streets, each house with its own garden.

Meanwhile the Lowthers, already rich from their coal-mines in other parts of Cumbria, were delving into the Whitehaven cliffs for more of the same. Their pit on the south shore at Saltom Bay was the first one in England to burrow out under the sea, and soon others were heading in the same direction. When Defoe paid his visit to Whitehaven, 30,000 tons of coal were leaving the port every year, most of it gratefully snapped up by Ireland, which had none of its own. The Lowthers got richer and richer: Sir James Lowther, who built Whitehaven Castle for himself at the top of the town in 1769, was said to have died 'the richest commoner in England'. Whitehaven was their creation, and they gave it some handsome buildings, among them the Assembly Rooms, more symmetrical streets of tall terraces and detached houses, and the church of St James perched up behind the town. At the same time, merchants were building their own large houses, and the Whitehaven bubble went on growing bigger.

By 1770 there were almost 200 ships trading out of Whitehaven – enough to make a tempting target for John Paul Jones when he sailed this way on 23 April 1778 in the privateer *Ranger* under the flag of his adoptive country, America. Jones, a Scots lad from Kirkcudbright, knew Whitehaven well, having trained here as a seaman. He had planned to slip ashore at dead of night with thirty companions and burn everything he could lay his hands on, but things went wrong. An unfavourable tide delayed the raiders' boats, half the task-force captured a pub on the Old Quay and settled down to some serious boozing, and the matches of canvas dipped in brimstone wouldn't light. In the end, Jones and his friends got away in broad daylight and under fire, having managed only to spike the cannon of the harbour defences and set fire to a single ship, the coal boat *Thompson*. Nevertheless, the *Cumberland Packet Extraordinary* had a splendid time in its next issue, firing off indignant phrases about 'diabolical work' and 'infernal bufinef'; and Jones is still remembered with admiration in Whitehaven. A vigorous coloured portrait of him hangs on the cliff wall south of the harbour, and one of the cannon he spiked points impotently out to sea just beyond.

The Whitehaven bubble swelled on into the nineteenth century, with more coal pits opening and a rash of Italianate buildings, stiff with columns and floral mouldings, breaking out all over. The Lowthers were by now the Earls of Lonsdale, and by far the richest family in the north-west; but even they couldn't stave off the effects of the new-fangled railways. Suddenly the transport of coal over moor and mountain was no longer an insuperable problem, and its passage by sea from mine to consumer began to look both costly and time-consuming. At the same time Liverpool was expanding into a port so large and so conveniently placed for Irish and American trade that Whitehaven simply couldn't compete. The tidal harbour, an expanse of mud at low ebb, found the enormous new iron ships too big to handle, and the shipyards found the demand for their traditional wood-built products slackening off. Even 'the coalworks, Lowther's treasur'd mines', for so long the mainstay of the town's prosperity, were getting too deep, their working faces too far out under the sea, to be as profitable as in the past.

There were other problems for Whitehaven, too. Sir John Lowther's beautifully regulated town had enticed thousands of Cumberland men and women away from their farms and villages to make and service ships, run pubs and boarding houses, build, dig and delve. The miners' terraces had crept over the cliffs round the pits at each side of the town, and down in the centre of Whitehaven those lovely back-gardens of the elegant Georgian houses had filled up, acre by acre, in a slow growth, with tiny, cramped, sunless hutches shared by several families, with no drains, lights or unpolluted water-supply. Visitors to the town commented on the pinched, white faces of the women and the rickety legs and ragged clothes of the children. Disease was rife in these drab courts and alleyways; and as the port began to sicken and the shipyards to die off, so the blight of dirt and decay spread through the town.

Perched on the south cliff above the portrait of John Paul Jones stands Candlestick Chimney, so called after it burst into flames having been struck by lightning. Candlestick Chimney was built to vent one of the shafts of the Wellington Pit that ran seaward from under the cliffs. For Whitehaven people it's not just a reminder of their industrial heritage, but a memorial to the victims of the worst accident in the whole history of mining in Cumberland which tore a hole in the already embattled community in 1910. On 18 May of that year there was an explosion in the workings which killed some of the miners outright and trapped others behind rock-falls nearly four miles out under the sea. Nothing could be done for them in spite of frantic efforts by would-be rescuers, and the final death-toll came to 136 men and boys. Very few mining families in Whitehaven escaped loss; soon the town was to be pushed further into misery by the loss of hundreds more of its men in the First World War. Then came the economic slump of the 1920s and '30s. The bubble had not so much burst as withered away.

Just along the clifftop from Candlestick Chimney are the pithead buildings and great winding wheels of the Haig Colliery, the last Whitehaven pit to be sunk and the last to close – it worked from the First World War until 1984. Some 750 men were employed there, producing about 470,000 tonnes of coal a year; and when Haig shut down it was the end of nearly a thousand years of coal-mining in Cumberland. Plans to establish a museum of mining in the Haig Pit buildings are currently under consideration. In the meantime there are many men in Whitehaven's pubs and streets who can show you their dust-blue scars and tell you what it was like to labour, half doubled over, at a coal-face under the sea which took an hour to reach from the pithead. Some well remember another terrible disaster on 15 August 1947 after an explosion two miles out into the haulage road of the William Pit. The scenes which followed were similar to those in 1910 – a rush of volunteers, fruitless attempts to reach the trapped men (dogs were tried, including Jet the Alsatian who had won a canine VC saving fifty lives during the Blitz), the slowly growing realization that the victims were beyond rescue, and another appalling list of 104 fathers, husbands and brothers lost to the community. Three men did manage to make their way out, and one of them subsequently worked underground at Haig Colliery. Asked how he could face going down the pit again after all he had been through, he replied simply: 'Big family – small wage.'

A huge lump of coal and the roll-call of those 104 names commemorates the victims of the William Pit disaster in the south chapel of St James's Church on the hill at the top of Queen Street. It is a spacious Georgi⌐

building with wide upper galleries flanking the nave and two relief roundels in Wedgwood blue and white on the ceiling; one shows an ascending Christ in a sunburst, the other a kneeling Virgin at the moment of annunciation, beneath angels strewing rosebuds and some very bouncy cherubs playing peek-a-boo among the clouds. The Italian sculptor took some historical licence by inserting into this pre-Christian scene a medieval church with a flag flying from the spire. Behind the altar is a treasure of a painting given by the 3rd Earl of Lonsdale, a Transfiguration scene by Giulio Cesare Procaccini (d. 1626). Among the memorial tablets is one to a schoolmaster, Joseph Wood, who died in 1827. With 'Unwearied Assiduity' he taught maths to Whitehaven children for almost half a century.

Walking down from St James's into the town centre, there are prospects over the open-topped canyons of the straight streets towards high green banks of countryside and cliff. The town's past prosperity through trade and the Lowthers is reflected in the architecture of the streets and in their names: Duke Street; Lowther Street, where stand the box-like new Civic Hall and town museum, splendid bank and post office buildings and the tower of St Nicholas's Church (burnt down in 1971) which now houses the tourist information centre; Tangier Street with its evocative name, full of the smell of spices; the Waverley Hotel which began life in the seventeenth century as Tangier House, a merchant's dwelling; the stone jetties of Sugar Tongue and Lime Tongue licking the harbour waters. Irish Street and Scotch Street are lined with Georgian buildings.

Near the harbour, Roper Street diverges from the straight, though not from the narrow. Here the old Market Hall and Golden Lion Hotel stand opposite each other in the market place at the bottom of King Street, a pedestrian thoroughfare these days. New Lowther Street on the waterfront has two superb terraces of the early eighteenth century. The end house on the right contains a travel office and the Dutch and Danish vice-consulates, exotic-sounding entities with a very practical task. Many seafarers from Scandinavia and Holland visit Whitehaven, and some have settled here. If they run into trouble, or need a bed or a ship or a quick or just a chat in their own tongue, it's to this little terraced house

rman Nicholson, the Lakeland poet, came to Whitehaven in 50s he found a shabby old town on its knees, 'the world of

Smollett and Rowlandson without the laughs', cowering between 'scarred cliffs, scabbed with coal and blood . . . a landscape as solemn as any in Cumberland'. The townspeople were rapidly losing both pride in their past and hope for the future. Shades of that down-and-out Whitehaven, product of half a century's slide into depression, are still to be seen in the many derelict terraces, the peeling hulk of the old Town Hall at one unfashionable end of Duke Street, and the crumbling sandstone public baths at the other end on the waterfront with cupola, pillared porch and dusty relief sculptures of a muscular Neptune and a plump, sexy, full-breasted mermaid with long tresses and a girdle of seaweed. But if recent trends continue, these sad places will probably be renewed by the time you walk this way. Whitehaven's scarred old face is rapidly getting a lift of heroic proportions. West Cumbria is a region of high unemployment and low expectations, but you'd hardly know it from the gleaming façades of Whitehaven's renovated streets and the freedom with which money and goods are exchanged in its old-fashioned shops. A century ago, Lowther was the name that ran the town; nowadays there are two, both tainted with controversy: Sellafield and Marchon.

Volunteers from Greenpeace and other watchdog organizations tend to get short shrift when they hand out their leaflets of facts and figures in the streets of Whitehaven. Trying to get signatures on any petition containing the words 'Sellafield Nuclear Reprocessing Plant' is a thankless task. Sellafield has been a fact of life here for three decades; it's taken the place of coal-mining as a job that goes down the family line from grandfather through father to son. Soon a fourth Whitehaven generation will be working at Sellafield. Familiarity has bred not contempt, but content. A lot of Whitehaven cars carry window stickers proclaiming 'Sellafield Is Safe', and many of their owners flatly refuse to believe in all this pollution nonsense. They don't see British Nuclear Fuels PLC as the owners of a time-bomb ticking away twelve miles down the coast, but as the providers of 7,000 jobs for which they may be truly thankful. As one resident told me, 'I've got a husband, father, two brothers and numerous uncles and cousins all working there, so I'm not going to be signing any bloody petition.' When Greenpeace try to put across their latest readings of radioactivity on the beach or in the sea, a large number of pragmatic blind eyes are turned. The Chernobyl reactor accident of 1986 caused ripples of alarm across the rest of the country, but it made little apparent impression here. Whitehaven people only have to look a few miles up the coast to Workington and Maryport, or down to Barrow, to remind themselves of what economic recession has done to neighbouring coastal towns, and they only have to survey their own streets to see what dramatic effects an enormous company budget can have on a slump town.

At the end of the 1960s, large sections of Whitehaven – whole streets in some parts – were mildewed, rotting, vandalized, boarded up and sagging earthwards. It wasn't a cheerful place to live or bring up children, and families were leaving. Then in 1969 the whole town-centre of Whitehaven was designated a conservation area. With large grants from the county and borough councils and the Department of the Environment, a programme of restoration got under way. The idea – a model for other such schemes – was not just to tart up the biggest and best buildings, leaving them as islands of elegance in a stagnant pond of decay, but to improve the whole area by renovating complete blocks. As the beautifully produced project booklet keeps reminding the reader, it couldn't have been tackled without the involvement – and massive cash input – of British Nuclear Fuels. The company bought up many of Whitehaven's crumbling old terraces to be restored as accommodation for their workers. They pumped in money and expertise, and thereby secured a lot of loyalty among local people reluctant to bite the hand that was feeding them so generously.

Sellafield lies well beyond St Bees Head to the south of the town, out of sight and out of most Whitehaven minds. The other big provider, Marchon chemical works, is likewise invisible from down in the town centre; but get up on to high ground north, south or east and you can't avoid confrontation. The works stand on the clifftop beyond Candlestick Chimney and the Haig colliery, a giant complex sprouting fuming chimneys. Marchon makes chemicals for detergents, soaps, shampoos and bubble baths, and an awful lot of remarkable smells. The cliffs and beach below the works are splattered a greasy black, the bay beyond a scummy white with Marchon's outpourings. People living in the shadow of the chemical works admit to itchy eyes, sore skin patches, chest troubles, vegetable gardens 'covered with white flakes, like there'd been a frost – only this was a fine summer's night'. They don't much care for the sight and the soapy stink of Marchon. But there are 2,000 jobs in there. The works are also the only concern keeping Whitehaven port from complete closure;

North African cargo ships bring in the phosphate rock used to make the phosphoric acid that goes into those detergents and toiletries.

With the coal pits gone, the only traditional industry left in the town is fishing. There's a small fleet, its boats marked WA for Whitehaven, which goes out for prawns, cod and whiting in season, but the harbour is used mostly by fleets from elsewhere, particularly Ireland. If the town-centre renovations succeed as Copeland Borough Council hopes they will, there could be a future in tourism for Whitehaven – but in the meantime the townspeople lift their eyes to the southern hills, from whence cometh their help. 'Sellafield and Marchon have put this place back on its feet,' I was told across a bar counter. 'If they go, we might as well pack up, too.'

Just above Candlestick Chimney stands a derelict old house on the cliff edge. In times past it served the colliers of the Wellington pit as the Red Flag public house, but when it was built, more than 300 years ago, it was known as Bowling Green House. Here for a few childhood years lived Jonathan Swift. Looking down today over the harbour and town that he knew as a bustling trading, shipbuilding and mining centre, he might have something pungent to say about the rope dance that Whitehaven is currently performing; sloughing off the scabrous skin of its past, with Sellafield and Marchon underpinning its hopes for a brighter future.

SCOTLAND

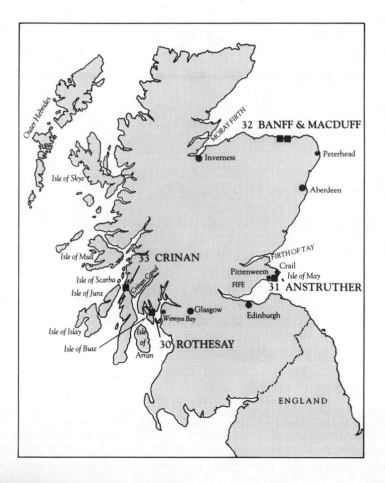

30. Rothesay

The Isle of Bute lies some thirty miles west of Glasgow as the seagull flies, slotted neatly into the angle formed by the Firth of Clyde and the Sound of Bute. The island has none of the craggy drama of Arran or the isolated romance of Islay – it's a subdued patchwork of fields and woods, not one of its hills reaching even 1,000 feet. Rothesay, its chief town, is little more than a dignified waterfront and a sprawl of inland streets, far removed in spirit from the out-and-out commercialization of thumping pleasure centres such as Blackpool. Yet Glaswegians are still firmly bound by ties of tradition to their island resort 'doon the watter'. The shipyard and factory workers may turn to the Malaga-bound jets for their main holidays; but, for many of them, especially those who can remember pre-war fortnights on the Isle of Bute, a summer without at least a courtesy call on Rothesay would be unthinkable.

There are two ferry routes to the island. The main one – the well-worn track of millions of Glasgow holidaymakers – leaves the pier below Wemyss Bay railway station's elaborate curve of ironwork to forge for half an hour across the Firth of Clyde to Rothesay. Most of the town is hidden from view until the latter half of the journey opens up Rothesay Bay to reveal the tall hotels, bars and boarding houses lined up in an impressive curve round the bay. The sight still brings a smile of pleasure to the faces of elderly Glaswegians who have seen it several times a year for fifty years or more – one of these views where buildings, water, woods and hills fit together just so. Back in 1903, when Wemyss Bay railway station was built, the journey from Glasgow was all part of the fun, the train ride to Wemyss Bay and the crowded steamer trip across the water building up to that slowly unfolding view of Rothesay along its waterfront.

The alternative ferry crossing to the Isle of Bute, a five-minute hop from Colintraive on the northern shore of the Kyles of Bute, lacks this sense of anticipation. The doors at one end of the Caledonian MacBrayne ferry have hardly closed before those at the other end are opening to let you off. But the shore-road drive through Port Bannatyne leads to Ardbeg Point and a prospect of Rothesay Bay just as striking and more suddenly revealed than the view from the sea. The buildings seem to stand straight up out of their own reflections in the bay, church spires rising above them, in front of a gently swelling green hill unspoilt since the early Victorian developers agreed to leave it be. Most of Rothesay is strictly limited to the little saddle of land inside the bay, with a line of houses running away along the shore road until it curves out of sight round Bogany Point. It's a charming, old-fashioned view, still retaining the flavour of the select retreat that Rothesay provided for well-to-do Glasgow industrialists early in the nineteenth century, before Bank Holidays and the shipyard workers arrived together some fifty years later.

Rothesay may have become the island paradise of Glaswegian manual labourers and their families, but that didn't stop the bosses and the emerging middle classes from coming here. As you reach the Esplanade, Rothesay's main waterfront street, either from the Wemyss Bay ferry or the shore road, relics of the golden decades each side of the turn of the century stand in view: grand Victoria Hotel right in the centre; the great dun-coloured Glenburn Hotel (built in 1890 as one of those classic Victorian health-and-leisure conglomerates, a hydropathic establishment) dominating the Bogany side of the bay; the ironwork, glass and gull-dotted dome of the Winter Gardens in a prime seafront position, where the pre-war entertainer Jimmy Cameron used to parade the stage, rasping 'It's ye Ah mean, wi' the wee flat hat' to packed and roaring audiences. There are ornate lamp-posts bursting with cast-iron foliage, palm trees, fountains and putting greens in the floral gardens. The whole effect is more Bournemouth than Blackpool, elegant holidaymaking in the shadow of fine buildings.

It's in the narrow streets behind the seafront that you begin to sense the struggle Rothesay is having to stay in touch with its long-term customers from across the Firth of Clyde. Lines of small shops fill these streets. You won't find a Marks & Spencer's, a Boots' or a Sainsbury's in Rothesay – shirts and skirts, corn plasters and groceries are all served over the counter in family-owned and family-run shops. Up the High Street are the Castle Bakery, the Shortbread Shop, a little old saddlery and The Brandane pub ('¼ Gill Served Here'), next to each other on the sloping roadway. Down on East Princes Street just back from the seafront is the Golfers' Bar, a pub like no other with its complete and untouched art nouveau interior. The shelves behind the bar are a forest of shapely pillars, peaked gables and old whisky brand statuettes. The deeply polished wooden bar looks out on to button-back benches, pull-the-chain heaters and a little snug booth with swirling frosted windows. Mrs Eva Murdoch, the proprietor of this comfortable, idiosyncratic watering-hole, swears she won't change a thing. This self-sufficiency and freedom from the uniformity of the big marketing companies is a source of pride to the townsfolk, and part of Rothesay's attraction for its visitors. But these days many of the little shops are dusty and grubby, their gilt lettering tarnished, their range of goods too limited for the sophisticated tastes of modern city-dwellers. Inland from the showroom window of the seafront there's a feeling of decline about the place.

The holidaymakers, too, are pretty thin on the ground. There are the strolling elderly couples who have always come to Rothesay and always will, and pinch-faced young mothers threatening to slap their dragging children; but very few of the teenagers out for fun or the large parties of workmates on their communal visits that in the 1930s would snap up every available bed in the town, months before Glasgow Fair and the holiday fortnight came around in July. In those heady days the boarding-house owners of Rothesay could expect a knock on the door and an advance block-booking of rooms any time from November onwards. Nowadays you can arrive unbooked in the middle of July and be sure of a bed, 'nae bother' – good news for foolish virgins, but not so good for trade. Loyalty and affectionate memories still draw many Glaswegians back to Rothesay, but the majority of these stay for only a nostalgic day or two. Most of their serious holiday savings go into the pockets of tour operators and Spanish hoteliers.

'The Clyde towns had their holiday fortnights starting in July,' Tommy Wilkinson told me across the counter of his newsagent's shop. Bute born and bred, he's a storyteller who sketches the differing characters of the Clydesiders in sharp, humorous phrases. 'Greenock was first away. That was known here as Greetin' Wains Fortnight – those Greenock bairns always seemed to be crying and wailing. Next was Glasgow Fair for the second and third weeks of July. Glaswegians were welcome here: they're always carefree, spend well and enjoy themselves. They're lovely people. Then came the Paisley folk. They had a reputation for being tight with their money. At the pierhead we had what folk called the Pointing Porters. They'd line up to meet the steamers, pointing at people and shouting, "Carry your case, mister?" The porters did well out of those Paisleyites, all weighted down with great heavy bags. They'd bring everything they needed for the whole holiday along with them – even their food – rather than have to buy it here.'

These visitors were the inheritors of the tradition that had brought

Clydeside to Rothesay through three or four generations, and they wanted much the same things: plenty of entertainment, booze and laughter, an escape for a few days from their hard lives at work and at home in the heavy industrial surroundings of Glasgow and its satellite towns. It didn't much matter if, in the words of the old music hall song, a single sneeze could 'waken half a million fleas in a single room in Rothesay-O'. A whole clutch of new entertainments opened within a few years of each other in the decade before the Second World War: the Pavilion ballroom and café with its glossy modern curves, the Regal cinema, the new swimming pool. The steamers arrived crammed to the rails, the Esplanade was thronged, there was plenty for even the most cost-conscious Paisleyite to do. But Rothesay's success attracted sharp Glasgow main-chancers who bought up blocks of houses to let out to the holidaymakers. By the time that those cheap package flights abroad were beginning to entice away the Clyde-siders, there were whole areas of Rothesay in the hands of people who never set foot on the island themselves and couldn't have cared less about the town's native community.

As you stroll round Rothesay and your eye tunes in to the signs of decay, it's plain that today's town is at a crossroads in its history. The once-beloved Winter Gardens have stood empty since the 1970s, victim of the thinning stream of customers. The large open square where the High Street and Watergate meet Montague Street, slap in the middle of the seafront and surrounded by handsome buildings, cries out for more imaginative use than its present function as a dusty, stony car park. There were three cinemas in Rothesay in its heyday, but they have all been shut down. The superb Victorian Aquarium on the Bogany side of the bay, refurbished as a swimming pool in the 1930s, has likewise closed down, the steel rods encased in its concrete walls corroded beyond repair by chlorine and other chemicals. Even the Pavilion, Rothesay's dance, concert, conference and show centre, struggles to attract tourists to such threadbare offerings as the 'Waggle O' The Kilt Show, featuring Johnny Adam and the Wagglettes'. People whose tastes have been turned around by slick television extrava-ganzas just don't want this kind of thing any more, a hard fact emphasized by the empty spaces on the Firth of Clyde ferries. There's still a taste of the old seaside resort atmosphere in Rothesay – children run raucously about in and out of the seafront shelters, there's more immoderate laughter and finger-whistling on the putting greens than would be tolerated on the golf courses of tight-lipped wee mainland towns. But these jackal calls of enjoyment stand out painfully against a background hush that never settled over summer season Rothesay in the good old days.

One place, however, is guaranteed to draw a faithful line of devotees: the rickety wooden end of the ferry stage where the fishermen sit or stand, blind and deaf to the outside world, their attention riveted as if life itself depended on it on their outsize weights, lures and hooks. It's a superb place to fish, with the deeply cut, rounded hills of the Corlarach Forest across the very blue water to stare at in between cast and bite. Here I saw a stout young Glaswegian in a denim jacket, watched out of the corners of their eyes by envious younger boys, sending his great lead weights and hooks lumpy with ragworm flying fifty yards out into the bay, then casually reeling in one wriggling pollack after another – a masterly exhibition.

People with an interest in getting Rothesay on its feet again as a tourist attraction are fully conscious of the slope down which the town has been steadily sliding since the 1950s. The organizing manager of the Pavilion is bitter about the inertia that caused a projected takeover of the town's facilities by Butlin's a few years ago to be 'knocked back', as was a scheme to build a bridge across the narrow waterway of the Kyles of Bute. He thinks the Tourist Board should be far more aggressive in its marketing, going out to grab the punters – particularly American visitors to Scotland – with kilt and bagpipe, flogging cheap holidays on Bute round the mainland for all they're worth. But James McMillan, the Isle of Bute's Tourist Officer, sees both sides of the problem from his seafront office on the ferry stage. Like Tommy Wilkinson, he's a native Bute islander, from a family accustomed to wielding influence in Rothesay. James can number three former Provosts among his forebears, and he's well aware of the need to consider the interests of the townsfolk as well as the tourists.

'Rothesay is changing year by year, one can't deny that. Back in the 1930s the town was vibrant – it was really jumping, and the Town Council was very progressive. Everyone approved when they built the Pavilion, the cinemas and the swimming pool. But these days, with the slack in the number of holidaymakers coming to Rothesay, there's a lot of argument about how money should be spent. Take the swimming pool, for example. When the engineers condemned it there was proposal after proposal for a new one, but for ten years every scheme was turned down. We're finally getting one on the meadows at the top of the town, but the delay turned a lot of custom away. Then the Winter Gardens – that's had £100,000 from the Historic Buildings Council for outside restoration, while the museum gets just £200 a year. That makes people angry. No one really knows what to do with the Pavilion, either – though everyone agrees something has to be done.'

Efforts are being made in other directions, however, to get to grips with the holiday trade and entice it back to Rothesay. James McMillan is enthusiastic about the popularity of the cruises on the motor vessels *Keppel* and *Gay Queen* round the islands and little coastal towns of the surrounding firths and waterways; and especially the paddle steamer *Waverley*, last of the line that once brought the crowds to Bute, which makes a long promotional trip round the southern coast of England every year, flourishing her 'Bute is Beautiful' banner wherever she goes. 'Caledonian MacBrayne sold her to the preservation society for one pound. That was a clever move – they sold them a whole bundle of trouble as well, and made sure Cal-Mac couldn't be accused of sending her to the scrapyard.'

There are plans to take advantage of the sheltered harbour by dredging it to provide a water sports area with deep water at all states of the tide; other plans to rebuild the landing stage and smarten up the town's shops in hopes of encouraging yachtsmen to use Rothesay as a staging post on their way out to Crinan, Tarbert and the Western Isles. Here, perhaps, is the target on which the aims of the various interested parties – tourist officers, entertainments managers, shopkeepers, hoteliers, townsfolk – are beginning to converge. Those Clydeside hordes are unlikely ever again to flock 'doon the watter' to Rothesay, but the wheel of fortune has meanwhile revolved almost full circle, to open up possibilities of the town becoming once again a favourite resort of the middle classes. Many commuters to Glasgow and its fringe towns already live here, taking their chances of rough winter crossings and a journey of an hour and a half to work, for the sake of living in the seclusion of lovely Rothesay. The town's housing association, formed in the 1970s, has already bought back much of the housing stock from the absentee landlords, and is busy converting the old buildings that once held five or more families in single rooms into desirable residences for half that number. The island has as many retired people – nearly fifty per cent of its population – living in and around Rothesay as it can cope with, and demand for manageable old folks' accommodation goes on growing. Several of the big old hotels have been turned into retirement flats. Boarding house owners, sensing the wind of change, are beginning to shake out their rooms and install showers, TVs and bars. The dark and dismal hulk of the Winter Gardens will, if present plans shape up, soon come back to life as a heritage centre with an exhibition of Bute past and present, the maritime history of Western Scotland, memories of Rothesay and the vanished glories of seaside entertainment – alongside bars, a cinema, souvenir shop, café and a small theatre. Only the expectation of a flow of new and continuing money could have given birth to such an ambitious scheme.

And Rothesay, despite its current low-key atmosphere, has all the right attributes to make a splash in the ever-expanding pool of up-market holidaymaking and commuter living. It can look back nearly 1,000 years to the building of its first castle – possibly by Magnus Barefoot, King of Norway – in 1098. The castle that nowadays stands modestly in among the inland streets of the town was put up in the thirteenth century, and boasts the wild tradition of raids, sieges and bloody skirmishes common to most Scottish strongholds until Norsemen, English and rival Scots all fell by history's wayside. King Robert III created Rothesay a Royal Burgh in 1401, and he and his descendants used the town as a kind of exalted seaside resort. Rothesay was entertaining blue blood with its sea-breezes and green hills for at least four centuries before those Georgian shipyard magnates began to appreciate the beauties of 'the Naples of the North'. Neapolitan the weather here is certainly not: Rothesay rains and mists are infamous among holidaymakers. But that damp climate made the town an important cotton-spinning centre early in the nineteenth century. Some of the small hand-loom mills still stand, as do the kippering sheds from Rothesay's herring-fishing boom of the same era (over 500 boats in the 1850s). The town has sadder associations, too, for it was here that many dispossessed Highlanders embarked on their one-way journeys to different, if not better, lives across the Atlantic. Local people say that Canada Hill, where the golf course now lies, was given its name by the families of these unwilling wanderers who would stand up on this high shoulder of land to watch their men sail away – often for ever. Rothesay is packed tight with such memorials to a vigorous life, not always revolving round the pleasing of Clydesiders. It has taken the recent downhill years to focus local people's attention on the richness of their heritage, but that inheritance is now beginning to be seen for what it is: the lifeblood of the place, something to gather local pride around as well as something to hold out to the tourists who have been slipping away. Outside the town, too, are assets that Blackpool would just love to own: unfrequented hills, woods and valleys; sandy beaches with plenty of leg-room, such as Ettrick Bay, ten minutes' drive away across the waist of the island; quiet lochs full of trout to the south, quiet hills full of nothing to the north; splendid views of mountains across water to all points of the compass.

'It's a lovely island, you know,' said Tommy Wilkinson warmly. 'Everyone knows everyone here. No one's a stranger on Bute. People have fond memories of this place – old folk who came here on Glasgow Fair, young couples bringing their kids as their parents brought them. Of course, the foreign travel has taken a lot of customers away. Nowadays you can choose to go to Spain if you want to – they've got the weather, which we haven't. But Rothesay has a charisma all its own. There's something about the place that brings people back here. Would I live anywhere else? I wouldn't dream of it.'

Rothesay is looking with cautious optimism to climb out of its present trough into another era of prosperity, its dingy shops and faded back-streets renovated, its history exhibited imaginatively in a revitalized Winter Gardens, its harbour full of yachtsmen and water-sporters. Both tourism industry and traders are groping towards what they see as a light at the end of a long tunnel. Whether the place will lose its friendliness and strong community spirit in a flood of well-heeled visitors and new residents – and the wine bars, delicatessens and smart shops that will follow them – remains to be seen. What seems certain is that new upheavals are on the way for a town that down the years has weathered more than its share of them.

31. Anstruther

The fishermen of Anstruther don't like to hear the salmon named. 'The red fish' is the way to mention it if you want to stave off bad luck. There are still men working on the most up-to-date boats who feel uneasy if they meet a church minister or hear of a pig or a woman on their way to the boat. These are no folksy affectations, but evidence of a tradition that has knitted together the fishing towns and villages of East Fife since these settlements were founded. Nowadays the Fife fishermen put to sea in less danger and with greater certainty of success than at any time in history. The very latest in radar, radio communications, computers and fish-finding gadgetry cram the wheelhouses of the boats, and modern weather forecasting means that only a freak of nature could bring down on the fleet the kind of disaster so often suffered in the past by the fishermen at sea and their families back on shore. But the superstitions continue, as do the broad Doric speech and the reluctance to accept outsiders into the community.

To call the Fife fishing communities self-sufficient is like saying that Robinson Crusoe must have felt a bit lonely from time to time. Isolated through the years in the corner of their wind-blown peninsula known as the East Neuk, the hard facts of life in daily contact with the dangers and uncertainties of the fishing made a strong, uncompromising enclave of the three neighbouring settlements of Pittenweem, Anstruther and Crail. These days, only a couple of boats fish out of Crail for lobsters and crabs. The village has declined – or risen, according to your point of view – to a haven for painters, potters and retired folk, a charming bunch of old cottages and houses above a tiny, picturesque and almost lifeless harbour. Pittenweem goes stolidly on, catching and selling fish, a working harbour with a thriving fish-market. It's at Anstruther, between these two, that you can see the fishing past in the process of sliding, with many a bump and backward look, into the tourist future. Unless there's an unlooked-for change in the attitude of the fishermen, the day is rapidly coming closer when they will have finished the business of stripping all the available sea of all its fish. Less pretty than Crail, less concentrated on fishing than Pittenweem, Anstruther is fixing lifelines for itself against that day.

From the end of the unevenly cobbled eastern pier in the harbour, the seaward view is spectacular. Five miles offshore, but seeming nearer, rise the sheer cliffs of the green Isle of May, a lighthouse sticking up on top. Away to the east an oil platform stands out of the water on thick legs, its flat top sprouting cranes. Behind run the miles of low hills along the southern shoreline of the Firth of Forth. Turning inland, the view is filled with buildings. To the east are the red roofs of Cellardyke, the harbour of Kilrenny village which is the oldest part of the settlement. The houses of Cellardyke rise over each other in cobbled 'wynds' or narrow lanes above a small enclosed harbour whose only craft nowadays are pleasure boats. Some of the fishermen's cottages here are several hundred years old, with cellars underneath (where the nets were barked in wooden tubs to strengthen them) and outside stone stairways up to the first-floor living quarters.

Separated from Cellardyke by the Culdees Burn, Anstruther Easter stands directly in front of you, facing the main harbour where large yachts moor in the outer section and the inshore fishing boats in the inner enclosure. The tall white and grey buildings here are grander than those of Kilrenny and Cellardyke, reflecting the growth of Anstruther Easter in the great days of fishing into a place where ships' captains and master mariners could live just sufficiently removed from the humbler homes of their employees. This is the main part of Anstruther today, while the medieval fishing centre of Anstruther Wester away to the left across the Dreel Burn has become a pleasant suburb, with splashes of green fields above and beyond its houses. All four communities – Anstruther Easter and Wester, Kilrenny and Cellardyke – were amalgamated into one Royal Burgh in 1929, each place contributing something to the newly created joint coat of arms. From Easter and Wester came an anchor and three fishes, from Kilrenny and Cellardyke a fishing boat – appropriate symbols for a town so rooted in the fishing tradition. Kilrenny's motto, 'May the hook always hang in your favour', might have been taken from any public bar wall, but Anstruther Easter's 'By well-doing, poverty becomes rich' could well be stamped in letters of gold across the bows of every Anstruther boat these days.

At the foot of the eastern pier stands the Scottish Fisheries Museum, a must for every visitor to Anstruther. If the idea of labouring round a small town museum makes you yawn, here's something to wake you up. It's more than just a superbly organized and presented window into Anstruther's bygone glories. Housed in a group of old stone buildings, the museum contains an aquarium where dogfish, cod, eels and flatfish cruise through the murky waters of seawater tanks. There's a layout explaining the extensive plans for the Maritime Heritage Area which Anstruther has been designated – landscaping of the harbour, new housing behind the town, smartening up of neglected streets and houses, a 'floating museum' of ships in the harbour. Anstruther doesn't intend to be left high, dry and redundant when the last of the fish are harvested. But the bedrock on which all these schemes are founded is the fishing: how it used to be, and how it has shaped and influenced the community. It's hard to imagine how this side of the display in the museum could be bettered. The complete wheelhouse and galley of the fishing boat *Brighter Hope III* stand in the cobbled courtyard as an introduction. Then there are reconstructed fishermen's net lofts full of patched brown sails and tarred wicker pots; cottage living-rooms of the 1900s laid out, down to the religious texts on the walls, granny and the bairn in the rocking chair; a patent gutting machine in which the fish were slashed open by a fearsomely toothed circular saw and disembowelled by a revolving whisk; lifesize models of the herrin' lassies who travelled as far afield as Lowestoft to meet the Anstruther fleet and gut and pack the catch; beautiful ship models and paintings by local artists; old boat nameboards, instruments, engines and gear.

Wandering round the museum, you grasp the essence of the fishermen's life in the nineteenth and early twentieth centuries when the herring fishing dominated the town. There are photographs of the Anstruther harbours when the fleet was in, the masts so closely packed that they look like a defoliated forest. At such times it was said that you could walk across the boats in the harbours from Anstruther Wester to Anstruther Easter and never get your feet wet. The herring made great, unpredictable mass-migrations from time to time, and during one of these they brought prosperity to the East Neuk fishing communities by deserting the west coast of Scotland and moving round into the North Sea. In late Victorian days, over 600 Anstruther men were employed in the herring fishery. In 1881 there were 221 boats in the fleet, meeting the herring in spring out beyond the Outer Hebrides and chasing them round the coast, down almost as far as the Channel by autumn. Scandinavia, Russia and the Baltic countries were insatiable consumers of Scots-caught herring. Before the herring departed as mysteriously as they had arrived, just before the Second World War, the steam drifters were making the most of the windfall, as the lines painted on one of the museum's walls recall:

> Drifters seekin',
> Fog, or rain, or shine,
> Surface veins
> O' th' ocean's silver mine,
> Drifters seekin' herrin'
> Fae the Shetlan's to the Tyne.

By the end of the herring fishing, the Anstruther boats were going many miles beyond these bounds, staying at sea for up to a fortnight. Over-fishing played its part in the disappearance of the herring, even in the days before echo-sounding devices and electronic navigation aids, when skippers still relied on hard-won experience and their noses to find the silver harvest. As the herring vanished, new trawling, seine-netting and purse-netting methods kept the fishermen in business. There was also the great line fishing – nearly twenty miles of line with 7,000 hooks to be baited by hand as they went out one by one into the water. It took eighteen hours to shoot these monstrous lines, using a steam machine, and two hours to haul them in and remove the catch, hook by hook. The roughest great line trips were out to the Faroe Islands, month-long voyages during which no one had time or inclination to wash or relax. Storm-force winds, mountainous seas and bitter, icing cold made baiting by hand a dangerous business. One slip with chilled fingers and a man could have those fingers or his whole hand ripped open, or himself be hooked over the side and into the freezing water. The rewards were catches of giant cod and halibut, some up to six feet long. The great line trips went on until 1984, but it became too expensive for the crew, who had to supply their own gear for a month away in some of the toughest conditions possible, and for the boat skippers, who had to buy and insure boats equipped to withstand such demands. The Faroese, too, began to make plain their objections to the working of their waters by outsiders. Anstruther, like its sister villages, turned wholesale to other ways of catching fish, especially purse-netting and the huge bags it scoops in.

George Milne, the harbourmaster at Anstruther, works from a tiny office on the waterfront, a room he nearly fills single-handed. A barrel-chested Edinburgh man with a luxuriant white beard, he moved into the village several years ago to run a hotel. In contrast to the friendly welcome that visitors get here, but in common with incomers who intend to stay, he didn't find it easy to become part of the community.

'I wish I had a pound for every time someone has said to me, "Aye, you'll not last six months in Anstruther." But you just have to ignore it and carry on. The families here are very strong, and they look after their own. Many of the locals have never been out of Fife – I had one girl of twenty-three working in the hotel for me who'd never even been to Kirkcaldy. The fishermen generally get a couple of weeks' lay-off in the summer. They could well afford to go abroad, but most of them spend it right here in the town. They don't like to be away from the gossip and the scandal, all the local news. I took a few of the fishermen with me down to London to see a football match, Scotland against England; but when I suggested going up to the West End after the game and seeing the sights, they didn't want to know. They couldn't wait to get home again.'

George has seen the Anstruther fishermen gaining rewards from their intensive farming of the sea that the old herring skippers never dreamed of. He explained how the profits are shared out.

'The boat comes in at the end of the week and sells its catch; maybe £15,000 or more on a really good trip. The boat's expenses are deducted, then the boat owner – probably the skipper – takes half of what's left. The rest is divided up between everyone on board, with the skipper taking his share of that. You can see why some of these owner/skippers are doing all right; their crewmen as well. A young lad might be getting well over £1,000 a week if he's got a good skipper. There's great competition to be top skipper and top boat. Everyone in the town knows how everyone else has done. The top skippers don't have to worry about getting a good crew next year; and a good crew means good profits. Some of these young boys don't know what to do with all this money. Fishermen always moan about how they're doing, but the best of the Anstruther men are coining it, there's no doubt about that.'

Almost all the Anstruther-owned boats are based not in the village but at bigger ports like Aberdeen. The crews commute by minibus in between trips, coming home for a couple of days with the family before setting off again. Some sell their catch through the fish market at Pittenweem, a mile along the coast, but with modern-day communications they can easily switch markets if they don't like the prices being offered. George Milne told me a story about one of the Anstruther skippers who had hit a shoal of prime haddock and scooped the lot – maybe 300 boxes or more. He knew he would be offered about £22 a box at Pittenweem fish market so, like any stock market speculator, he checked out the competition on his ship-to-shore radio.

'This man found he could get £60 a box at Aberdeen, so when he landed his catch at three o'clock in the morning he just borrowed a flat-bed lorry from a friend. He had the whole lot in Aberdeen and sold before the Pittenweem buyers knew he was in.'

Such skippers are the fish barons of Anstruther, but there are others occupied with inshore fishing who have more of a struggle to make ends meet. Down on the harbour shore a thirty-foot 'creel boat' (or lobster and crab vessel) was having her hull scoured with a hose by her skipper, Davie – not his real name, but he was not keen for the other fishermen in this closest of communities to know his views on the way things are going. The *Ann Mary* – not her real name, either – a wooden-hulled, steel-decked boat built in the 1930s and owned solely by Davie, provides a reasonable living for him and a couple of crewmen. In summer she cuts across the heart of Scotland to the west coast by way of the Caledonian and Crinan canals to fish for lobsters and prawns round the Western Isles, Davie and his two colleagues getting home for a short visit every ten days or so.

'These top purse-net skippers have really struck gold since all this modern equipment came in,' Davie said rather sourly. 'They can get anything they find, the whole bloody lot, with no bother. So they do.' He jabbed out a finger towards the green hump of the Isle of May. 'See that island out there? The waters round it used to be full of dogfish – it was a good breeding ground. Well, a couple of years ago they went out and caught every fish round the island, big and small. They didn't leave one. There's no dogfish there now. And they're doing the same a hundred miles out. The quotas came in for a short while, but the skippers just went on catching beyond their limit and dumping the smaller stuff as they caught bigger and better fish.'

Davie's inshore creel work puts him in a different league from the all-devouring purse-netters. It isn't just sour grapes that makes him bitter about the greed, as he sees it, of the top skippers. He foresees the day when the golden eggs will all be gone and the goose well and truly killed off.

'Ach, they're cleaning out the sea. There are flashy cars in Anstruther these days, young lads wandering round the pubs with £1,000 in their pockets. They're well informed about conservation of the fish stocks, but a lot of them don't want to believe it. It doesn't suit them right now. In a few years' time they'll have ruined the fishing and Anstruther will be a tourist town.'

The top Anstruther skippers and their crewmen are high on the hog just now. But when the day of reckoning comes, the town is well placed to take on its new role. The Scottish Fisheries Museum is not the only tourist attraction on offer. Opposite its doors is moored the retired North Carr lightship, a great stark iron cage painted a ferocious pillar-box red from stem to stern, now housing an exhibition on the lonely, dangerous job her crews carried out all year round between 1933 and 1975, before automation put an end to that hermit-like way of life. Beside her in the harbour is a restored Shetland fishing boat, the first step towards Anstruther's 'floating museum' of various kinds of ships. The East Neuk Outdoors Centre in the High Street lays on all sorts of activities for youngsters during the summer, from canoeing in the pool at Cellardyke to boardsailing, archery, trampolining and bird-watching trips to the Isle of May. One or two gift shops are already creeping in among the small bakeries, butcher's and grocer's in the narrow streets above the waterfront of Anstruther Easter. The town doesn't have the dimity charm that Crail can offer, but there are many fine old buildings in the heart of Anstruther from days of past prosperity – the present riches, however, haven't expressed themselves in stone and tiles, but in Volvos and videos. There's a strong sense of the town, or at any rate those who run it, gearing up for a different future.

Whether the Anstruther people themselves are so keen on this impending change of role is another matter. When the Spanish galleon *Gran Grifon* limped into the harbour in 1588, another casualty of the storm-battered Armada, her captain and crew were well received, fed, looked after and sent home. That was probably the operative point, then as now: they weren't going to stay. A few did; and the chances are that they found, as incomers buying up pretty little cottages in Cellardyke do today, that it took fifty years to be accepted as part of the community. Until now, the continuing fishing tradition has kept Anstruther alive and individual. There's something both hopeful and ominous, however, in the promise held out by the display in the Fisheries Museum of 'many opportunities for small-scale speciality shops, additional catering and infill housing development which would strengthen the town's vitality as the east coast's major maritime visitor resort'. This could easily translate into a profusion of knick-knack shops, arcades and carelessly planned new housing estates

251

and chalet parks. These last are already in evidence above and behind the town. Balancing old traditions and new influences will be a ticklish business in Anstruther, with powerful forces pulling both ways. There are a few years yet to play with before – if Davie's forecast proves accurate – the moment of change is upon the townspeople, whether they want it or not.

One tip: a few boats still land line-caught fish at Pittenweem market. Unlike the fish taken by the purse-netters, harried and crushed in the crowd squashed into the giant nets, those brought on board attached to individual hooks retain their shape and flavour. They cost a few pence more, but it's worth paying the difference. Roll a line-caught Pittenweem haddock fresh out of the sea in egg and breadcrumbs, and you have a dish fit for the angels.

32. Banff and Macduff

'Banff has its past,' goes the saying, 'but Macduff has its future.' Rivalry between these two neighbouring small towns was always strong, especially during the last century when Banff's harbour silted up and the silver harvest of herring was grabbed enthusiastically by Macduff, its younger neighbour. After all, Banff had been a prosperous member of the Northern Hanse trading league back in the twelfth century, 600 years before the money and influence of James Duff, 2nd Earl of Fife, brought into being that other place round the bay. Upstarts to a man, those Macduffers.

Banff and Macduff lie side by side looking north into the Moray Firth from their rocky coastline of low cliffs, separated by the mouth of the River Deveron as it flows under Banff Bridge. Macduff, the town of the future (which is already here, in the shape of the seine-netters and the fish they bring in to market), is out of sight round the corner of Banff Bay as you stand on the bridge; but Banff's fine buildings, domed gently over their hill ahead, breathe past prosperity from every handsome town-house, inn and merchant's dwelling. It's a lovely setting for a town, not picturesquely perched on high cliffs but stylishly descending and filling the slope of the hill. Banff people are immensely proud of their well-preserved, orderly town with its wealth of elegant architecture. It copes, as all attractive seaside towns do, with the demands of today's visitors, though the bulk of these are kept at arm's length in caravan parks outside Banff. But the pulse of the town beats more strongly in its Preservation Society than it does in its tourist office.

The best way to get the full flavour of Banff's history is to sit on the seat outside the Town House at the northern end of Low Street. Here you find yourself on a paved area known as the Plainstones in the heart of the old trading town, with Banff's story through the centuries laid out all round you. On the pavement stands the Mercat Cross, a few feet from its original position in the middle of the market square. The seventeenth-century shaft reaches up nearly twenty feet to an eroded crucifix on top, at least a century older, which somehow escaped the image-smashing zeal of the Reformation. To your left as you sit here are lichen-green stone carvings in the wall of a house, a Stuart Royal Coat of Arms dated 1634 and a simian-looking Virgin and Child of 1628, along with another figure weathered beyond recognition. To your right is the oldest inn (and almost the oldest building) in Banff, the Market Arms, which carries high up on the inner wall of its archway a sinister mask of a face with a thin, cruel handlebar moustache and sunken eyes, dated 1585. Round the corner on the corner of High Shore stands a merchant's dwelling built in 1675 with three storeys of small windows and a side-turret under a pointed hat of a roof. A few steps from the Plainstones bring you beside this handsome old house to a view across High Shore into the abandoned kirkyard of St Mary's. The sixteenth-century church was demolished in 1797, but the vaulted Banff Aisle still stands among the gravestones sheltering the tomb of Sir Walter Ogilvy and his wife, Alison. This looks like a blackened fireplace, full of broken bottles and chip papers – unusual sight in house-proud Banff. All these buildings and structures speak of the hey-day of Banff's trading with the Baltic, the Mediterranean and the Low Countries, when the town's harbour was deep and the world its oyster.

The Duffs were sharp operators. When local families who had supported the Jacobite cause fled to the Continent as William of Orange arrived, the Duffs moved in to buy up the land left behind. By the time James, 2nd Earl of Fife, was in the saddle, Banff had turned from a declining trade to a new role as a fashionable winter resort for local nobility and gentry. Something smaller, cosier and more manageable than their cold stone caverns of castles was what they were after. Returning to your seat on the Plainstones, you can see just how effectively they were serviced by the Adam father-and-sons dynasty, John Marr, John Mitchell and the other eighteenth-century architects who rebuilt Banff so splendidly. Behind you James Adam's fluted, octagonal steeple is joined to the huge, plain block of the Town House. James Reid, the self-styled 'squarewright', designed this – and had to wait two years before his twenty-guinea fee was finally handed over. Low Street runs away south from here, lined with Georgian buildings; and there are more up the bank along High Street which you can reach by walking up the steep and narrow Strait Path. Pause before you begin the climb, however, to admire the crowned, crocketed and flying-buttressed Biggar Fountain in the centre of the square, a wonderful exercise in Victorian over-elaboration. On this spot stood the gallows where, in 1701, one of Banff's favourite black sheep went unabashed to his death. James Macpherson was a well-born lad gone wrong, equally keen on playing the fiddle and robbing people at the head of his gang of gypsies. Waiting for the hangman, he penned the song that Robert Burns later re-wrote as 'Macpherson's Rant':

> Farewell, ye dungeons dark and strong,
> The wretch's destinie!
> Macpherson's time will not be long,
> On yonder gallows-tree.
>
> Sae rantingly, sae wantonly,
> Sae dauntingly gae'd he:
> He play'd a spring, and danc'd it round
> Below the gallows-tree.

Having played his last song to the crowd round the gallows, Macpherson smashed his fiddle into pieces and offered his neck to the halter.

The Georgian masons' skill is on show everywhere in Banff. The stones of the house-walls are cut every imaginable way, from completely smooth faces in High Street to the walls of Low Street where blocks side by side are cut on opposing diagonals to present a surface that seems almost alive. All through the town the Victorian architects carried on the excellence and grandeur of design: the Fife Arms Hotel and the splendid County Hall at the south end of Low Street; the large, imposing churches; the long classical façade of Banff Academy, with six great Ionic columns high over the town, looking out over the bridge and river – perennial distractions for teenage daydreamers with desks near the classroom windows. In a way, Banff suffers from too many splendours. The apple-shaped plaques of the Banff Preservation Society hang on many walls, but there's so much for them to do with their limited resources of time, money and manpower. They haven't yet got round to updating their little guidebook *Royal and Ancient Banff*. It will be rather a pity when they print colour pictures in place of those black-and-white photographs full of 1960s' hemlines and Hillman Minxes by the kerb.

Banff's pride in itself shows in small details as well as on the grand scale. The museum in High Street contains a moving account of the life of Thomas Edward, its curator in mid-Victorian times and a self-taught natural history enthusiast. 'Discouraged by his experience of school as he had been expelled for bringing his beasties', Edward never learned to read or write well, and at one point of his life was so depressed by everyone's lack of interest in his natural history collection that he went down to the seashore, bent on killing himself. 'While about to end his misery he was attracted by a flock of sanderlings among which was a stranger that fascinated him. He forgot his misery and began to think over matters.'

These reflections led Edward, by trade a shoemaker and a hard-up one, to plug the hole in his pocket by selling his entire collection for twenty pounds – it couldn't have hurt him more if he had been selling a child of his. Local fishermen went on bringing him the waste dredgings of their nets and lines, and in time the collection had re-seeded itself. Edward became Curator of Banff Museum in 1862, and for the next twenty years devoted himself to the job. 'When no longer able to wander over nature's domain as was his wont, he turned to other things such as the antiquities of Banff.' He died in 1886 aged seventy-two, to the end 'able to appreciate and admire the beauties and wonders of nature in the incomparable works of the Creator'. In most other places, an obscure museum curator of the last century such as Thomas Edward would have long been forgotten, but here he is fondly and proudly remembered.

While you are looking round the museum, your children can be on the stairs that lead up to it, admiring another of the treasures of Banff. Each tread of the stairs carries a picture at either end, leading young explorers up through the alphabet from anchor, bugle, cannon, daisy at the bottom to whale, xylophone, yak and Zeppelin at the top. These beautifully executed works of marquetry in different colours of lino were laid on these stairs by the local traffic warden a few years ago when the library and museum building was a schools' museum. He's still to be seen around Banff's streets today. Maybe he'll reveal to you what neither the lady at the desk nor I could work out – the identity of the 'x' on the right-hand side.

Banff's Tourist Information Centre, by the car park at the top of Low Street, is housed in what appears to be a small Greek temple. This is Collie Lodge, built in 1836 as a fitting entrance to Duff House, the great baroque mansion of the earls of Fife that stands behind the trees down beyond the golf course by the River Deveron. William Duff had it built when he was plain (or fairly plain) Lord Braco, to the design of William Adam; but he never lived there. Work began in 1735, but the squabble that took place between owner and architect over the enormous cost of the house – £70,000 in all – so soured Lord Braco that he lost interest in the whole enterprise. His son, James, 2nd Earl of Fife, added to the pile and also built a mausoleum in the park woodland. James Duff was painfully aware of the shaky claims of his family to historical importance, and much of his building and development work in the area was carried out to bolster up this insecurity. He had a knight effigy removed from the tomb of Provost

Douglas of Banff in St Mary's, and re-erected by the south wall of the mausoleum – and wasn't at all displeased when local people took it for Robert Bruce, and Bruce himself for a Duff forebear. Duff House is open to the public, and it's well worth putting aside a morning to tour the house and park.

James Duff's most useful and enduring monument, however, is Banff's twin town of Macduff. The little village of Doune that his father bought up in 1733 had struggled along on fishing throughout its existence, but the 2nd Earl set about it with a will when his turn came, half a century later. On to the old fishermen's cottages he grafted a whole new town and named it after himself. The fine harbour that he had built for his new creation in the 1760s was extended by later earls of Fife in time for the herring when they arrived in undreamed-of numbers around the turn of the eighteenth century. Gutting and curing yards were set up, and 100 years after its foundation Macduff had grown into a town of a size to rival the fashionable resort across the river. In the 1820s there were almost 100 herring boats in Banff's own fleet, but in the middle of that century the course of the River Deveron shifted. So did the balance of power between the two towns, Banff settling into gentility while Macduff rolled up its sleeves and went on catching herring in ever-increasing quantities. In the 1870s a North Basin was added to Macduff's original West and East Harbours, followed in 1921 by the Princess Royal Basin, and in 1965 a new fishmarket.

The fishmarket by the East Harbour (now renamed the Outer Basin) is a fine place to watch the catch being sorted in the early hours of a blustery morning. Outside, the narrow entrance to the harbour is blocked by successive green waves that come slapping and surging in, to race round the West Harbour and thump against the inner wall, throwing sheets of spray all over Shore Street. It's all fish here. Along Shore Street opposite the fishmarket stand the premises of the Banffshire Fishselling Company; also Paterson's, Ship's Chandler and Fishsalesman. Spray and low clouds blot out the view of Banff across the bay as the seine-netter *Aurica*, registration number BF 474, wallows and pitches into the harbour to join the other boats rocking gently in the calm, sheltered water of the Outer Basin. Their names are those of a century ago, picked out in gold on the bows: *Ocean Challenge, Delightful, Venture, Opportune*. The crews, in jerseys or yellow oilskins, get the week's catch into the fishmarket shed as soon as they can, smothering the boxes in ice and pulling more fish out of the holds. Most boats are based at Peterhead, Aberdeen or Fraserburgh, but the Macduff men like to bring their catch back with them to unload in their own home market before they speed off in minibuses, in cars or on bikes for a reunion with their families.

Inside the long stone shed of the fishmarket the buyers prowl round the boxes, licking pencils and jotting down notes. The catch stares up glassily out of the ice blankets: codling, haddock, dab, plaice, skate with their gristly whip of a tail, hideously grimacing and grinning monkfish, shark-like dogfish and puffy-cheeked, blandly smiling catfish. The larger fish are gashed open up the belly, the smaller ones gape pinkly from a neat cut in the throat. Everything's grist to a seine-netter's mill. Those fish that can't be sold for human consumption end up in animal feed, or dried and ground into fertilizer powder. The sheer variety and quantity taken by the boats with their modern fish-finding equipment gives the most casual onlooker a signal that isn't hard to read. Macduff's fishmarket is small stuff compared with the great clearing-houses of Aberdeen and Peterhead. Fish of every description are pouring in week by week in their thousand upon thousand. How much more of a hammering can those precious stocks still out there take?

Aurica's white shelter deck sits high on her rounded black hull, the steel wheelhouse carefully painted to look like wood – a link with the bygone fishing boats that most skippers like to maintain. Everything on board is very plain and practical. Thick layers of blue and orange paint cover the deck and walls. Great cable-drums fill the well of the deck, forward of the wheelhouse. Aft stands the winch for hauling in the bright orange, plastic-meshed seine net which now lies piled in its open-topped locker. Everything smells of salt, wet metal and fish. Inside the housing there's a tremendous clutter, at the end of this five-day trip, that would appal a respectable Banffburgher. Boots, papers, ropes, fish corpses, soggy bits of sandwiches and unwashed pots of cold tea lie piled on the floors and tables. There's a tiny lavatory with a hand-operated seawater pump, an equally tiny galley and a vertical flight of steps leading down to the stuffy little glory-hole where the crew are cramped cheek by jowl in their few hours of relaxation at sea. To get into their bunks they crawl through small elliptical openings in the walls of their room, to be cocooned inside against the wildest roll. The furnishings are spartan, to say the least: lockers, a central table with a raised 'fiddle' round its edge to stop crockery sliding on to the floor. In theory the men are supposed to eat at this table, but no one does. Carrying hot dishes down that perpendicular stairway in rough weather isn't on. Everyone eats in the galley, squeezed tight up against the next man, where food has to travel just a few inches from cooker to table.

Up above all this in *Aurica*'s wheelhouse are the electronic devices that give a shoal of fish, once in range, practically no chance of escape. When you discover a good hunting ground, you record its position on tape. Feed that tape into your automatic direction-finder on your next trip – or at any other time – and up on the screen pops a map of Scotland, with a course set from wherever you happen to be to the target area. Arrived there, you monitor the contours of the seabed on your echo-sounding wire graph machine to pinpoint the boat over the exact spot where you previously hit good fish. A thick black smear on the paper means you're in business. Now the fish-finder takes over, telling you in colour code how big the shoal is, the direction it's travelling, its distance from the boat and even – miraculously – what kind of fish you've found. If they are worth taking, you put a marker over the side, move downwater to intercept the shoal, shoot your net and return to the marker. Up comes the big orange bag with a week's wages thrashing about inside. Of course, it's not always as straightforward or productive as that. Jim, the crewman who invited me on board *Aurica*, described February trips into sleet and high wind as he stood in the wheelhouse. In short, clipped sentences he drew the framework of a lot of rough experience.

'Winter it can get dangerous. There's a lot of gear about the boat these days for you to foul yourself on. Ice is bad. We can get on each other's nerves, too.'

Jim patted the square box of the fish-finder.

'Aye, I'm not too expert on this. The skipper kens what kind of fish it's showing. Things have changed a lot since I started. That was twenty years ago. In them days everything was done by hand. Now we've all this new machinery, it's an easier job. Want to see the modern machine we use for killing fish?'

He grinned, displaying a tarnished old pocket-knife in the palm of his hand.

'We catch a lot of fish. All kinds. Our catching power – there's no comparison. We do all right, ken. The skipper takes half for the boat, and we share out the other half. Other boats are doing all right as well. Most families fish around here. There's very little else in Macduff.'

Macduff has one or two attractions, apart from its fishing activities, that might hold a tourist's attention. There's a fine open-air swimming pool along the seafront at Tarlair, golf, bowling and sea-angling trips. But it's essentially a working place intent on filling that fishmarket week by week. Macduff owns the practical present, Banff the stylish past. Both places are doing all right, ken.

33. Crinan

'To the man of business who must spend the greater part of the year among the din and bustle of the city, no pleasanter retreat could be recommended than the village of Crinan. To the tourist anxious to behold the beauties of nature – the splendour of land and sea – no place could be chosen that possesses these in more pleasing and picturesque variety.' Henry Grunewald, the proprietor of the Crinan Hotel in late Victorian days, knew how to turn a seductive phrase. His self-penned guidebook *Crinan and its Neighbourhood* went into raptures about the beauties of this remote corner of Western Scotland as it promoted 'the large and well-built hotel that has just been erected. This is a splendidly designed Scotch baronial building. In front of it is Crinan Bay, upon whose rippling waters a tiny craft is now sailing with the breeze. To the west is a panorama which in all Scottish scenery cannot be surpassed. Here lie the hills of the Northern part of Jura, made more beautiful by the distance, and as the summer sun lights upon them no more pleasing sight could be imagined . . . Still farther off rise the distant and lofty hills of Mull, and, as the whole view breaks upon one's vision, we mutter, "Surely this is the gateway of an island paradise".'

Paradise isn't a bad description of Crinan. You can pay a lot to enjoy a superb seafood meal in the top floor restaurant of the Crinan Hotel, or a lot less for a bar snack at ground level; but the views are equally stunning from either location, or from a picnic spot on the grassy banks outside. On sunny days Loch Crinan is shot-silk blue as it stretches out west round the long, flat islets in the fairway of the Sound of Jura. The bare back of Jura, rock screes and thin green patches, rises to fill the far view ahead, with the sharply cut outlines of the mountains on Mull further off to the north. A filmy blue haze lies between the mainland and the large islands, emphasizing their isolation and putting the shimmer on the surface of the loch into soft focus. Cormorants fly heavily among the fishing boats, gulls more gracefully over their heads. The sense of being on a remote edge of land is absolute as you look out westward to Jura, Scarba and the mountains of Mull, framed by one of this coast's spectacular sunsets.

Across the loch from the hotel, Duntrune Castle rises from the rock above the water's edge, now tamed into house shape with a pitched roof and chimneys, its tall, square walls carrying eight centuries of history. From the castle the view sweeps inland past a line of low hills into the flat floodplain of the River Add, known as Mòine Mhór or The Great Moss.

The first Scots came to Mòine Mhór from Ireland in AD 498 to found a kingdom from the rocky knoll of Dunadd that rises from the marsh beside the river. If you climb Dunadd you'll see the symbols those settlers cut in the summit rocks nearly 1,500 years ago: the outline of a foot, denoting kingship; a scooped-out bowl symbolizing the washing of kingly feet; a hump-backed boar, the sign of royal lineage. From this high place the newly crowned rulers of the Dalriadic kingdom could look westward towards their origins and eastward into their future. Dunadd was the source of their earthly power, as Iona was of their spiritual strength. The Dalriada held sway for over 200 years, until the Picts settled their differences with the invading Angles and drove the old rulers back across the Irish Sea. But Dunadd and the Dalriada remained powerful tokens for Western Scots for many centuries, symbols of 'the Celtic heart of Scotland' in its earliest and purest state – a kind of landbound Atlantis.

Monuments of the distant past are scattered all over the hills and fields in the district around Crinan. Standing stones rise in rough circles from the corn near Dunchraigaig, three miles to the north, the rubble of Bronze Age burial cairns heaped nearby. There are incised handprints on an outcrop of rock near Barnakill Farm to the east, cup-and-ring marked rocks at Cairnbaan, remnants of the chapel built by St Cummine, the seventh abbot of Iona, on the hillside at Kilmahumaig, just south of Crinan. All are reminders of the influence this outpost of the mainland exerted for thousands of years on the lives, mythologies and religious feelings of past civilizations. But it was a severely practical construction, the Crinan Canal, that brought the modern world to Crinan at the beginning of the nineteenth century.

Just off the A816 road from Oban to Lochgilphead stands the Cairnbaan Hotel, a steam trawler painted on one end-wall. Cairnbaan is where you embark on the final approach road to Crinan, with five miles of birch, oak, Scots pine, spruce, larch and rowan on one side and the River Add on the other, gradually snaking closer through the peaty plain of Mòine Mhór to empty into Loch Crinan. Sticking closer than a brother to the road runs the dark waterway of the Crinan Canal, a slash across the neck of the Knapdale and Kintyre peninsula. It's a four-hour journey through the eight and a half miles and fifteen locks of the canal from Ardrishaig on Loch Fyne across to Crinan, but the yachtsmen and fishing boat skippers are only too glad to avoid the 130-mile trip round the stormy Mull of Kintyre that those wanting to get from Loch Fyne to the waters of the Western Isles had to face before the canal was built. It was authorized in 1793 and begun a year later in response to the fast-growing trade between a quickly expanding Glasgow and the Western Isles. At that time the Highland clans were being uprooted and thrown off their lands to make way for Cheviot sheep, and it wasn't easy to assemble a competent workforce out on the extreme west coast. Money, food and materials were in as short supply as men; but somehow the Crinan Canal was completed by 1809, just as the herring were beginning their great invasion of the coastal waters. When the Caledonian Canal was opened in 1822, fishing, cargo, trading and passenger boats could all speed from the Clyde through Loch Fyne and the Crinan Canal, then nip up the west coast to Loch Linnhe and the Caledonian Canal's dead-straight run of sixty miles right across the face of the Highlands into the North Sea at Inverness – a sheltered journey of some 130 miles in preference to the 600-odd miles of storm-blown seas round the outer coastline. Suddenly Crinan was a boom town, not in size but in its strategic importance to cargo owners and herring boat skippers.

On the wall inside the Crinan Hotel hangs an account from *The Argyllshire Advertiser* (a.k.a. 'The Squeak'), printed in the 1890s, of the canal's finest hour – the visit of Queen Victoria in August 1847 as remembered after half a century by 'a charming old lady'. In 'regular Queen's weather' the royal party was drawn through the canal on a barge, before disembarking at Crinan to the tumultuous cheers of the assembled locals. A tartan carpet led down to the beach and their waiting boat.

'I remember a little fellow about ten,' reminisced the old lady to the 'Squeak' reporter, 'who, just as the Queen approached, managed to pop his head through between two men in the front, gasping out, as he struggled, in a strong Highland accent, "But

I WANT TO SEE THE QUEEN."

Her Majesty cast on him a smile of intense amusement.' That was the smile of a sweet young Queen, not yet thirty years old and madly in love with her handsome Prince Consort. Her flunkeys were not so amused by the antics of the blacksmith of Bellanoch, who became

'SO CARRIED AWAY BY HIS ENTHUSIASM

that he patted the Prince of Wales on the head, exclaiming "What a clever wee bit chappie you are!" For his loyal zeal he had a rap on the knuckles from the polished baton of a blue-coated functionary.'

When they came on the scene, towards the end of Victoria's reign, the increase in size, power and seaworthiness of the big steam-driven trawlers and passenger boats put an end to the Crinan Canal's century in the sun, but it remains very much the lifeblood of Crinan village even today. Just about everyone who lives and works there is involved, directly or indirectly, with the canal and its daily traffic of small fishing boats and pleasure yachts. The water comes through the final land lock of fifteen into a small basin below the Crinan Hotel where the boats can tie up, manoeuvre, take on supplies and put off refuse. The inner wall of the basin is usually crammed with fishing boats, the view across them a criss-cross mesh of masts, yards, rigging, ropes, blocks, pulleys, chains and cable-drums, all recalling a scene from some great herring port of the last century. CN (Campbeltown), BA (Ballantrae) and TT (Tarbert) are the commonest registrations, though boats from East Coast ports base themselves here, too, at certain times of the year. They go out on a Sunday evening or Monday morning and stay away all week, fishing the inshore waters for crabs, clams and prawns. All the boats are under contract to big selling concerns, so the skippers don't have the worry of seeking a market for their catch; it's unloaded at Crinan into refrigerated vans that speed it overland to Glasgow and the buyers. The boats fish an area clean of prawns and move on elsewhere, returning a few months later when the stocks have built up again. Prawns regenerate quickly, luckily for them and their consumers. Each boat is equipped with electronic fish-finding gear; but the atmosphere on board is far removed from that on the largest East Coast trawlers. Out here the operation is small-scale – small boat, small crew – and the skippers, unlike the almighty demi-gods of Aberdeen and Peter-head, work alongside their crew members, mending nets and gear and often taking advice about sea conditions and choice of fishing grounds.

Along with the commercial traffic, the canal handles an increasing number of private yachts, as pleasure sailors discover the freedom and excitement of cruising the unfrequented waters round the Western Isles. Crinan is no blah-hah, gin-and-tonic skippers' bolt-hole – yachts in the basin tend to be crusted with salt and rust and well battered by bad weather. Converted fishing boats lie alongside the bigger, smarter craft. The bar of the Crinan Hotel fills up at midday with the members of this rough-and-ready club, all talking technicalities. They smell of beer, sweat and engine-oil rather than of champagne and after-shave. Yachtsmen and fishermen co-exist, each acknowledging the dividing line between work and play.

Every boat, working or leisure, enters and leaves Loch Crinan by way of the sea lock. A small community of lock-keepers lives permanently at Crinan, their white-painted cottages grouped on neatly trimmed lawns. The head lock-keeper and his assistants work hard, as their predecessors did, always on call to operate the heavy bars of the lock gates. These are swung by electric control nowadays, but things can still go wrong if boat skipper and lock-keeper don't work in harmony. The lock-keepers tend to be self-sufficient men of few words, like lighthouse keepers – which is another duty they undertake, maintaining the little hexagonal light-tower beside the head keeper's cottage.

Just up the road from the hotel stands the large corrugated shed of Crinan Boats. Inside is a clutter of trestles, wood shavings, chunks of polystyrene and paint drums lying under the fishing boats and small motor dinghies awaiting repair. The slipway that runs down to the loch can be hired by boat owners who want to carry out minor repairs, or they can bring their vessels up into the yard for major surgery. Humphrey Massey left his directorship of a Clyde shipyard to take over Crinan Boats in 1968. He loves his work out here in the west.

'Hard work, enjoying what you do and not being too greedy – not taking too much money out of the business – that's the secret of success in this line. We haven't built anything for many years. You need a run of several boats of the same type to make it worth while. It's a question of a learning curve for the men – the first one always takes twice as long as the next. But out here things are so bitty that you can't expect more than two the same.'

Mr Massey would like to have seen a recently proposed scheme get off the ground: a plan for a marina of about 100 boats in the old Crinan harbour, half a mile to the west. A narrow lane runs down a gently falling valley to the wide curve of the harbour, still used as a sheltering place by a handful of small fishing boats and yachts. It's guarded from north and west winds by Eilean da Mhèinn, a flat island right in the mouth of the harbour that all but blocks off the view out to Jura.

'The scheme wouldn't have hurt anyone, hidden down there under the hill,' said Mr Massey decisively. 'Someone was prepared to put money into it. But the plan leaked out' – great scorn filled his expression – 'at an Edinburgh cocktail party. People who hadn't been consulted and others who had berths in the harbour marshalled their objections, and that was the end of that. Personally, I think it would have been a *tremendous* success.'

In spite of this disappointment, he counts himself lucky to have exchanged the Clydeside shipyards for the wilds of Crinan. 'Living here is heaven. I love it, especially on those still winter days when we get a red fire of bracken on the hillsides, the blue of the loch and white of snow on the Mull hills.'

The Crinan Hotel stands at the centre of everything that goes on here, a large white block exuding permanence and importance from its over-stepped upper storeys, rounded front bays, little cylindrical corner turrets and baroque doorway. It's an imposing place, built to dominate the canal's seaward terminus. Couples with a good deal to spend – generally overseas visitors – stay in its individually designed bedrooms and eat in that expensive seafood restaurant in the glow of sunsets over Jura. But it's not just the extremely well-heeled who use the many amenities of the Crinan Hotel. Yacht owners and passengers drink in the bar, tourists eat light lunches or take tea in the coffee shop overlooking the canal basin which was once the stable block for the barge horses. The coffee shop contains an eccentric and beautifully polished collection of early petrol-engined agricultural machines, and a glass display-counter full of unimaginably heavy, sickly and delicious cakes. (NB – Estimate the number of these you think you'll want, then halve it: you won't manage more unless you have the digestion of an anaconda.)

In winter the hotel closes, but the bar stays open. During these bad-weather months most of the yachts are laid up elsewhere, and Crinan's waterfront becomes home to a shifting community of fishermen who put into the harbour and canal basin in stormy conditions. They kick their heels, mending gear, overhauling their boats on the slipway at Crinan Boats and drinking and chatting in the hotel bar until the weather allows them out again. Hotels in remote parts of Scotland are different creatures from the 'pay up, eat up and go away' establishments of English resorts. They come into their own during the long, snow-bound winters as havens of warmth and light, gossip-shops and social centres, cheerful caves out of the storm. The Crinan Hotel has been functioning in this way since it was established back in the time of Henry Grunewald, the author of that enthusiastic guidebook. Fishermen, wildfowlers, lock-keepers, yachtsmen, anglers, hikers, tourists and travelling salesmen pass through its doors, along with the paying guests. It's the nerve centre of Crinan, all things to all people.

Crinan village has a permanent population of fewer than sixty. It's surrounded by some of the most thinly populated, lovely and historic countryside in Scotland. It has lochs, islands, woods, hills and sunsets all on its doorstep. The scenery is lush and green – plants and trees flourish here on the coast in what for Scotland is a mild climate, a delight to the eye and spirit after the rugged bareness of so much of the interior. It's the sort of place where you can spend an entire day lazily watching the boats going in and out through the sea lock, in a pleasant daze of relaxation. For anyone who is aware of what usually happens to places like this, the first reaction is to wonder how on earth Crinan has escaped a litter of holiday homes, caravans, bungalows and gift shops. After all, it's only a morning's drive from Glasgow, and there's no shortage of prettily sited building-plots.

The answer lies in the diversity of interests that make up the life of Crinan. Several communities work side by side here, interconnected but separate, like a set of cog wheels. The Crinan Hotel; the lock-keepers and their employers, the British Waterways Board; the fishermen; the yachting enthusiasts; the boatyard; the villagers – all these have their own interests to consider, while engaging at some point of their operations with all the rest. They watch each other like hawks. Developers come to Crinan from time to time to make astronomical offers to one of the parties, but invariably the others make common cause and see the interloper off. The marina scheme was a case in point. It's a system of checks and balances. No one does what the majority don't want. And it's fair to say that, when it comes down to brass tacks, they all want the same thing – to keep Crinan as it is, undeveloped and within bounds.

The lady in the tartan skirt selling prawns to tourists on the sea lock wall put things neatly into perspective, speaking for small communities under threat from development all round the coasts of Britain: 'Here it is just the fishing and the forestry, along with these yachts. We don't like change here. I wouldnae want to see this place being developed. Other places have already got a lot of incomers in this part of the world, and I have tae say they don't do much for the community. We're maybe a bit careful wi' strangers hereabouts. We're hanging on to our tradition, and we dinnae want to see it go.'

But the last word rests with Henry Grunewald, his fanfare of praise for the quiet pleasures of Crinan: 'With its picturesque and sublime, its beautiful and oftentimes majestic view it is an ideal spot for the lover of nature. With its exhilarating sea and mountain breezes it will give renewed vigour to the traveller and tourist. With all its charms it must surely command a place among the most attractive beauty spots of our dear Auld Scotia.'

Amen.

INFORMATION AND
FURTHER READING

Information and Further Reading

Few of the publications recommended here are major, book-length works. Almost all are inexpensive local pamphlets, booklets or walking trail guides, obtainable in the town or village concerned, that will help you to find your way round while pointing out items of interest.

* related walk described in *Coastal Walks in England and Wales* by Christopher Somerville (Grafton Books 1988)

1. Holy Island
Museum: Church Lane
Nearest Tourist Information Centre (12miles): Castlegate Car Park, Berwick-upon-Tweed tel: (0289) 307187
Reading: *Holy Island* by Frank Graham (Butler Publishing)
   In St Mary's Church, many pamphlets on St Cuthbert, monks of Holy Island, Lindisfarne Gospels, etc.

2. Easington Colliery
Nearest Tourist Information Centre (4 miles): 20 Upper Chare, Peterlee tel: (0783) 586 4450
Reading: *Easington Colliery* – booklet produced by the National Coal Board (now British Coal)
   Save Easington! – Easington Colliery People, Past and Present – compilation of writings, poems, photographs and art work by local residents
   Easington District Council have many booklets (NB their 'People Past and Present' series of verbatim interviews on tape and in script, and *The Easington Colliery Disaster* by Steve Cummings), as well as a superb collection of photographs, at their Council Offices, Seaside Lane, Easington, Peterlee, Co. Durham. SR8 3TN tel: (091) 527 0501

3. Robin Hood's Bay
Museum: Fisherhead
Nearest Tourist Information Centre (6 miles): New Quay Road, Whitby tel: (0947) 602674
Reading: *Robin Hood's Bay: a practical guide for visitors* by E. Gower (Dalesman)
   Robin Hood's Bay As It Was by J. Robin Lidster (Hendon Publishing)
   Three Fevers and *Foreigners* by Leo Walmsley – set in the town

* Walk No. 36: Robin Hood's Bay to Ravenscar.

4. Scarborough
Museums: Museum of Natural History, Wood End (the Sitwells' old house)
   Rotunda Museum, Valley Road
Tourist Information Centre: St Nicholas Cliff tel: (0723) 373333
Reading: *Scarborough: a practical guide for visitors* by Jean Curd (Dalesman)
   Scarborough As It Was by Bryan Berryman (Hendon Publishing)
   The Scarborough Heritage Trail (Scarborough Borough Council)

5. Flamborough
Exhibition: Heritage Information Centre, South Landing
Nearest Tourist Information Centre (4 miles): Prince Street, Bridlington
tel: (0262) 673474/679626
Reading: *Flamborough* (Dalesman Mini-book)
   Look at Flamborough (Bessacarr Prints) – available from Heritage Information Centre

* Walk No. 37: Flamborough Head.

6. Skegness
Museum: Church Farm Museum, Church Road
Tourist Information Centre: Embassy Centre, Grand Parade tel: (0754) 4821
Gibraltar Point Nature Reserve:
tel: (0754) 2677
Reading: *Skeggy! The Story of an East Coast Town* by Winston Kime (Seashell Books)
   Bygone Skegness by Winston Kime (Bygone Grantham)
   Discovering Skegness – Three Town Walks – available from South East Lindsey Teachers' Centre, Pelham Road, Skegness PE25 2QX

7. Cromer
Museum: East Cottages, Tucker Street
Tourist Information Centre: Town Hall, Prince of Wales Road tel: (0263) 512497
Reading: *Poppyland Papers* by Clement Scott (copy in Cromer Library)
   Poppyland – strands of Norfolk history by Peter Stibbons and David Cleveland (Poppyland Publishing)
   Poppyland in Pictures (Poppyland Publishing)

* Walk No. 42: Cromer to Sidestrand through Poppyland.

8. Southwold

Museum: Victoria Street
Sailors' Reading Room: bottom of East Street
Tourist Information Centre: Town Hall, Market Place tel: (0502) 722366
Reading: Southwold (out-of-print, outdated and fascinating guide)

    Guide to Southwold and District (published annually by Southwold and District Chamber of Trade and Commerce)

    Discovering Southwold by Alan Bottomley, John Hutchinson and Christopher Chestnutt (Southwold and Reydon Society/Suffolk Preservation Society)

    – all available from Town Hall

* Walk No. 43: Walberswick to Dunwich.

9. Southend-on-Sea

Museum: Victoria Avenue
Tourist Information Centres: Civic Centre, Victoria Avenue tel: (0702) 355122
High Street Precinct tel: (0702) 355120
Reading: Southend's Heritage – Georgian and Victorian Terraces (Southend Society)
Southend – a Seaside Holiday 1750–1950 (Southend Museums Service)
Southchurch Hall by Leonard Helliwell (Southend Museums Service)
History of Prittlewell Priory by J. W. Burrows (Southend Museums Service)
Porters – Civic House and Mayor's Parlour (Borough of Southend-on-Sea)

10. Ramsgate

Museums: Maritime Museum, Clock House, Royal Harbour
Ramsgate Library and Museum, Guildford Lawn
Tourist Information Centre: Argyle Centre, Queen Street tel: (0843) 591086
Reading: A Walk Round Regency Ramsgate (Ramsgate Society)
Royal Harbour of Ramsgate – Historic Harbour Trail (Thanet District Council)
Maritime Thanet ed. Robert B. Matkin (Thanet District Council)

11. Brighton

Museum: Church Street
Royal Pavilion: (0273) 603005
Tourist Information Centres: Marlborough House, Old Steine tel: (0273) 23755

Sea Front, King's Road tel: (0273) 23755
Reading: An Architectural Walk in Brighton and Hove

    Children's Brighton
    A Walk about the Best of Brighton
    The Buildings of Brighton
– all available from 68 Grand Parade, Brighton tel: (0273) 673416

* Walk No. 3: Brighton: Palace Pier and the Pavilion to Kemp Town.

12. West Wittering

Nearest Tourist Information Centre (8 miles): St Peter's Market, West Street, Chichester tel: (0243) 775888
Reading: Witterings Then & Now by Keith and Janet Smith (Mill Press)

    East Head/West Wittering Nature Walk (National Trust)

    Chichester Harbour – The Thirteen Villages by Jill Dickin (Chichester Harbour Conservancy)

    History and Management of Chichester Harbour by Geoffrey Godber (Chichester Harbour Conservancy)

* Walk No. 4: Chichester Harbour: East Head to West Itchenor.

13. Swanage

Museum: Tithe Barn Museum, Church Hill
Tourist Information Centre: The White House, Shore Road tel: (0929) 422885
Reading: Swanage Town Trail (S.E.P.)

    Swanage Rediscovered by Stewart and Danielle Borrett

    Old Swanage – Quarry Port to Seaside Spa by Rodney Legg (Dorset Publishing Company)

    Story of Swanage History from Early Times by David Lewer (Harewood Publications)

    Curiosities of Swanage, or, Old London By The Sea by David Lewer and J. Bernard Calkin

    Purbeck – The Ingrained Island by Paul Hyland (Gollancz, 1978) is an excellent general book on the area

* Walk No. 5: St Alban's Head and the cliffs of Purbeck.

14. Lyme Regis

Museum: Philpot Museum, Bridge Street
Tourist Information Centre: The Guildhall, Bridge Street tel: (029 74) 2138

Reading: Three Town Walks by John Fowles
A Brief History of Lyme by John Fowles
Lyme Regis Walkabout
Lyme Bay Fossils: Beach Guide by Nigel J. Clarke
The Axmouth/Lyme Regis Undercliffs National Nature Reserve by T. J. Wallace
Landslips near Lyme Regis by Muriel A. Arber
– all these available from Serendip Fine Books, 11 Broad Street, Lyme Regis, Dorset

* Walk No. 7: Lyme Regis to the Axe via the Undercliff.

15. Dartmouth

Museums: Town Museum, The Butterwalk
Henley Museum, Anzac Street
Tourist Information Centre: Royal Avenue Gardens tel: (080 43) 4224
Reading: Exploring from Dartmouth (Dartmouth and Kingswear Society)

* Walk No. 9: Little Dartmouth Farm to Blackstone Point and Dartmouth.

16. Lizard Town

Museum: Apply Gweal Crease, The Lizard
Tourist Information Centre: Carnebone Farm, Wendren, Helston tel: (0326) 40899 – May until end of September. At other times telephone Kerrier District Council's Tourism Office tel: (0209) 712941 for 24-hour information service
Reading: 100 Years Around The Lizard by Jean Stubbs (Bossiney Books)
A Week At The Lizard by Rev. C. A. Johns (available for study in Local Studies Library, Redruth tel: (0209) 216760)
The Lizard Peninsula Tourism Association publishes a local guide, widely available in and around Lizard Town

Walk No. 12: Around the Lizard.

17. Padstow

Museum: Padstow Institute, Market Street
Tourist Information Centre: Council Offices, Station Road tel: (0841) 532296
Reading: Padstow and District by Donald R. Rawe and Jack Ingrey (Lodenek Press)

Padstow's 'Obby 'Oss and May Day Festivities by Donald R. Rawe

* Walk No. 16: Rock to St Enodoc's and Polzeath.

18. Clovelly

Tourist Information Centre and Exhibition: Visitor Centre, Clovelly tel: (023 73) 781
Reading: Clovelly and its Story by Nancy Ruthven (Aycliffe Press)
Down A Cobbled Street by Sheila Ellis (Badger Books)

* Walk No. 17: Clovelly to Mouth Mills and Brownsham Farm.

19. Appledore

Museum: North Devon Maritime Museum, Odun Road
Nearest Tourist Information Centre (3 miles): The Quay, Bideford tel: (023 72) 77676
Reading: 'The Crake', from *Tales Of Moorland and Estuary* (Macdonald Futura)
Chapters 4–6 of *Salar The Salmon* (Faber)
– both these contain some of Henry Williamson's best writing on the Appledore of the 1920s

20. Lynton and Lynmouth

Museum: Lyn and Exmoor Museum, St Vincent Cottage, Market Street, Lynton
Tourist Information Centres: Town Hall, Lee Road, Lynton tel: (0598) 52225
National Park Information Centre, The Esplanade, Lynmouth
Reading: They Took The Lifeboat Up The Mountainside by William T. Baker
The Lynmouth Flood Disaster by Eric Delderfield (ERD Publications)
Lynton and Lynmouth Cliff Railway (Salmon Mini-guide)
A Walk Through Lynton and *A Walk Through Lynmouth* (Exmoor National Park Authority) – both available from Lynmouth Information Centre

* Walk No. 18: Lynmouth and Lynton to the Valley of Rocks.

21. Southerndown

Tourist Information Centre and Exhibition: The Heritage Centre, Seamouth, Dunraven Bay tel: (0656) 880157

Reading: The History of Dunraven by Stan Bevan

The Wreckers of Dunraven and The Story of Dunraven (Glamorgan Heritage Coast leaflets available from the Heritage Centre, Seamouth)

22. Oxwich

Information Centre and Exhibition: Oxwich Nature Reserve Centre tel: (0792) 390320
Reading: A Guide to Gower (Gower Society)

A Guide to Gower – the Seashore by Julia Berney (Culver House Press)

At the Reserve Centre, a wide variety of leaflets on dragonflies, flowering plants, birds, butterflies, ferns, sand dunes, etc.

* Walk No. 22: Oxwich to Port-Eynon Point.

23. Tenby

Museum: Castle Hill
Tourist Information Centre: The Croft, Tenby tel: (0834) 2404
Reading: The Story of Tenby by Margaret Davies (Tenby Museum)

Tenby Town Trail (Tenby Civic Society)

24. Aberystwyth

Museums: Ceredigion Museum, Pier Street Old Coliseum, Terrace Road
Tourist Information Centre: Eastgate tel: (0970) 612125/617911
Reading: Aberystwyth Town Trail by Douglas B. Hague

* Walk No. 26: Aberystwyth to Borth.

25. Barmouth

Museums: Maritime Museum, The Quay Exhibition, Tŷ Gwyn yn Bermo, The Quay
Tourist Information Centre: The Library, Station Road tel: (0341) 280787
Reading: Exploring Barmouth (Barmouth Publicity Association)

* Walk No. 27: Fairbourne to Barmouth.

26. New Brighton

Tourist Information Centre: The Bathing Pool, Marine Promenade tel: (051) 638 7144
Reading: Yesterday's Wirral No. 4 – Wallasey and New Brighton by Ian and Marilyn Boumphrey

New Brighton Seashore Nature Trail (Merseyside County Museums)

Many other interesting publications on New Brighton and the Wirral available from The Study Centre, 88 Market Street, Hoylake, Wirral, Merseyside L47 3BD tel: (051) 632 3084

* Walk No. 30: Hoylake to New Brighton by Mockbeggar Wharf.

27. Blackpool

Museums: Incredible though it may seem, there is no museum in Blackpool
Tourist Information Centre: 1 Clifton Street tel: (0253) 25212/21623
Reading: There is a hugely glossy Holiday Guide to Blackpool, but no Town Trail or guide to the town's history. Spot the market gap!

Best of the rest: Seven Golden Miles by Kathleen Eyre

The Blackpool Story by Brian Turner and Steve Palmer

* Walk No. 31: Blackpool's Golden Mile between the piers.

28. Grange-over-Sands

Tourist Information Centre: Victoria Hall, Main Street tel: (044 84) 4026
Reading: Around Morecambe Bay by the Oversands Route by W. R. Mitchell (Dalesman)

Sand Pilot of Morecambe Bay by Cedric Robinson (David & Charles)

One Man's Morecambe Bay by Cedric Robinson (Dalesman)

Grange and Cartmel: A practical guide for visitors (Dalesman)

Hampsfell Nature Trail guide

A Walk Around Old Grange by G. R. M. Webster

Natural History of Grange-over-Sands and District (Grange and District Natural History Society)

* Walk No. 32: Crossing the Sands of Morecambe Bay.

29. Whitehaven

Museum: Civic Hall, Lowther Street
Tourist Information Centre: St Nicholas Tower, Lowther Street tel: (0946) 5678

Reading: *Whitehaven – a unique conservation project*,

Whitehaven – an outline history by Harry Fancy and *Whitehaven Walkabout* all available from Tourist Information Centre

Many informative sheets and pamphlets on Whitehaven Harbour, Jones's raid, fishing, shipbuilding, nautical superstitions, coal-mining, Whitehaven sewerage system, etc., available from Whitehaven Museum

* Walk No. 33: Whitehaven to St Bees.

30. Rothesay
Museum: Stuart Street
Tourist Information Centre: The Pier tel: (0700) 2151
Reading: *Treasure Isle – The Buteman Guide to Rothesay and the Isle of Bute* (Bute Newspaper Ltd)

Wish You Were Here – a Picture Postcard View of Edwardian Bute by John MacCallum

31. Anstruther
Museum and Tourist Information: Scottish Fisheries Museum, Harbourhead, Anstruther tel: (0333) 310628

Reading: *An Historic Walk around Anstruther* by Stephanie Stevenson

Auld Anster by Alison Thirkell (Buckie House Gallery)

Salt-sprayed Burgh – a View of Anstruther by Forbes MacGregor (Pinetree Press)

32. Banff and Macduff
Museums: Banff Museum, High Street Occasional exhibitions, Macduff Town Hall
Tourist Information Centre: Collie Lodge, Banff tel: (026 12) 2419
Reading: *Royal and Ancient Banff* (Banff Preservation Society)

Duff House by A. A. Tait (HMSO)

Macduff and its Harbour ed. Robert Henry, James McPherson and Alastair Patterson

33. Crinan
Nearest Tourist Information Centre (8 miles): Lochgilphead tel: (0546) 2344
Reading: *Crinan and Tayvallich* by Màiri MacDonald (West Highland Publishing)

The Crinan Canal by Lesley MacDougall (Famedram)

INDEX

Index

Aberystwyth, castle, 190; chapels, 192; Coliseum, 192; geographical position, 190–91; railway, 192; sea frontage, 191; spa town, 191; University College of Wales, 193, 194; Welshness, 190; Welsh Language Society, 194

Adnams family of Southwold, 60, 63

Anning, Mary, 110

Anstruther, East Neuk Outdoors Centre, 251; fishing, 245–51 passim; museum, 246–8, 251; Royal Borough, 246; seaward view, 245–6; superstition, 245

Appledore, estuary, 150; Henry Williamson, 148–9, 156; incomers, 155; shipbuilding, 150–55; waterfront, 149

Arnold the cup-bearer of Ogmore Castle, owner of Dunraven Castle, 171

Austen, Jane, 77, 109

Ayckbourn, Alan, 26

Banff, Duff House, 256–7; elegant architecture, 253; Georgian buildings, 254–5; historical buildings, 253–4; museum, 255–6; Thomas Edward, 255–6

Barmouth, Afon Mawddach, 198; effect of visitors on, 199; Guild of St George, 195; modern-day life, 200; quay, 200; sand, 197; viaduct, 197–8; views, 195–7

Beatles, the, playing at New Brighton, 208

Betjeman, Sir John, 124

birds, Crinan, 261; egg-gathering, 37; Flamborough Head, 31; Gibraltar Point Nature Reserve, 46; Grange-over-Sands, 218; Holy Island, 10; Oxwich, 181; Pegwell Bay, 81; West Wittering, 98

Bispham, 210

Blackmore, R. D., 157

Blackpool, Bispham, 210; Golden Mile, 212–13; Pleasure Beach, 215–16; tram journey into, 210–11; Stanley Park, 214; survey of visitors, 214; visitors, ix, 213

Blogg, Henry, coxswain of Cromer lifeboat, 53–4

Borrow, George, 190, 196

Brighton, Brighton Centre, 89–91; conferences, 84, 90; Kemp Town, 26, 88; The Lanes, 85–6; marina development, 50, 83, 90; museum of vintage slot-machines, 88–9; Palace Pier, 88–9; Pavilion, 86–8; prosperity, 90–91; Queen's Park, 91; Ramada Renaissance Hotel, 84; Regency architecture, 86; Steine, 85; Tussaud's waxworks, 84; violence, 90; West Pier, 88, 89

British Nuclear Fuels, involvement in renovation of Whitehaven, 232

Broadstairs, 74

Brontë, Anne, 26, 29

Brunel, Isambard Kingdom, 151

Burns, Robert, 254

Burt, George, bringing curiosities to Swanage, 103–4

Butlin, Billy, 45, 46, 47–8, 96

Caledonian Canal, 263

Carleon Cove, 129

Caroline of Brunswick, Princess, 69, 77

Cate, Albert, 'Weep for Wittering' poem, 99

Chichester Harbour, 98

Churchill, Sir Winston, staying at Cromer, 53

Clovelly, car park improvements, 142; Clovelly Court, 146; Clovelly Estate, 144, 145, 146; disadvantages of living in, 144–5; donkeys, 143; fishing community, 141; Hobby Drive, 141; prettiness, ix, 140; unchanged, 142

coal-mining, Easington Colliery, 12-13, 15, 18; Whitehaven, 226, 227, 228–9

coal-picking, 11

cobles, Flamborough, 31, 32, 35; Robin Hood's Bay, 22; Scarborough, 26, 27

Coleridge, Samuel Taylor, l157, 161

County Durham, 11, 15

Crinan, beauty of, 261; Crinan Canal, 262; Crinan Hotel, 261, 263, 266–7; Duntrune Castle, 261; early settlers, 262; fishing industry, 264; lock-keepers, 265; monuments of distant past, 262; permanent population, 276; proposed marina, 265–6; undeveloped, 267; working and leisure boats, 264–5

Crocombe, Jack, coxswain of Lynmouth lifeboat, 162

Cromer, architecture and streets, 49; cliffs, 49–50; 'Cromer Crabs', 50–51, 53; incapable of further development, 55; lifeboat, 52–3; middle-class devotees, ix; 'Poppyland', 52; Quaker squirearchy, 51–2; sea-encroachment, 49; work prospects, 55

Cuthbert, St, 5–7

dancing, Flamborough Sword Dance, 33; May Eve in Padstow, 133–4

279

Index

Dartmouth, Bayard's Cove, 121; Butterwalk, 119–20; The Cherub, 118; Dart bridge, 122–3; fishing, 119; museums, 120; river, 117; Royal Naval College, 118, 119; Royal Regatta, 121, 122; St Saviour's Church, 120–21; shipowners, 118; Station Restaurant, 121; steam pumping engine, 119; streets, 120; traffic problems, 117; Yacht Clubs, 122; York House, 121

Davidson, Harold, Vicar of Stiffkey, mauled by lions at Skegness, 45

Defoe, Daniel, Aberystwyth, 191; battle of Sole Bay, 62; Scarborough waters, 25; Southwold, 58, 59; Whitehaven, 226, 227

Dickens, Charles, 74, 141

Duff, James, 2nd Earl of Fife, 253, 256–7

Duff, William, Baron Braco, *later* 1st Earl of Fife, 256

Dunraven Bay, 169–70

Dunraven, Caroline, Countess of, 172

Dunraven and Mount-Earl, 6th Earl of, 172

Dunwich, 58, 59

Durham, St Cuthbert's remains, 6

Dutch, the, battle of Sole Bay, 61, 62

Easington Colliery, coal mining, ix, 12–13, 15; coal-picking, 11; disease, 13–14; Hawthorn Dene, 14; miners' strike, 16–18; streets, 13; unemployment, 15–16, 18; working community, x

Easton Ness, 58

Edward VII, King, at Cromer, 52; as Prince of Wales, at Crinan, 263

Farne Islands, 5, 6

Fiennes, Celia, Scarborough, 25; Lyme, 108–9

Fife, Earls of, *see* Duff

fishing industry, Anstruther, 246–51 *passim*; Appledore, 149, 150; Barmouth, 197, 199; Brighton, 85; Clovelly, 141; Crinan, 264; Cromer, 49, 54–5; Dartmouth, 119; decline of, 85; Fife, 245; Flamborough, 35; Grange-over-Sands, 217; Holy Island, 7–8; Lizard Town, 129; Lyme Regis, 109; Macduff, 257–60; oysters, 68; problems, x; Ramsgate, 76, 78–9; Robin Hood's Bay, 21, 22; Rothesay, 241; Scarborough, 26, 27, 28; Southwold, 58, 59, 62; Swanage, 105; Whitehaven, 233

Fitzherbert, Maria, 77

Flamborough, Castle, 34; customs and traditions, 33; egg-gathering, 37; fishing, 35, 38; Flamborough Head, 31–2, 34, 38; Heritage Information Centre, 38; holiday camps, 34; lifeboat, 35–6, 37; St Oswald's Church, 33; superstitions, 34–5; village, 32

Fowles, John, connections with Lyme Regis, 109, 113

Frith, William Powell, paints *Ramsgate Sands*, 77

Gainsborough, Thomas, paints Lynmouth, 161

gardens, Grange-over-Sands, 219, 220; Scarborough, 25, 29; Skegness, 43; Southerndown, 171; Stanley Park, Blackpool, 214–15; Tenby, 186

George IV, King, 79; as Prince of Wales, Brighton's 'Prince of Pleasure', 77

Glamorgan Heritage Coast Project, 170, 171, 173

Glyndwr, Owain, 190

Gogh, Vincent van, 78

Goodwin Sands, 76

Gosse, Philip, writing on Tenby, 185–6

Gower Peninsula, 176

Grange-over-Sands, appeal of, 219; climate, 218–19; clubs and societies, 221; elderly population, 221; Furness Railway, 220–21; Hampsfell hospice, 222–4; nineteenth-century building, 220; plant life, 219; sands, 217–18; views from Hampsfell, 217; young people, 222

Greenpeace, lack of enthusiasm for in Whitehaven, 231

Griffiths, Philip, lighthouse keeper at the Lizard, 128

Hamlyn, Christine, ruler of Clovelly, 145–6, 147

Hassall, John, designs the Jolly Fisherman of Skegness, 41

Hawley, John, Chaucer's 'Shipman of Dertemouthe', 118, 121

Henry Tudor, *later* King Henry VII, at Barmouth, 200

Herbert, Sir George, involvement with Oxwich Castle murder, 179

Heritage Coast, Flamborough, 38

Hill, David, serpentine worker of Lizard Town, 129, 130–31

Index

New Brighton, in decline, 204–5, 207–9; early twentieth century, 205–6; ferries from Liverpool, 204, 207–8; Ham and Egg Parade, 207; landmarks, 205; Marine Parade, 207; rock music fans, 203; Tower ballroom, 205–6; Victoria Road, 208

Newcomen, Thomas, steam pumping engine at Dartmouth, 119

Newnes, Sir George, benefactor of Lynton, 160

Nicholson, Norman, on squalor of Whitehaven, 230–1

Oxwich, camping park and bungalows, 176–7; difficulty of access, 176; dunes, 180–81; marsh, 181; nature reserve, 180–82; Oxwich Bay Hotel, 176, 177, 178; Oxwich Castle, 178, 179; smuggling, 178; village, 177

Padstow, Abbey House, 139; May Day, 136–9; May Eve, 133–6; 'Obby 'Osses, 135, 136–7, 139; museum, 135; shipping, 135

palaeontology, 110

Pegwell Bay, 80, 81, 82

Pembrokeshire Coast National Park, 189

Pilgrim Fathers, departure from Dartmouth, 118–19

pollution, 14

Porlock, 162

Purbeck Stone, 100, 101, 105

Quakers, taking over at Cromer, 51, 52

quarrying, lime, 7; serpentine, 130; stone, 101

quicksands, 218

railways, Aberystwyth, 192; Barmouth viaduct, 197–8; Brighton, 88; Cromer, 52; Dart Valley, 121; Furness, 219, 220; Lynton & Barnstaple, 157, 160; New Brighton, 206; Robin Hood's Bay, 21; Skegness, 43; Southend, 69; Southwold, 60; Whitehaven, 228

Raleigh, Sir Walter, departure from Dartmouth, 118; collecting dues at Padstow, 137

Ramsgate, Albion House, 76; Albion Place, 77; architecture, 78; buildings, 75–6; in decline, 74–5; fishing, 78–9; harbour, 76; Harrison's Cafeteria, 74; history, 76; hovercraft service, 80; marina development,

50, 80, 81–3; maritime museum, 80–81; Royal Crescent, 77; Royal Harbour, 75, 79, 80; Royal Parade, 80; Smack Boys' Home, 79; visits by paddle-steamers, 80; waterfront, 78–9; Wellington Crescent, 77; World Wars, 78, 79–80

Regent, Prince, *later* King George IV, *q.v.*, influence on Brighton, 86–7

Remington, Thomas, poetical Vicar of Grange-over-Sands, 223

Robin Hood's Bay, appearance, 19–20; Bay Town museum, 23–4; fishing, 21, 22; second-home owners, 22–3

Robinson, Cedric, Sands Guide of Morecambe Bay, 218

Rothesay, absentee landlords, 240; assets, 244; buildings, 238; changing use of properties, 242–3; cotton-spinning, 243; entertainments, 240; ferry routes to, 237–8; optimism over future, 244; shops, 238–9; signs of decay, 240–41; trans-Atlantic emigration, 243; visitors, 237, 239

Rous, John, director of Clovelly Estate Company, 146

Royce, Henry, living at West Wittering, 97

Ruskin, John, social experiments at Barmouth, 195, 197

Russell, Dr Richard, effect of sea-water cure tract on early Brighton, 85

Sandwich, 76

Sandwich, 1st Earl of, fighting madness at Battle of Sole Bay, 61–2

Saundersfoot, 189

Savin, A. C., on Coxswain Henry Blogg of Cromer, 53

Scarborough, attractions, 25–6; castle, 26; Eastborough, 28; growth and development, 26–7; mineral spring, 25, 27, 28; walk through, 28–30

Scarbrough, 9th Earl of, development plan for Skegness, 43

Scott, Clement, originator of 'Poppyland', 52

seals, grey, 5

second-home owners, Appledore, 155; Cromer, 55; Holy Island, 8–9; Lyme Regis, 111; Robin Hood's Bay, 22–3

Sellafield, nuclear reprocessing plant near Whitehaven, 231, 232, 233

Shackleton, Sir Ernest, 53